Nightwing:
Reflections of a Traditional Shaman

Nightwing:
Reflections of a Traditional Shaman

Roberta Lee / Nightwing

BAST CAT / TEMPE, AZ

Copyright © 2016 by Stephanie deLusé

All rights reserved. No part of this publication may be reproduced, distributed, or transmitted in any form or by any means (graphic, electronic, or mechanical, including photocopying recording, taping, or by any information storage retrieval systems) without the written permission of the publisher except in the case of brief quotations embodied in critical articles and reviews. While we are generally happy to share, do touch base with us if you want to use the material so we can keep track of that. And do let us know, please, if you write an article or review about this book so we can share it with others.

Bast Cat Enterprises, a division of Mindful Living Companies, LLC
P.O. Box 27783
Tempe, AZ 85285-7783
480-829-6770
Support@MindfulLivingCompanies.com

To reach Roberta, please contact the publisher above.

Publisher's Note: This non-fiction memoir is true, as remembered by Roberta Lee, though some names have been changed. The intent of this book is not to dispense medical advice or prescribe the use of any particular technique as a form of treatment for physical, emotional, or medical problems, either directly or indirectly, without the advice of a physician. The only intent of the author is to tell her story and, along the way, it might offer information of a general nature to help others on their quest for well-being. In the event you use any of the information in this book for yourself, which is your constitutional right, the author and the publisher assume no responsibility for your actions.

The book cover design, Universal Serpent (on back cover and page 232), and Bast Cat logo are by Christy Van Deman. The front cover owl is by Ekaterina Druzhinina. The "Barn Owl in Flight Tattoo Sketch" on the frontispiece is courtesy of tattoobite.com. The "Barn Owl Flight 4" on page 12 is courtesy of NefaroStock. The barn owl illustration on page 186 is by Jaclyn Morace. We thank them all. The remaining images are personal.

Nightwing: Reflections of a Traditional Shaman / Roberta Lee. -- 1st ed.
Physical edition
ISBN-10: 1-943193-08-8
ISBN-13: 978-1-943193-08-0

Ebook edition
ISBN-10: 1-943193-09-6
ISBN-13: 978-1-943193-09-7

Publisher's Cataloging-In-Publication Data
(Prepared by The Donohue Group, Inc.)
Names: Lee, Roberta, 1938-
Title: Nightwing : reflections of a traditional shaman / Roberta Lee/Nightwing.
Other Titles: Reflections of a traditional shaman
Description: 1st ed. | Tempe, AZ : Bast Cat, [2016] | Includes bibliographical references.
Identifiers: ISBN 978-1-943193-08-0 | ISBN 1-943193-08-8 | ISBN 978-1-943193-09-7 (ebook)
Subjects: LCSH: Lee, Roberta, 1938- | Women shamans--Anecdotes. | Shamanism--Anecdotes. | Shamanism--History.
Classification: LCC BL2370.S5 L44 2016 (print) | LCC BL2370.S5 (ebook) | DDC 201/.44--dc23

To all who have sat across from me, for I have learned much from each. There is nothing that will teach you so much as teaching.

To Larry for helping me persevere and living through it.

To Stephanie, Stanley, and Nichol for making this book possible.

"If you are not outraged you are not paying attention."

—ROBERTA LEE / NIGHTWING

Contents

2016 Foreword by Stephanie deLusé xi
2005 Foreword by Gordon Mustain xv
Chapter 1—Just What Are We Talking About? (Or: Bones and Feathers Do Not a Shaman Make) 1
Chapter 2—Early On: The Eagle Egg 13
    The Eagle Tries Its Wings 16
    Teachers Arrive 19
    Our Hometown 23
    World of Law and Order 23
    Not All Shamans Are Native American 29
    The First Americans? 33
Chapter 3—Illusion, Realities, and Rationality 35
    World of Illusion 35
    Realities 37
    Ordinary Reality 37
    Non-Ordinary Reality 38
    Shamanic Reality 40
    Rationality 45
    "Irrational"? 48
Chapter 4—Healing 53
    Broken Woman: A Physical Healing 56
    Physical and Mental 58
    Shamanic Neurosurgery 62
    Vietnam 67
    Exorcisms 71
    A Jump 75
    Hallucinations 80

Changing History 82
Chapter 5—The Dead and Dying 87
    Belief Systems 94
    Hauntings 96
    Medium Pizza 105
    The Brothers 107
    A Murder 110
    Suicides 113
    A Ghost Story 114
    Dying 118
    Traumatic Deathing and Ethos 126
Chapter 6—Soul Retrievals 135
    A Physical Healing and Soul Retrieval 135
    Past-Life Soul Retrievals 140
    Kidnapping 146
    Vietnam 150
    Are You Prepared To Die For It? 155
    Power of the Name 158
Chapter 7—Curses 163
    Multi-Generational Curses 166
    Past-Life Curses 169
    Troubled Sites and Houses 171
    Control and Balance 175
    Postscript 177
    A Prehistoric Spider? 183
Chapter 8—Danger, Judgment, and Protection 187
    Judgment 190
    Protection 194
Chapter 9—Evil and Shadow: Walking on One Leg 199
    Shadow: Darkness, Night, and Winter 210

The Black Man 212
Poltergeists 216
Chapter 10—Hand of God and Shamanic Spirits 223
Chapter 11—UFOs and the Faire Folke 233
    Implants 247
    Angels and Demons 251
    Real Demons 253
    A Coven of Owls 254
    A Vision 257
Chapter 12—Teaching and Learning 261
    Eduardo 264
    The Smoking Pipe 268
    The Shamanic Practitioner 275
    Medicine Men and Women 276
    Channeling 277
    Find Your Teacher 281
Chapter 13—The Failed Shaman 283
Chapter 14—Fakes, Frauds, and Fools 293
Chapter 15—Totems and Power Animals 303
    Animals Are Our Teachers 305
    Protective Animal Essences 309
    Preconceived Notions 313
Chapter 16—Guilt and Karma 319
    Re-Weaving the Fabric 326
Chpater 17—Foreseeing: Predictions and Prophecies 331
    Predictions 331
    Schlepping Around in the Past 340
    World Prophecies 346
    Postscript 357

Chapter 18—The Meaning of Life, the Nature of God, and What Is Prayer 359

    Prayer 366

    Living Without a God.. 370

    Meditation 377

Bonus Content—Walking Hawk 383

References 403

About the Author... 405

Roberta's cabin, RavenHouse, in 1995.

Foreword

2016

I am probably not the sort of person you'd think would be writing a foreword for a book by a shaman. Beyond being raised in a religion that taught me to think that anything that had to do with spirits was probably demonic—and thus to be avoided—I grew up to pursue a very western, quantitative education that largely looked down upon any experiences or phenomena that couldn't be easily explained by current standards of science and the scientific method.

Yet I felt drawn to seek out this shaman I'd heard about in southeastern Arizona who, by all reports, had an interesting skill set and helped people. At the time, Roberta Lee/Nightwing lived in RavenHouse—a rustic one-room cabin on a mountain in a very remote area (the southeastern foothills of the Dragoon Mountains) where she had no running water, no electricity, no "utilities" of the sort to which most of us are now accustomed. What she did have was beautiful oak, juniper, pine, and manzanita to live amongst at 5,400 foot elevation, as well as all sorts of wild animals and birds, and other rescued animal companions of a wide range of species (including emu) that she cared for, and considered among her teachers.

She could only be contacted through traditional letters sent through the U.S. Postal Service and she only collected those letters once every week or two when she made the trek into a distant small town where she kept a Post Office box. I wrote her and we exchanged a few letters until we agreed I'd come camp outside her cabin for several days to meet her and have her "journey" for me, etc.

I approached her and the experience with objectivity for I believed that despite the advances of modern science there was still much we could not yet—and might never—fully explain. It seemed to me more than a bit short-sighted, and even arrogant, to dismiss other ways of knowing just because they didn't currently—or might never—meet a certain discipline's evidentiary standards, or that they didn't fit within a certain "acceptable" religious system or worldview. So I went with a certain amount of skepticism, to be sure, but not with cynicism.

Trust me, while I was open-minded I was not empty-minded. Having taught undergraduates in my university psychology classes about the tricks our eyes can play on us, I was vigilant to make sure I wasn't fooling myself with simple idiosyncrasies of our perceptual system as Roberta went on spirit journeys. I would look away in various manners and look back again, testing myself in the moonlit darkness. Additionally, let me make it clear again that Roberta lived "in the middle of nowhere." She had no phone and no electricity to secretly project images somehow. I even looked around for battery-operated devices. Upon close inspection, there was no way there could be "tricks" in what I saw. There was no alcohol, no drugs, and no other explanation—beyond that it was really happening—that could account for what I witnessed.

Though I would not claim any expertise in fully explaining what I saw or how, I can simply report that I did experience unusual phenomena and that it was quite real.

What I saw and experienced opened up more questions than it offered answers, but I at least realized that, indeed, however removed we are from nature in our modern lives, nature is not removed from us. And I realized that though I valued looking through the eyes of "science" those eyes would not be the only way I looked at the world from there forward. I had a new set of things to consider, new lenses through which to start seeing. I was sufficiently intrigued to engage in extensive interviews with Roberta which she kindly indulged because I respected her, and still do.

I felt more people needed to hear about this ancient part of the fabric of a community, of life, so I managed to persuade her to come up to Tempe (part of the metropolitan Phoenix, Arizona sprawl) where I lived and arranged for her to give lectures on "What is Shamanism?" and a workshop on "Midwifing Death" in our university town where I was sure there'd be curious minds. When people heard she was coming, I got requests for personal appointments with her and I arranged these meetings that ran late into the night as she desired to help as many as she could during her brief time here. She allowed me to attend all of these private sessions so I could observe and learn more.

The lectures and sessions were a success, but being in a relatively loud, polluted, highly populated area was hard on her. Being removed from the hustle and bustle of "society" is definitely Roberta's preference and she stayed on that mountain as long as she could, until age and the loss of her husband (who hauled water out to her regularly) made it impossible to continue there. Her husband, Larry, died in 2011 and as his decline became apparent Roberta, her apprentice, and her friends went to great efforts to find homes for her 90 bird and animal friends in preparation for her reluctant move to Tucson. That same year Gordon Mustain, the author of the 2005 Foreword to this book, also died. This series of heart-breaking losses was hard on any who knew Roberta, but of course they were hardest on her.

I first met Roberta/Nightwing in 1997 and we have stayed in touch off and on over the years. We were in touch enough, long enough, that when she wrote this book in 2005 I was one of the first to read the manuscript. With all she had on her plate and with living so remotely, it was a challenge for her to pursue publication in a time when phones, emails, fax machines, and social media were common tools—things she didn't have ready, reliable access to living in the wilderness. So the manuscript languished for some time. Finally, a couple of years ago she gave me the gift of the manuscript with the request to publish it to share the insights it holds.

I accepted the gift and the responsibility to share it with others as this mind-expanding information will be useful to many, but I also accepted the opportunity to respect and honor this rare woman who cares so much about All Life and teaching. I set about getting the book published while Roberta Lee still walks in ordinary reality to see it. At this writing, she still lives in Tucson and I look forward to presenting her with a copy of her own book! Much time has passed since she wrote the book—there are so many more lessons and anecdotes that could be added—but we agreed to leave the book "as is," as it was written back in 2005, at this juncture lest there be any more delays in it reaching the public eye. Perhaps the future will permit another edition or for me to share other of Roberta/Nightwing's writings.

I hope you both enjoy and learn from Roberta/Nightwing's book, as well as from the thoughtful preface by Gordon Mustain. At the very least you will find the perspective, the candor, and the anecdotes thought-provoking and entertaining…and any lessons you learn just might change your life, or death.

~ Stephanie deLusé, PhD
2016

Foreword
2005

The manuscript you are about to read is a unique and important contribution to the existing body of literature regarding shamans and shamanism. To understand its importance it is necessary to see it in context, and to do that it is necessary to understand a couple of fundamental concepts.

The word "shaman" is a Siberian word chosen by anthropologists of the early twentieth century to describe a peculiar but nonetheless powerful social figure who lived on the fringes of every tribal culture they studied. This figure, regarded by members of the tribe with a mixture of respect and awe-bordering-on-fear, could be defined in broad strokes as the tribe's spiritual ombudsman, the interface if you will between members of the tribe and the mysterious and dangerous forces of all the invisible realities surrounding and influencing the everyday life reality of the tribe.

Eventually, anthropologists everywhere, encountering the same figures in the tribal groups they studied, adopted the word "shaman" as the label of choice for such individuals. They also discovered, as they compared their ethnographic studies, that there were certain commonalities across tribal cultures in how shamans described the world, what sorts of practices they followed, and what sort of services they provided. These commonalities came to be the core of what is meant today by the word shamanism.

There are plenty of readily available scholarly texts which delve into these commonalities in detail, but for our purposes we need only examine one, really: shamans' commonly held perception of the world. Uniformly, they see the world, the universe, and everything in it as alive, conscious, and in many cases sentient. They see the matter-energy-space world of everyday tribal activities as but one manifestation of a much greater, more powerful, and more mysterious reality, the invisible beings and forces of which continuously interact with and influence, for good or ill, that everyday tribal reality.

That is the core perception at the heart of what is known as shamanism. Notice, I did not say core belief. Belief or faith has little to do with shamanism. For the shaman it is not a matter of "believing" the world and everything in it are alive and sentient, or that the universe is far more vast and mysterious than everyday reality shows. It is a matter of having directly and repeatedly perceived through personal experience that these things are so.

And this brings us to a fundamental truth common to all individual shamans no matter their culture: somehow, by birth, trauma, or experience, a shaman becomes a shaman through the process of having their perceptions expanded and altered in a way that leaves them continuously aware of that vaster, more mysterious reality and the forces and beings in it. Other tribal members may sometimes get glimpses of it, or momentarily encounter manifestations of it, may even learn how to intentionally temporarily access it on occasion, but what makes the shaman unique is that the shaman lives in it continuously, has no way to "turn it off," and ultimately has to struggle to learn how to live amongst members of a society who do not share that continuous perception. This struggle is especially difficult, as Nightwing makes clear, for shamans who live in a culture which for the most part denies (as most monotheistic cultures do) the "reality" of that vaster reality in which the shaman lives continuously.

Aldous Huxley, in *The Doors of Perception*, his seminal work on the effects of psychotropic drugs such as LSD and peyote, uses the analogy of a faucet to describe the effects. He maintains we are surrounded and bombarded by a continuous influx of sensory data and impressions far too vast to process in any rational fashion. He describes the mind as a kind of faucet evolutionarily installed between that influx and our consciousness, and that it is usually kept mostly closed to hold that influx to a volume of information which can be processed rationally. The effects of the drugs, he maintains, are to open that faucet up way beyond what we can rationally process, thus overwhelming the mind and letting those perceptions straight through to consciousness with no intervening processing.

I don't believe it is too great a stretch to apply that analogy to the shaman. Something has opened the faucet of their perceptions far beyond the ordinary, and in the process their rational minds are to greater or lesser degree overwhelmed. The success or failure of an individual shaman in any culture is in large part dependent upon their ability to develop a substitute for that overwhelmed rationality, a logic and rationality which holds within the über-reality in which they exist but which also can be understood in the everyday reality of the tribe at large. In short, their success in the society is directly dependent upon their ability to mediate between realities, which is—in itself—a pretty good job description for a shaman.

And that brings us to why *Nightwing: Reflections of a Traditional Shaman* is such an important and unique document. A survey of the literature on shamans and shamanism reveals plenty of anthropological ethnographic studies; plenty of "as-told-to" stories about individual shamans; lots of works by scholars of shamanism on shamanic practices and techniques; books by self-described shamans who make their livings off their writings and workshops and lectures rather than their shamanic work; and a scattering of work by "debunkers" who set out to disprove the reality of the shamanic world view and to depict shamans as societal con artists living off the public's gullibility. But nowhere in my research and reading have I run across a first person manuscript by a practicing shaman about their life and work.

I suspect there is a very good reason for that. Writing, as a practice, is sort of the supreme rational act. Outside of poetry, writing requires the application of logic and rationality if it is going to successfully communicate. Since shamans do not live in a logical or rational universe by everyday reality standards, any attempt to reduce that non-rational universe to a rational and logical written description is a daunting task at best, and perhaps near impossible for the most part.

What Roberta Lee has managed in *Nightwing: Reflections of a Traditional Shaman*, is really quite astonishing. It is not a description or analysis of shamanism, per se. Nor is it a linear recounting of her life experiences. A practicing shaman in an unreceptive and even hostile culture, what she has managed to capture are a series of experiences, impressions, relationships, internal transformations, and thoughts about them, all of which combine to produce not a story, but like a mirror, a reflection of the reality that is being a shaman.

In contemplation of that reflection we find our perceptions of shamanism, shamans, and, most importantly, ourselves and the universe around us altered in significant ways. Whether those changes in perception are positive for us or negative depends on what we do with them. They are our perceptions, after all, which have been changed. I suspect Nightwing would say that was the case with all shamanic teachings.

~ Gordon Mustain
2005

Chapter 1

Just What Are We Talking About? (Or: Bones and Feathers Do Not a Shaman Make)

The shaman's world and life is comprised of riddles, paradoxes, and metaphors. It is Illusion deeply anchored within Reality. In all ages, the shaman has lived apart from the community, while living only for it. The sole purpose for her existence was, and is, to serve as liaison between humans and Nature, to keep those she serves as part of the All Life until such time as humans return to that condition. The world of the shaman is despised by humanity. It is the unsolvable mystery; the shaman herself is so natural as to be unnatural to the human condition.

I recently quizzed a visitor to my cabin, a Tibetan Buddhist monk, regarding Tibetan shamans. I have seen videos of these shamans, usually depicted as mad, as they are cared for by monks, since they appear incapable of caring for themselves. It is a frightening concept, to live in utter madness. However, I am aware that such divine madness is the ultimate in shamanic life. My friend responded to my question somewhat uncomfortably.

"There are basically three types of shamans in our culture," he stated, and went on to describe people who are so average in appearance and deportment that one is unaware of their role. In each case, he described the shaman as being *neurotic*.

I bridled a bit, but he went on.

"They serve as *mirrors to all they come into contact with*," he mused. "That is their part in it all."

As I digested this, I realized that shamans *appear* to be neurotic to others. However, under further consideration, I wonder just who is neurotic? Just which side of that mirror is mixed up?

Several years ago, I found a copy of Holger Kalweit's, *Dreamtime and Inner Space*, (Shambhala, 1988), which I highly recommend to anyone wishing to study the shaman. I found myself in these pages and experienced a "coming home" sense: someone *knew*. Kalweit cites Plato's "Parable of the Cave," which is a nearly perfect description of shamanic ecstasy, and for the matter, human spiritual awakening.

Briefly, the parable describes a people who have lived deep in a cave for generations. One day, a man finds his way to the mouth of that cave and sees life outside: trees, blue sky, birds, the sun. Of course, he is forever altered. He can never again dwell happily deep in the cave, cut off from all this … life. When he brings this news to his family and tribe, he finds no words or drawings to communicate this "life" to anyone. Nor can he ever be content cut off from its wonder. In my case, as a born shaman, I was born outside the cave, yet yearned to be with my family and tribe. Thus, I've come to dwell in two distinct worlds.

As I have abandoned myself to my shaman identity, I have often embarked upon tangents during which I attempt to become a nicer person, a sympathetic person. All my life, I've wished to be a saint. I want desperately to be a good person, kind and loving to all. Instead, I have been placed into the undesired role of shaman. I strive to sanctity. But when my head is bloody from being beaten upon that wall, I am reminded that

I am not here to live as a saint, but as a shaman, and shamans are not particularly nice people. Indeed, we are exhorted by our incorporeal teachers to be *pitiless* in order to work effectively. Much of my life is now lived out in *outrage* over the outrageous actions of our species. Pitiless, but filled with enormous compassion for Mother Earth and all her children.

Modern times and the "New Age" have turned shamanism into a fad, confusing shamans with medicine people, though these are two wholly different existences, despite how complementary they may be. As ever, the shaman remains an illusory, elusive being. I have described us, in modern terms, as being of an autistic nature. That is to say, ordinary reality startles us, resulting in a constant fight-or-flight response to life, as the shamanic reality causes to human beings. Each reality is essential for the other to survive: we are inter-dependent. Describing how I interact with life about me, I suggest that shamans not only see everything from all points of view, but *from the inside out*. As children, then, we begin early to discern methods of being acceptable, of quickly interpreting and integrating the two realities, and behaving *as if we dwell within ordinary reality*. As we become successful in this, we become stronger and quite versatile—absolute requirements for our lives as shamans in the terrifying World of Illusion.

An acquaintance once suggested to me that today's psychology can be compared to the Inquisition of the European Middle Ages in that it determines what is normal human behavior. The shaman in no way fits into such parameters, but instead is something else. From childhood, the shaman diligently does everything possible to display normalcy, to "fit in." This causes extreme responses expressed through serious illness, both physically and emotionally. Childhood and youth become for the shaman as the rat in a maze, moving all about, testing every place and thing in order to please.

Shamans are born, not made. There are, today, shamanic practitioners who are taught and use shamanic techniques to effect healing. In many cases, such healers seem to be effective in a broader sense than the shaman, who remains at most an incomprehensible specialist.

Shamans are magicians in the truest, most ancient tradition ... masters of illusory reality. Mircea Eliade (*Shamanism: Archaic Techniques of Ecstasy*, Pantheon books, 1994) has entitled shamans "technicians of ecstasy." The shaman's world overlaps, or intersects profoundly within the OtherWorld, a place where All Life has its deepest roots. It is a place and space containing all answers—and all questions—where everything originates and continues to be in its greatest Truth and Illusion. It is also a place populated by all Light and Dark, by greatest Good and deepest Evil, where all is the same, where dark *is* light and where evil *is* good.

The OtherWorld is populated by the essence of everything, including species the human mind cannot recognize. The shaman must not only recognize these truths, illusions, paradoxes and essences, but must interact and relate with them fully. So you see, resilience is paramount for the shaman's survival, and of course, in order to be of any use.

At what cost? As I have just described, shamans all experience terrible health difficulties. Our bodies are, from birth, dying each moment in very physical ways. It is an awful strain on the mind and body. I have been officially pronounced dead three times in hospitals. The line between life and death is nearly negligible to us. We often endure seizures, neurological explosions and intense pain, especially as we come into our power. We survive frequent coma-like periods, most often during childhood. We feel helpless within our bodies, which react abnormally even to simple foods, medications, vitamins and herbs. While young, we are fed foods which are good for people. Our bodies revolt, but we continue, as part of being acceptable, until a sort of tolerance is created. It is through these sufferings that we become fully at one with our super selves where, as Kalweit describes in *Shamans, Healers and Medicine*

Men, Shambhala, 1992: "we may enter into a psychic emptiness; a space that is without the frame of reference of human existence—the absolute." Our reactions to normalcy are also demanded by our shamanic spirits, who are intent upon killing out the persona to make room for the shaman to live. It is non-personal. These non-human, non-animal spirits which run our lives are simply focused on the shaman, to the exclusion of everything and everyone else. Strength is gained in that process of tolerance. Avoidance of discomfort weakens us all.

Shamans are generally found in poverty. A mystery. Those people purporting to be shamans, holding their huge and overpriced seminars, during which they promise to make their attendees into shamans, simply are not shamans. This is not to say that shamans should not expect to make a living for their work. Of course, it is valuable work! But shamans are not glitz and shine and shimmer. They are poor folks. So do not look for them among the mansions in town—that is illusion of a different sort.

One of my favorite saints is the great mystic and intellect, Saint Teresa of Avila. She was not only deeply into her personal mystical experiences, but also founded a number of convents across Spain in the 1700s, while carrying on a tremendous volume of correspondence with Saint John of the Cross and others in a time prior to computers. This is a story about her.

In order to maintain the integrity and discipline of her order in her convents, St. Teresa had to travel among them often, and much of this travel took place in inclement weather. On one such journey, when she was older and suffering from arthritis and other pains, it had rained and rained. The roads were mush, the lodgings in between her convent houses were lousy in the truest sense of the word, food was bad, she was cold, and one day it was just too much. Her mule had slipped in the mire and she had fallen into this deep, cold muck. Looking up into the watery heavens, she cried out to her God.

"My Lord, why do you treat your child thus?"

God is said to have replied, "My daughter, this is how I treat my good friends."

"Alas, Lord," Teresa wept in frustration, "that is why you have so few."

Shamans have a profound and uncontrollable sense of the ridiculous, of silliness, of foolishness, of the absurd. Absurdity is sacred. Everything is absurd. This is not to say we are not serious—everything is serious also. But do expect us to be absurd. In fact, that extends to yogis, medicine people and real gurus, all adepts. Life may be serious business, but we are all so damn silly!

Shamanism was the first human spiritual expression. Prior to that, humans were one with Life and had no need of spiritual experience, since we *were spiritual experience*. When we drifted away from that One-ness, shamans happened. Through the shaman, those who wish may return to that One-ness. That is our role. Sub roles include acting as priest, seer and healer. I have healed people for years, but what I really am here for is to serve as guide back to the At-One-Ness that Is. Yes, I foretell the future, we can tell the hunter where the herds are, and we comfort and re-weave the fabric of individual and community, but we exist to make ourselves obsolete.

Shamans are referred to as psychopomps, a term coined by Eliade to describe one who leads the dead to their appropriate place. This is likely the greatest calling for the shaman, and within this body of work, I would include soul retrieval and reunification of soul parts, as well as spirit rescue (a sort of ghost busting). All shamans are mediumistic: it is natural and essential. Simplistically, the shaman has always been the arbiter of death. When someone died, he and his family were assured that he would be taken by their shaman to the appropriate space on the "other side." There were no lost souls and no ghosts, as there are today. Shamans heal the dead as well as the living, there being little difference.

Traditionally, the shaman, once identified, was and is cast from her family, shunned by all except other shamans (with whom they competed and so kept an uneasy relationship). They lived outside the community, consulted there and were brought in only for emergencies or special cases. They were cared for by the tribe but kept apart. On the face of it, it may seem cruel but there are good reasons for this, and it is this way today. Shamans live apart, and during the years of their Work, generally alone, unable to maintain any sort of intimate relationship with fellow humans. Shamans must be celibate. Korean shamans, who are almost exclusively female, may continue to live with their husbands, but no longer have any conjugal relationship with them. It is impossible, if for no other reason than the protection of the spouse or mate, who are emotionally, spiritually, and physically attacked by those beings which are responsible for the emergence and functioning of the shaman. Since so many of our society show great concern regarding celibacy considering such a life style to be an abnormal sacrifice, let me add that although I enjoyed an exciting and active sexual life previously, when Power took me and I began entering this ecstatic work, sex became dull by comparison.

Once you have sat in the presence of a shaman, you begin to understand how uncomfortable it can be to be in day-to-day proximity with them. Things occur about the shaman's person which cause people to respond in anxiety or discomfort. I have learned to control much of it, but I sleep, and there are times when I am tired and just do not want to make the effort. Making that effort for any great length of time usually results in impatience and "testiness" born out of exhaustion and even pain. Then there are those spirits in my life who cause discomfort in their presence. Some of these entities are of such alien species that no one wants to be near.

As I spent years traveling to various cities to heal and teach, I reminded the people there that I was Shaman, often considered despicable and who teaches by provocation and even aggravation, whatever it takes to break down one's ego in order to break through to receptivity. Invariably, people would become angry and most often stay that way. I have been virtually run out of two towns! And in both cases, by the people who received the greatest healing and professed the hardest that they understood the way of the shaman. Irony of the shamanic type.

Thus, a separateness and inclusion is established, and was, in older days, tended with some care. The leader of the community and the shaman often consulted. Shamans work closely with medicine people and other priests. I suggest that discomfort and fear kept the shaman outside the village, but this was also recognition of mutual responsibilities and loyalties.

All races have shamanic roots. All people come from aboriginal foundations. Our ancestors were all native peoples. Anthropologists have found that commonality for all peoples on this planet. My ancestry is Anglo/Celtic: Scot, Welsh, English, and French. Going back still further, one is aware that the British Isles became quite a melting pot early on. There are no "pure" races. France includes Slav, Teutonic, and Spanish peoples. Going back still further, the Spanish peoples are mixed with African tribes, the Slavs with Asians.

The fact is, our *species*—including all races—lived very *similar* lives until Roman Christianity, a comparatively modern occurrence. Thus, we each hold deep genetic memory of the shamanic lifestyle. This is why there has been such a modern-day emergence of the Wannabe Tribe—people emulating Native Americans. Hopefully, that is but a step toward one's own ancestral identification and pride. What we seek is a return to the balanced shamanic-oriented lifestyle, or rather, bringing that Way forward. Shamans are inappropriate to society as it is. Shamans may be described also as another species residing in apparent human form with the ability to demonstrate reason. This results in great conflict, but conflict is a tool of the shaman.

NIGHTWING: REFLECTIONS OF A TRADITIONAL SHAMAN

Far from being the serene guru, seated upon silken cushions with esoteria emitting from his lips, shamans are the embodiment of clumsy, foolish passion. We are puppies, whales, the tree which looks like a dragon, or simply a tree; we are the stone which you could swear moved of its own accord; we are the holy fools, and our life role is to be as we were created to be.

Observe a shaman. What you see is real, but whoops!—no it isn't, it's something else. The shaman makes inane statements. But are they truly inane? Do not forget them, they hold meanings which become apparent when you least expect to recall them. They live in poverty. Perhaps the house is not too clean, cluttered. Or is it? They are also most organized. Nicely coiffed? Fashionable? Likely not. Why should they be? Irritating habits? Absolutely. Do these mannerisms distract you? Too bad. You are being provoked.

You came a long way, and at some sacrifice, to meet with this shaman, and you are feeling a bit disappointed. Just another weirdo? The shaman speaks to you, but it is merely about her goats or the weather or come help collect firewood. Hey, listen up! Pay attention! Each "inanity" holds truths and answers—yes—and questions, more often than not such things you do not even know to ask as yet. The whole "mystical" shaman thing is packaged within the most mundane wrappings. That is a shaman.

Serge King, the Hawaiian shaman, in his book *The Urban Shaman (Simon & Shuster, 1990)*, describes two types of shamans: the warrior and the adventurer. The warrior shaman, he tells us, "tends to personify fear, illness, or disharmony and to focus on the development of power, control, and combat skills in order to deal with them. An 'adventurer' shaman, by contrast, tends to depersonify these conditions ... and deal with them by developing skills of love, cooperation, and harmony." I think of medicine people as being "nicer" in their approach than shamans, yet I cannot define the shaman's work as not nice. It just is. I suggest that there exist no definitions of good or bad, nice or not nice, love or hate in the world of the shaman.

I have had a few people come to me for counsel and healing who leave feeling that my approach is negative. One young man persisted during his two-day visit seeking my help by lecturing me on how I should work within love, rather than as I do. He felt that meeting loathing with love is the only answer. I experience that loathing and loving are out of the same One-Ness and that only our separateness from that One-Ness causes us to experience a difference between such "opposites." Rather than consider opposites, I urge people to consider "others" and "alls." We lose most of life by viewing it in an either/or framework. However uncomfortable it may be to us to know that good and evil may be the same and that love and hate are also out of One, whether we wish them to or not, we must embrace it, as well as all the light and dark patterns in between the two contrasts.

In writing this collection of anecdotes, I feel that I inadequately describe the experiences. I usually do not have a visual during the work. My eyes are closed to avoid distraction. An analogy: you find you can fly and so leap from a tall building to do so. All goes well until you open your eyes and look about you. You get caught up in the birds flying alongside, the scenery below, clouds—all of it. You lose your focus and fall! Our eyesight is limited and often gives us information which is irrelevant, confusing, or even false. By this I mean that eyesight goes through the brain, which has a limited capacity, since it is, after all, a physical organ. True "vision" then is comprised of all senses—and other. Putting aside the eyesight/retinal thinking limitation enables us to see more clearly.

As I wrote this book, I found that these intense, highly charged sessions and experiences came into telling in a manner which seems vastly "flatter" than as they occurred. Why? To relate them requires some reasoning, and this work is not reasonable. Any attempt to place a shaman or true shamanic experience into a rational niche fails miserably. *Power is always irrational.*

Likely, you will approach this book in one of two ways: through a rational curiosity or, setting reason aside, perhaps you will hurl yourself complete with your wondrous power of imagination into the experiences here. As I always suggest to clients, the most amazing things may happen, and at the very least, it will be wildly entertaining.

A barn owl, an animal with whom Roberta deeply identifies.

Chapter 2

Early On: The Eagle Egg

One of my earliest memories is of my "crazy" aunt, Willa, screaming in pain in a dark room as the rest of her family pretended it wasn't happening. While it frightened me, I also felt that I was experiencing that pain with her. Willa was a shaman out of time, in a space where she had no way to express her power. Willa was my father's sister, half Welsh, half English. Mother was half Scot, half French.

Willa had the raven hair, laced with silver, of many of the Welsh people, who have a tendency to appear more Native American than many people indigenous to this continent do. While I do not resemble her in any way physically, it is from Willa that I inherited the Shaman. Fortunately, it has become possible to express that power, and, although I share her intense physical pain and the agony of Power owning myself, I am not as mad as she. Yet. For Power does create madness.

I also inherited the all-American family, Methodist (when we bothered), Republican, and white. This inheritance is important insofar as it required me to go to great lengths to overcome it. I worked unimaginably hard to be accepted by all. That was my great goal in life—to be acceptable. That beginning, and especially the struggle necessary to free myself of it, strengthened me in a way that I was able to survive being taken by Power.

I (Roberta) was born on December 25, 1938, exactly ten months following conception during a major flood in Fresno, California. It was a year of floods, earthquakes, and pre-war madness. Since I arrived on Christmas Day, it was difficult to locate the doctor. Thus, the nurses at the maternity hospital bound my mother's legs together, preventing my birth until the Lord Doctor's arrival (probably from the golf course). This has ascertained my exact astrological position, while resulting in a crushed neck and upper back. The heart problems were already there, and it was this that caused my death shortly after birth. Brought back to physical life, I spent my childhood years seeming to leave once again. Rheumatic fever, scarlet fever, polio, migraine, and epilepsy furthered my tenuous hold on this life. During each of these episodes, which began at age two, I was taken to the brink of death. I became most familiar with death and those who occupy that space.

The epilepsy and migraine stretched the fabric of my neurological makeup, furthering my ability to interact freely with persons and other species not of this physicality. Many shamans and mediums suffer from these conditions. Of course, other people do, too, but that does not mean they are all shamans. If you have migraine, do not panic. As a child, I had trouble differentiating between living and dead people, until I got punished often enough for talking with the dead ones. Dead people aren't as clearly defined as living ones, and seem to live by other laws. Most live people do not walk through walls.

We had a poltergeist at our home, too. I abhor them; they're illogical, having no human personality to lend logic to their actions. I hate them because they're so physical. I probably despise them because they frightened me intensely as a child. I sat out on the back stoop while spoons whirled about the kitchen, skidding across the sink and flying back into the air, much like carnival rides, only small. As I recall those days now, I am grateful that it was only spoons—forks and knives might have presented real danger. I suspect that spoons were a deliberate choice.

Chairs rocked to and fro violently, doors slammed so hard I was always surprised to see them still hung. Objects flew about the place, but usually returned to their "home" sites, oddly. There were times that I felt I could not bear to continue living in that house. It was worsened by the awareness that somehow it was my "fault." I didn't know why or how that could be, but I did know that it was.

Intense emotion caused trouble for people around me. My sister received bruises (always on her arms) when I was angry with her. I never touched her, but I knew they had come from me. She and I would stop fighting to watch them appear and spread. "Oooh," we would sigh. Feeling resentful of my father being served first at dinner, when I was hungry, his artichoke rotted. It's probably a good thing that no one in the family believed it had anything to do with me, or I would have paid dearly. I still feel guilty for ruining daddy's artichoke.

As it was, without teacher or understanding of how and what to do about it, knowing that it was "bad," I controlled these things the best way I could think of, by hurrying to a corner and sitting there, allowing that energy to flow into the corner ... and bouncing back into me. The migraines and seizures increased accordingly. To this day, I have to remind myself that if people are dumb enough and nasty enough to me, they can take the lumps, rather than turning it all inward.

I had a normal Southern California childhood and adolescence. In fact, for the most part, an ideal one. There was strict discipline, which I still thrive upon. But great freedom to be with friends, to learn, to have time alone. Still, my greatest need was to be acceptable in all ways—typical of young people in the '40s and '50s. The way children grow is with opposition, which is stimulation. If all agrees with their basic natures, they just float along. With opposition, they stretch and become resilient. Opposition thus provides great challenge to the growing person, especially when that child is not allowed to act out rebellion.

The Eagle Tries Its Wings

During the last part of my typical teen years, I met Kenneth Hill. He was dark, handsome, and had the cutest Texas accent you ever heard. We fell in love instantly. One evening, as we were returning from a date, a "vision" struck. As I exited the car, I saw Ken dying young—at age thirty—violently, and leaving me. I couldn't breathe or move. He asked what was going on; I would not respond. I spent several long nights after that, deciding what to do. We married a few months later, but the "warning" was never forgotten. It lived in my heart and close to my thoughts for the thirteen years we were together, when he died at age thirty-three, as a suicide. He left me with two wonderful kids, Burton and Doyne. And he didn't really leave me, after all, since he has worked with me until just a few years ago. He visited the children often also, and actually physically saved my son's life on a rock-climbing trip with friends who witnessed it.

Other odd things happened all the time. The people in the hallway howled and moaned and begged for attention. It was awful. It was every night. I was now Catholic and this wasn't supposed to happen. It scared the kids silly. It scared me. I knew I was supposed to take care of it, but I didn't know how or what to do. I am describing here something many psychic people endure. Not only do they suffer from it, but their families do too. Clocks stopped when I entered rooms. We had to have our alarm clock on the opposite side of the bedroom, and it had to be replaced often. The kids were jumbled wrecks from the ghost activity in our home. My personal electromagnetic system was completely out of whack. No control. Sitting in corners no longer stopped these phenomena. Even having company over was an ordeal, for we didn't know what would take place. It wasn't all bad, however, since Ken had found that it was pretty trippy to have a bedpartner who exuded blue lightning when excited.

Levitation was another matter. That just isn't done. Especially by housewives trying so hard to be ordinary. For quite some time, I carried a stone around with me. It made me feel as if it would help keep me on the ground. The feeling of falling up was very intense. During meditation, I was often sitting above the chair. That's why I did it when everyone else was gone. Still, we strove with all our collective mights to keep these embarrassments secret. Carrying stones is easy to conceal when women carry purses. My stone was the size of a baseball. I had converted to Catholicism during this time for various reasons—one of which being that the church apparently accepted and even prized people who saw non-people, communicated with saintly dead folks, foresaw the future, had a deep mystical nature, and levitated. However, I soon found that the church only accepts these fine folks after they've died. That was not acceptable to me. I continued in my faith for several years, until one day when I took my concerns to Monsignor. After a very nice long chat, he suggested that I leave the Catholic Church. I am still grateful for his courtesy and kindness. But how many people are invited to leave a church? At least, I wasn't excommunicated!

Still, what was happening to me did cost me friends. For instance, Sheryl was preparing to go out of town for some really difficult surgery, and she was at our place while I got her laundry and ironing caught up for her in preparation for her trip. She was to have surgery to repair an aneurysm which lay between her pelvic bones and her unborn child. The doctors had advised her to abort, but she would not. The surgery was not a guaranteed deal, but it was her best bet to survive.

Suddenly, as I was ironing and she and I were talking about her trip, I began speaking from deep inside.

"You will do fine. You will give birth in just over six months to a baby girl with red hair, who will weigh six pounds seven ounces. But while you are recovering in your hometown, someone you love very much will die of something like what you have."

Silence. Stony face.

"Oh god, Sheryl, I'm sorry. I don't know where that came from. It doesn't mean a thing."

"Don't worry about it," Sheryl responded graciously. "I will pretend I never heard it."

While she was in her hometown, a few days following her surgery, which was successful, her father fell dead in the kitchen of a brain hemorrhage—from an aneurysm. Sheryl gave birth to a baby girl, red headed, six pounds, eight (oops) ounces. She never spoke to me again.

Ken was angry about the incident and several others similar to that one. He reasoned that people just wouldn't like us if I continued being a "witch."

But it continued. I was pretty upset about something I had just found out was happening to the kids in the first grade of our parochial school as I knocked and entered my friend's kitchen after dropping all our children off at school. The kitchen was to the left of the door, the family room to the right, so I noticed her beautiful Christmas tree, decorated and all lit up.

"Hi, Nancy, I just found out ... hey, nice tree you have there," I blurted.

She saw it too. Nancy, hands in dishwater, was staring at me. "It's not plugged in."

"But ..."

She let me tell her the bad news about the school, but once again, I had lost a friend.

Since those days, I have heard many stories about people who have these problems: toasters burning up, irons turning on alone, televisions blowing up, power outages, refrigerators ... you get the idea. It's all about control. Having no teacher to help me, I had to find, by trial and error, a way to stop these phenomena. And fast, before we went broke replacing appliances!

Teachers Arrive

In the nick of time, Sudy and Barbara entered my life, and for the next three years they hammered me into shape. We met daily during this time. Using the twelve-step program of Alcoholics Anonymous, we dissected my life, my very being. I gained incredible insight and a strong sense of discipline, which is essential to shamanic work. They let me get away with nothing, performing surprise visits to my home, nosing into all the closets and cabinets to see just where I was in all ways. If I were being utterly honest, my home would reflect that honesty; if my mind was becoming orderly, the closets would be orderly. How did I do the dishes? That was also how I lived my life. Was I careless in cleaning? Careless in living. Humility was big with my teachers. True humility, which they defined as utter honesty. None of this false modesty nonsense. Ego? That was the biggest thing they dealt with—in all senses of the word. We tackled my ego the day we met and never ceased our work at rooting it out.

Sudy and Barbara also introduced me to an open-minded research project into comparative religions and belief systems. We read, discussed, and attended workshops on various spiritualities. What doors that opened for me! And doing this simultaneously with the intense work on integrity—there was nothing better for me then and for my future. The electrical accidents were slowing down radically and finally ceased as those three years flew by.

Even as shaman, I realize that I cannot teach as much about throwing blue light around a room as I can—and must—teach about self. All I can do is to build the framework in which Power will come to reside. If the framework is not knowledgeable about her true self, not totally honest, not on the road to ego-free; if she is still playing the victim to life, unwilling to fiercely face herself and deal with that, Power will not reside, but brush over, possibly harming and even bringing the aspirant to the door of death. Or worse, produce a megalomaniac.

We have thousands, perhaps millions, of people who join the armed forces and undergo basic training—freely, of their own volition. Very, very few people will undergo similar basic training in shamanism. It is tough, harsh, and ego-destroying. As basic training must be. It is only after ego is stomped into bits that we can face and work with the true person present under all that trash. In the armed forces, ego is trashed so that one becomes a team person. In shamanism—as in all spiritual callings—ego must be trashed in order to become a team with Power. When we get into the ego-work, people start crying out "cult," "mind-control," and so forth. Not so. It is only to abolish lying, controlling ego that we work so hard at putting it from us and our students. America today is so caught up in individualism being supreme that everyone expects to be a leader, leaving us with no followers to lead. Thus, both leaders and followers are of little account, poor in quality.

Because shamans must be virtually ego-free, they are born with stronger egos than most. Again, that opposition-bringing-growth idea. So the apprentice approaches me with a mess of ego, willing, he or she says, to do *anything* to work with the great Nightwing, to become the best possible shaman—to serve humanity and Mother Earth. What rot. And that sort of attitude ceases in mere days.

I am grateful every day for my first teachers. Even when I did not understand what they were telling me, when they explained what scum I was and why, I knew they had the Truth for me. I was obedient for three years. When a person becomes your Teacher, even when she is wrong, she is right. They made many mistakes, but they were always right. One day, I questioned their teaching. They left me. I begged. They suggested other people. It was over.

Life is like that. One day, we run out of another chance. Ask people who are completely paralyzed. One day it's done. Ask people who have had someone they love die. It's over. No last few hugs or kisses or forgiveness or just one more sunset to watch. Done. My teachers quit me. Since then, I have quit several apprentices, and many more have quit me. It's hard work. It means facing some ugly truths about ourselves. Why should we have to do this when Jane Smith doesn't? Well, I really don't care if Ms. Smith faces herself or not; I don't know her, and she is not called to tough work. Power does not claim her to serve it forever. And she doesn't ask to live a life of integrity.

Life went on for me, without Sudy and Barbara. I still think of them often. They are still my heroes. Since then, I have had other human teachers, both living and dead ones, and many non-human teachers, who are *really* tough. Although you may not see my teachers today, they are here, and they are real, and I have to answer to them—they have great expectations, too. They laugh at me, call me names, hurt me physically at times, allow me to make a fool of myself, mislead me, and persuade me to make awful mistakes. At times, I suspect the latter is for their amusement.

As I was undergoing initial training(s), I also had to support my children and myself, and I did so in various jobs and in various cities. We had an adventurous life together, the kids and I. We made exciting friends. We moved a lot, which was hard on them but made them resilient and strong and quick. We have developed quite different lifestyles since.

What I regret, and can do nothing about, are the years of fear they endured, living with me. It got better as time went on, but there were always ghosts about and problems of psychic natures. Burton's girlfriend was upset to tears when she found that we carried on silent conversations. No, actually, they were half conversations—he would think a question to me and I would answer aloud, and vice-versa. To be fair with us, let me hasten to add that we were unaware that we did this, and only after the girlfriend situation did my daughter inform us of its veracity.

His new wife and her family were appalled when I called them long distance one evening to tell them to make sure that Burton took aspirin, his asthma medication, and more liquids. He had a bad fever and it was affecting his asthma. How did I know? When he awoke to them trying to get more liquids in him, he explained. Then I got the phone call from him saying he was better.

"And, Mom, please don't do that again," he asked me. "They just don't understand. They think it's weird."

Weird? What's weird? But I began that day to back off hard, to disconnect from them both. Doyne didn't like the "others," those dead people in the hallway. They scared her, and she couldn't sleep when they were whining. She didn't like it when someone I accidentally called in via the Ouija Board (don't do it) got loose and I didn't know how to get it back out. That one even dried up our mommy cat's milk! It was weeks before we were free from that.

Neither of the kids liked it that I always knew when they—or any of their friends—lied. That's been a very uncomfortable side effect of being psychic. Who cares if someone's lying? It's not my business if people lie all the time. Even people who know I know continue to lie to me. But the kids knew "the look" I got on my face when they lied. I didn't see why I should confront people about their lying, but I also could not free myself of the knowledge. It is still a real onus. Teenagers live by lies, I think. But "the look" usually got the truth from them. They learned, before long, that if they wanted to put one over on me, to just avoid being in my presence. They still do that.

By and large, it wasn't too bad for them. But sadly, both are afraid of psychic phenomena. Sadly, because both are born shamans and neither will learn, prepare, or practice. They have developed lots of little tricks to enable them to avoid ghosts and situations that are not "normal." I don't blame them. Their young years were with someone who had no control, and I doubt they can imagine how much better it is *with* control. What talent. Perhaps someday ...

Our Hometown

When I was transferred to Tucson, I was jubilant. At last, I felt I was coming home. We moved here when the kids were older teenagers. It has a hometown feel about it, too. But Tucson is also a place where people come to grow and learn. This is why there are so many who leave also. Growing and learning are hard. Tucson has been the grindstone with the finer finish on it, polishing me into Shaman. Southeastern Arizona is our home, no matter where else we may travel. Even when I have traveled to work in other parts of the country and Canada, I used to be so homesick that it was physical. It got better, once I learned to live the moment fully. But this is where my spirits insist I dwell, and here I am. We live just two hours out of Tucson now, on a mountain.

Once the kids grew up and left home, I was in the space where it was time for me to find my life's work. Living as Shaman. Now. Living it, not theorizing. Was it fun and games? Let's see.

World of Law and Order

After several other careers, legal work called. The way in this door was long and winding, so we'll cut to the chase. I ended up doing quite a bit of transcribing pre-trial interviews conducted by criminal attorneys, and working primarily for one. Nat Schaye is a genius lawyer. He is the man you want when you've been accused of doing bad. But as such, he also has some real bad people as clients. Well, our Constitution not only allows for the best possible defense of *alleged* wrong-doers, it requires it. Working there honed my skills at turning off receptivity.

During this time, I met some fine people on both sides of the "fence." Many wonderful lawyers, their support people, courthouse workers, police officers, and private investigators. Eventually, some of my "other" talents came out, and I found that I was popular as the downtown "seer." Most of this was personal—Tarot readings and counseling—but frequently lawyers asked me to "check" on clients or opposition for them.

I received a call from some people whose sister had disappeared while jogging one Sunday morning. I had a reputation for finding lost people, so would I help them find their lost sister? They came over.

"Are you prepared to learn the worst possible from me?" I queried. I have learned to ask this question each time, after a bad bit once.

"Oh, yes. But you will find her for us?"

"What if I find her not living?" I asked, gently.

"But you will, we're sure she's alive."

"If she's not?" I insisted.

They decided that whatever fears I might have, for me to proceed. I did.

I found the woman, Emily. Her body was in an unofficial dumping site on the southwest side of Tucson, at the base of a slope.

"She's anxious for her body to be found quickly, because there is evidence that ..."

They cut me off. "She's alive there."

"No, she is not alive. She was killed ... oh, on Sunday, prior to being dumped ..."

They left, angry that I would lie to them.

I called my unofficial contact at the Sheriff's Department. The Sheriff had made it next to impossible for psychics to work with the department in an open way. And this is why I refuse to do such work to this day.

"Jack," I said when he answered his home phone, "the woman who went missing last Sunday, the jogger?"

"Yeah? You got her?"

"Yes, and she won't let up. She's on me each time I take a moment to rest. She's a very strong woman, determined that she be found and her killer arrested."

"Okay, let me have it."

"Jack, her body is in that old dump area way southwest of town. It's at the base of an alluvial. There are white trash bags all about her, not black. She says to stop looking for vultures. There are clouds of ravens."

"We've been out there. No go."

"Jack, she's insistent. Look, it's about time for her. She is pregnant. Just. Told her fiancé and he killed her. He's some religious fanatic. Everyone thinks he's such a nice guy, Christian and all, but he's not. He's fanatic, and although he had been sleeping with her, pregnancy would reveal him for the hypocrite he is. She's not far pregnant, and it's important she be found before the fetus is gone. That's how she believes he will be convicted of her murder."

Jack sighed. "I don't know what to do about it. Can you get some people and go out there and search yourself?"

"I'll try, but I doubt it. Jack, it's a huge area, and it's June. It'll be over 100 degrees before ten a.m.! How many people do you think I can find who will go out there?" I was pretty disgusted by then.

They found her skeletal remains months later, arrested another man for the crime. He was found innocent before they arrested the fiancé and were able to prove that he was guilty. Her killer is now in Arizona Department of Corrections for many years.

That was just about the last time I did any work for law enforcement. It just doesn't work, and that's a shame, because the information flows in, even when I'm not asked. It's hard work, since I experience the death of the person in question—each nasty detail. But I thought it was important to do. I still would, if we were treated with any real respect and consideration.

It was mid-afternoon when I got the call from Joyce, a woman I used to work with in Denver. It didn't sound like the usual convivial Joyce. Would I be available for a telephonic consultation right after work, at the office? A dear friend of hers and Susan's, an undercover police officer, had just been taken to University Hospital with a severe injury. Would I please help them? I hemmed and hawed. Talking to dead people over a telephone isn't easy, but they were distraught. At 5:15, we were on a conference call, the two women trying not to sob aloud. They gave me his name and just said he had been hurt on duty.

The man came in like a flash. He gave his full name. I saw him, Scott, in the hospital. I saw how it had happened. He was riding a motorcycle, a chopper, and had been run into a median by an automobile, striking his head on the hard edge of the curb "... right here." I described where and in what line.

"There is practically no chance for Scott. If he makes it, he will be bedridden forever," I told them.

"No, no. He didn't hit his head," one of the women said. "Perhaps you have the wrong man."

"This man has an accent; Texan, I believe, and was born and grew up in ... near Dallas, no, Ft. Worth."

"Yes, Scott was. But ..."

"He has one son, and is a bigot," I described. "His wife's name is Sally."

"Yes, that's right. Say, I'll page my husband; he's waiting at the hospital right now."

She did, and he confirmed the head injury. I proceeded with the contact. I entered Scott's head to view the injury. With me was Walking Hawk, one of my old friends I channeled for years. You'll learn more about him in the Bonus Content.

"We are approaching the bed and Scott sees Walking Hawk and is reluctant to have the 'damn Indian' come near."

"Scott," said one of the women, "quit being such a bigot. These people are here to help you."

"Susan," I said, "maybe you'll tell him to lighten up on me, too, he's not fond of women in charge."

Susan "spoke" with Scott and we went on in our work. Walking Hawk stood at the head of Scott's bed, amid all the machinery and beeps and tubes. There he was, all of five feet tall, half naked, his abdomen ridged with old age, his face drawn from his paralysis, hands on either side of Scott's head. What a sight. I described that to the women as we worked. There were doctors also working on Scott, or at least in attendance. Oh, they were physically alive doctors. Anyway, we went into Scott's brain. It was terribly damaged. We relieved some pressure from the swelling in the lower right back of the skull, but it looked like a week-old stew in there. We also bonded with Scott's mind and soul, explaining what had happened and his options. We told him that he would need to decide whether to live or not, and soon. We took him "out" of his body to view the room and activity. Then we replaced him, told him we would help him with the pain during the night, and left.

All this was related to Joyce and Susan as we worked. I was firm with them to be prepared for Scott to die the following day, that they would likely find him brain dead by morning and the "plug" would be pulled. I further told them that while we were working with Scott, there was some brain activity because of our work. They checked the time. We said some nice-nice and hung up.

The next morning, I entered the office late. No messages. A few moments later, I began humming the advertising ditty for Oscar Mayer.

"Oh, I'd love to be an Oscar Mayer wiener. That is what I'd really like to be ..."

I placed a call to her office in Denver and asked for Susan. "She cannot come to the phone right now," was the reply.

"Tell her it's Roberta and I know what has happened," I suggested. Susan came to the phone, weeping.

"Susan, you just found out. But you have to know this—he just came in and sang the Oscar Mayer wiener ad song to me."

Susan sobbed and laughed all at one time. "That was his nickname on the force. Oscar Mayer for hot dog—you know, so often undercover cops are called hot dogs," she laughed.

"He just died within the past hour, didn't he?"

"Yes, Tony just called me and told me. Oh, and Roberta? While you and Walking Hawk were working on Scott, Tony was watching through the glass door. There was sudden brain activity at that time!"

"Thank you, Susan. Oh, and Susan, you are friends with Scott's wife?"

"Yes."

"Be close to her for a time, now. The force will find that she is not entitled to the full insurance because he was officially off duty at the time of the accident. He was going home."

And that's what happened.

Also during this time, I worked days and spent nights holding what I called "Tupperware seances" for people who gathered a group of about a dozen people. That was fun, but following each one, I seldom slept, so I would go back to the law office exhausted in the morning. In between, I read the Tarot cards, which I had laid hands on in 1970. The Tarot was a way for me to be psychic acceptably.

I left the law offices when a client of ours killed a friend of mine. That's all. I almost left the Tarot business that same month, when two more clients I had become close to over the years were killed by their ex-husbands, after I had foreseen that and warned both to leave the area and hide. One of these women was actually shotgunned within hearing distance of our home, where she was at work. Larry, my husband, helped me by reminding me forcefully that people came to me when they were in trouble, and that foreseeing it didn't really mean being involved. They didn't take my advice, so ...

It still bothers me when I think of those two women, both mothers and so full of life and hope.

Larry and I met on jury duty. That's right. A murder trial, lasting three weeks. We didn't get together until about four months following the trial. He's quite a bit younger than I am. We were counseled by other couples where one is a known psychic and one serves as support. It can cause real conflict. But twenty years later, as I write this, he's still my good friend despite it all. It is uncommon for shamans to be or stay married, for the spirits are, indeed, jealous, and because practicing shamans are celibate. But it works out for us. I am careful not to depend upon him too much, and he is careful not to anger a certain few of my non-human spirits which would attack him in a heartbeat, despite my attempts to come between. After all these years, we have enough trial and error behind us to do okay. And it is wonderful for me to have such support from him. He also makes me laugh.

Not All Shamans Are Native American

I am not Native American. That has been one of the first comments or questions from strangers. It seems we associate shamanism with Native Americans, although shamanism is completely cross-cultural. We also confuse shamans with medicine people, as I pointed out in "Chapter 1: Just What Are We Talking About?"

I met some great grass-roots Native Americans in Tucson about the time I left the law office work. Dorris was at a seance I did for a psychologist one evening, and we hit it off. Through her, I met some spiritual people who happened to be Native American in background. They would never discuss their other ethnicities, however, which bothered me greatly. It seems they were ashamed to have European ancestors. I hope that has passed. It is a common belief among the Native Americans (they call themselves Indians) that people of European nationalities have a harder, if not impossible, time being spiritual. Many equate any "white" person with the Bible. That seems one-dimensional to me. These fine people adopted me, but really didn't know what to do with me or about me, since I was a powerful, spiritual white woman. But we had a lot of fun, and I learned a great deal from being with them.

Let me suggest, to any of you who are considering it, that you do not join the "Wannabe Tribe." Yes, yes, you may remember past lives as Indians (it would be odd not to); the spiritual ways of indigenous peoples call to us strongly, the earth spirituality and all. The leather, feathers, and beads are cool. But, folks, we each have our own genetic memories to draw upon, and they are *all* earth spirituality. We all come from indigenous people. My background is Welsh, Scot, English, and French. When you think about what you read of history and pre-history, it is clear that all Europeans have Mediterranean roots. In fact, we all derive from the African gene pool one way or another. Then our ancestors began moving about, trading, conquering, whatever, and soon most places became melting pots, as America is today.

In the British Isles, we find that all European countries were there at one time or another, bringing an enormous genetic selection with them. Still, the British Isles was a pagan or country/earth religion land until the conquest by the Romans. The history of that is violent and awful—in all ways similar to the conquest of the native peoples on this continent. But I don't hate Italians. I do not hold them responsible for my ancestors' disenfranchisement. Admittedly, I wish I had a closer contact with my earlier ancestors there.

Being around Native American spirituality *reminded* me intensely of my own roots. It awakened me to the pre-Christian times, when Mother Earth was honored above all else. Many medicine people today are helping us awaken and then suggesting that we find our own paths through our own ancestors, realizing that when we do, we will be more at one with them and All.

I was introduced to the Sweat Ceremony and the Pipe Ceremony by John and Dorris and a few others. First, they invited me to attend and participate (on the side) in a Sun Dance being led by a man I consider to be the greatest living medicine man in the United States: Leonard Crow Dog. This was being held on the Black Mesa area of the disputed lands of the Navajo and Hopi in northern Arizona, and it was one of four annual dances there. It was Crow Dog's way of finding a spiritual solution to the dispute, which the U.S. Federal Government had been interfering in and stirring up worse. Because we were with one of the dancers, we were allowed to camp within the dancers' encampment. We got odd looks until Tony came into our camp on his way to the dance and asked me to comb out his hair. After that, our neighbors there were friendly.

The Sun Dance was a major turning point in my life. All day we fasted as we sat in the arbor set up for witnesses, being a part of the drumbeat, chants, the prayers and the public suffering of the men and women who had dedicated themselves to this four-year sacrifice. I danced under that arbor, and I cheered the men as they tore themselves free of the tree.

At night, as others slept, I sat up completely taken over by the water drums of the Peyote tepees, which I could not enter. These nights were some of my earliest shamanic journeys. When we left, I had to be helped into the pickup. I was a shaman, and had no idea what that was. But I was soon to learn.

I suffered in the sweat lodges of these good friends. I learned from them that medicine people and shamans suffered more greatly than other people. And I did. The sweat lodge brought me, on my knees, to my ancestors. I "remembered" their sweats. I "recalled" their Pipe Ceremonies.

A sunrise sweat ceremony was scheduled. John led it. As we exited the lodge at exactly sunrise, he reached his hand down to assist me, and growled at me, "Look to your ancestors." I was stunned. But I also knew that John often reminded us white folks that our people had injured his and that we should be doing something in reparation for that. Coming out of that powerful ceremony, however, I decided that it could mean much more.

I spent the day alone in the desert, walking, continuing my fast, meditating, awaiting my ancestors. Wulf came to me there. He is an ancestor from approximately seven thousand years ago, in Western British Isles or Wales. He was a shaman in his tribe, a teacher, a priest. He was my ancestor as surely as the good school teachers and ministers and politicians of more recent times were. He taught and I learned. It was the beginning of my ministry. As I met his spirit, a coyote walked into my immediate area, sat down and watched me closely. Coyote became my teaching power.

I wanted a sacred Pipe, but didn't know how to go about it, since John and the others assured me that only an Indian could carry one. Time passed, as did those good friends, and some women bought me a Pipe as a gift. I still was unsure about it, not wanting to intrude upon anyone else's spirituality. As I rested from a healing session in the back of the bookstore in Southern California, I heard someone enter the front and speak with the proprietor.

"I'm looking for a red haired woman with a Pipe."

"She's in the back, resting. She's here to lead some workshops, do some heal ..."

The curtain opened and there stood Frank Green. He had been ordered by the man who had dedicated him to his Pipe to find me and dedicate me to mine. He was Shoshone and had come all the way from

Idaho. Where was the Pipe, and let's get it done, he had to return home that evening.

I brought out my Pipe to the table, created an altar around it, while he set up his Pipe and sacred items. We went through a beautiful ceremony. As we sat quietly afterward, I pondered what to give him in return.

"I do not know why this had to be done," he said to me. "You are qualified to carry a Pipe. But perhaps it is to protect you from those who believe whites may not do so. I was told to do this by my teacher, and have done so. You know how that works. I wish you well."

He got up to leave. I gathered together all the foodstuffs I could find in that room, bagged them and got them out to his camper truck, the only gifts I could think of. It could never be enough.

After John and I moved along our diverse ways, I began sweating people in our own lodge, built in a different way from theirs but humble and sacred. The Sweat Ceremony is a powerful teacher, and I learned on my knees at the door of that lodge. I learned from each person who entered the lodge. My lodge ran the sweat, from the fire to the feast. In that lodge, I—and many others—reconnected with our ancestors in a most profound way, through genetic memories.

The First Americans?

Years later, Marcia came to me for a journey about her grandmother. She was visiting Tucson from Newfoundland and had attended one of my workshops.

Marcia's grandmother had immigrated to Newfoundland from Wales. Once there, the local native tribe adopted her as a medicine woman with great ability. Marcia wanted to strengthen her bond with that woman.

I journeyed. "She left a fur coat to you. It's what she wore when she went 'out' and worked in the meadows, taking plants and herbs for medicines."

"Yes."

"She also left you a smaller item, one you have wrapped in a piece of silk and in a leather pouch."

"Yes."

Good. I had the correct person. Back to the journey, I saw this woman coming out of the east to the coast of Newfoundland. She was coming home. What would that mean? I went to the place in the OtherWorld for the ancestors and called hers out to me. They came, and among them were Inuit people! They showed me that very long ago, some Indian men sailed eastward, eventually arriving at Wales. They lived there for a few years, intermarrying. When some of them decided they wanted to return west, some of the wives accompanied them. Some of the men remained in Wales.

This is especially interesting to me since there is a part of my family from Wales with strong Native American features. While most Welsh are quite fair, many are very dark, with black eyes, high strong cheekbones, and an epicanthic fold eyelid. I had always wondered.

I brought this information back to Marcia, who was slightly surprised, but admitted that it answered many questions she had had for a long time. Native Americans visited English territory long before Erickson visited the West, and quite long before Columbus blundered onto the West Indies. They went to visit and returned!

So let us go on with my story.

Chapter 3
Illusion, Realities, and Rationality

World of Illusion

Illusion holds major Truths and also contains the Deceivers. In the World of Illusion, we find that we cannot trust any of our day-to-day senses. What appears to be one way is actually another, and when we get that, it turns around and appears to be the first way. Or other. Many things in Illusion are those we have never experienced previously and are thus utterly incomprehensible. Our beliefs count for nothing, since there are no beliefs in Illusion.

We cannot count on things being opposite—up is not necessarily down. It may be something altogether different, even a "direction" which does not exist. There is no up and down in Illusion, unless it is there to confound us.

Perhaps you can see the difficulty here in preparing someone to enter Illusion. Think of distortion which is distorted yet again. Facades, masks, mind-bending suggestions, something waiting for our guard to be down even momentarily. What can happen? Death? It's not so simple. As Serge King, the Hawaiian shaman declares, "there are many worse things than death." That is true, both prior to death and afterward. And many of these worse things dwell in the World of Illusion.

Entering the portico of Illusion is good for most of us. Illusion rounds out reality for us. We enter this world briefly and gingerly on visionquest, where we find that the world is not exactly the way we had thought it to be. Illusion, taken in small doses as on visionquest, becomes our teacher; it stretches our comprehensions, allows us to see beyond the tiny realities we have been taught are finite.

Tom Cowan, in his book *Fire in the Head: Shamanism and the Celtic Spirit* (Harper Collins, 1993), tells us that Illusion, like the Zen koan, places us into "initial confusion, resulting in the stretching of mental limits, which in turn increases the elasticity of the imagination." He admonishes us to have "faith in ambiguity and enigma, and to learn to be comfortable in the twilight state where all things are possible." We must surrender our puny attempts at controlling Nature and What Is and allow ourselves to be opened to the great Ocean of possibilities and probabilities. We must give up our demand to be taught that old "Dick and Jane" way and learn from life and from the experiences of our teachers.

Part of today's shaman fad incorporates the seduction of Illusion, to enter the World of Illusion as does the shaman, with impunity. Do we really enter that world with impunity? That has not been my experience. The World of Illusion is holy to us, a place of infinite power, surely. A world of great mystery and even fascination, but a world which will kill us, or worse. Whenever I enter that world for a client, I make sure that those present are aware that I am in a life-threatening situation and demand that each person behave accordingly. I must not be distracted. Does the shaman fear to enter the World of Illusion? We are foolish if we do not. Yet, we cannot enter there afraid. That takes a few moments of inner preparation. If one is fearful, one is sure to be trapped there forever, or to make hideous errors, perhaps resulting in permanent harm to all involved. There are times I insist on removing all animals and children while performing such work, since they seem more susceptible to harm.

Delusion is not to be confused with Illusion. Delusion is a lie that we are being "fooled" by. Many people, including psychiatrists, seem to think the two are at least similar. I don't believe it. I do not work with delusion except in that some of my clients are deluded and wish to become enlightened. As with everything else however, one can find delusion within Illusion. Be wary.

Here is a simple practice to taste Illusion and its truths. Look out into your backyard in the daytime. Study its features carefully. Then, that night, look at it again in the darkness. You will notice that everything looks different. You might tell yourself that it is the same, but simply appears different because of the light. Not so. It *is* different. It has become part of the World of Illusion, and many "others" now dwell in the same backyard which looked so normal and familiar in the daylight.

Realities

In shamanic journeying, we work with three basic realities, each of which is *real*. Michael Harner describes realities from his perspective as an anthropologist in his book *Way of the Shaman* (Bantam Books, 1980). He also teaches forms of shamanic journeying quite different from my methods. Prior to any journey, however, let us discuss the realities involved.

Ordinary Reality

As I describe this in class, ordinary reality is the state we are in when we live our day-to-day existences, driving a car, on the job, whatever. People who drive their cars in any other reality are not clever; they are dangerous, no matter what they say. We *want* people to stay in ordinary reality while driving or waiting on us in a store or serving our meals in a restaurant. This state is that which most people refer to as reality, omitting the other realities, or even the reality of Illusion.

Non-Ordinary Reality

This is what we enter when we trance, heal, use our intuition, meditate or journey. One cannot refer to this as any kind of ordinary, when we meet up with a giant spider, standing over us in a journey, waiting to teach and protect us. It is not ordinary that we would dance with that spider or ride upon her back to amazing places.

While teaching journey work, I listen to quite rational people return from their first or second journey and relate such an incident calmly and with great belief. The other thing that is so amazing about this is that all those present accept this story of non-ordinary interaction calmly and matter-of-factly. Not only do they accept this information as real, but in these classes, in this non-ordinary state of being, they share the experience in many ways—they "see" the incident as it is being related, often seeing parts *before* they are told. This is also true of most people present as I work: they see and sense where I am and what's going on. For example, as the client and I sit across from each other in semi darkness, those observing see a blue light connecting us just as we do, indeed, connect.

The hardest part of teaching journey work is to impart fully to the student that what is happening is *real*, not metaphor or dream or imagination, although all of those are realities also.

Being a certified hypnotist, I can easily place anyone into a state of non-ordinary reality simply by talking with them. While discussing any subject quietly, I can help the other person slip gently into non-ordinary reality, and soon we can be much deeper into subject matter which might be difficult for the person to grasp or to even believe when in ordinary reality.

For this book, however, we will stick to journey work. While I cannot make a person a shaman, nor would anyone wish that, I can teach shamanic methods to people who are highly motivated to use such methods to counsel, heal, and foresee.

Generally, I use a drumbeat to journey. Various drumbeats, actually. I have often remarked that it is interesting that rock and roll has a distinct shamanic beat. My first shamanic trance was in 1969, to the early hard rock song, *Inagaddadavida*. And I bet many of you were with me. Today, I can easily tune out lyrics and journey to a rock and roll tape recording. Occasionally, we use a tape of the *Om* chant to induce nonordinary reality. This is not shamanic journeying, however.

As ever, some people insist on some sort of purity in shamanic work, as if there were a rule or law governing such things. Many folks insist that a drumbeat or rattle be used at a certain rhythm and nothing else will suffice. Not so. This attitude is excluding millions of shamanic people throughout pre-history and history who have been journeying with and without drumbeats of whatever rhythm for thousands of years. Just as it isn't only people with brown skins and black hair who are shamans and hold the wisdoms of Mother Earth.

I am a traditionalist, but I have found much of my tradition through a great deal of searching my ancestral memories. The rules here are, as always and in everything we do: keep it sacred and respectful and maintain integrity. For example, I am appalled and disgusted by some of the antics I have heard of in sweat lodges erected by people who are playing at this spirituality. The same type of thing occurs in shamanic journeying. Some people insist on using sacred plants to journey. That's a shortcut which invariably distorts the realities. Using marijuana, for instance, to journey is for wimps who haven't the motivation to journey the real way. I hope that's not too subtle.

Using a certain drumbeat to journey alters our brainwaves and places us in non-ordinary reality, where limitations are lifted greatly, where we can dance with giant spiders and burrow through Mother Earth with worms, all without the fear and disgust we might have in ordinary reality. In non-ordinary reality, we are able to tap into the future, bending ourselves into time; we are able to effect healings for people, present and far away; we are able to see the reality of how we live and how we might alter that to be more effective for us and what our souls hope to achieve in this lifetime.

We can soon learn to slip into and out of non-ordinary reality quickly and smoothly, using this ability to help others, as well as ourselves, often without drumbeat. Once we work with drums or rattles to effect reality changes, we can meditate, shrugging off ego and ordinary reality easily, perhaps going further within.

Shamanic Reality

Now, we're closing in on the World of Illusion. Shamanic Reality takes us further into journeying, into the OtherWorld, into areas where there is the ultimate in danger, distortion, and worse-than-death. It is in this world that the shaman performs soul retrievals, for example. I have not taken people into this reality, but I can permit advanced students to observe as I enter, enabling them to see all that I see as I see it, to witness the battles with creatures and concepts which populate this OtherWorld.

Jan had studied with me for years as apprentice shaman. She was born to it, she had worked pretty hard, and was medium good at journeying for clients. She felt she was ready to perform soul retrievals. I agreed to allow her to enter Shamanic reality with her as backup. She was excited as the moment neared. We journeyed simply once just to set the tone, to warm up our journey muscles, if you will. Then I told her to go.

I watched her entering the OtherWorld. It was tense for me. What would happen? Would I be agile enough to pull her out if something overwhelmed her abilities? Soon, however, the work had taken me from fear into the work itself, into the OtherWorld, Illusion. And she was already in a mess.

I brought her back. She was rattled and sore.

"What's the matter? I was doing okay."

"You were not. Look at what was *really* going on."

I went back to her situation, leaving her to watch at the "doorway." I cleaned up the mess she had caused and returned. Jan was still angry.

"This is a trick to humiliate me."

"If you were more humble, this may not have happened," I gently agreed.

"I was doing okay!"

"That nice man you were interacting with, turning your back on and generally behaving as if he were your long lost sister, was neither a man nor nice," I retorted, less gently.

"That's not true! I knew what I was doing."

I left the room. Students do not talk to their teachers this way, and I also had to protect her from being a prize ass. We would discuss and process this work after she had control of herself and could behave properly.

Later on, she still claimed to me, "I was sure that I was doing all right."

"Well, I saw what was really going on, and decided not to allow you to be worse-than-killed," I responded. "You were lollygagging about in that place, assuming that things were as they appeared. How many times have I told you that nothing is as it appears in that portion of Illusion? I am disappointed in your first work in this area. After we process this, I suggest that you go and do some real deep thinking about what you really want to do here."

"How do you know I was wrong?" she whined.

"Well, just from what I've described to you, doesn't it sound to you that I was in the same place you were, at the same time?"

"Ye-es. Yeah, you had it all. But how did you do that?"

"Right, get me off the subject. Nice try," I laughed. "Let's get back to what was really going on in there."

"I do good journeys; you've told me so yourself. What's so different about this? I've dealt with Illusion before."

"Baby stuff," I snorted. "Beginner's luck. You got away with it as any ingénue would, probably because you weren't worth messing around with at the time. Now that you're entering deeper into the World of Illusion, you are becoming a threat and are being treated so.

"And ... let me tell you that it will get much, much worse, and you will fail, and I think we should go back to basics, back to shamanic kindergarten."

Jan did not go forward. She quit. "This stuff is too real and too hard," she complained. Jan went farther into Illusion than any student I have had.

The World of Illusion and shamanic reality and the deepest part of the OtherWorld are similar to the point of being basically the same place and space. Let us continue our journey into these worlds.

Another example of shamanic reality took place while I was visionquesting some people deep in bear country in some mountains in southeastern Arizona several years ago. One of the women had quested previously and was a serious student of mine—not someone who is likely to be foolish or whimsical. The second night out, it rained most of the night. As is my custom, I rested in my tent but slept little, staying in tune with the questers. Suddenly, I sat straight upright, close to screaming. Chaz's hand was in the mouth of a bear! I could feel the tongue, moist heat, teeth, and the fur. I sent protection to her and sat up the remainder of the night, frozen by fear for her. On quest, each is told that although they have a whistle for emergencies, they will not need it because I will know if there is a true emergency before they know it. Each is also told not to even try to blow it at night, since moving about in the darkness is dangerous to me, my assistant, the wild animals, and the questers. I had to wait until morning.

At first dim light, I dressed and dashed to my assistant's tent, unzipping it and snapping, "Get up quickly, Chaz is in real trouble."

"I didn't hear her whistle," came the sleepy reply.

I was almost dragging her out and dressing her myself. "Hurry. She'll blow any minute now. Hurry!"

Dina tells the story well. How it was to awaken to find a mad shaman entering her tent and dragging her out of her nice warm bag. But she dressed quickly and we were headed down the trail to Chaz when we heard her whistle blast. She was seated in a puddle of cold mud and water. The tree she was under was lower than some of the area around her, and everything was soaked clear through. Could she have some fresh dry clothing and a new sleeping bag? Oh yes. Dina headed back for the dry articles.

As we set Chaz back up in a different site, she began telling us what had occurred during the night.

"This is going to sound crazy, and I know how you hate the word bizarre, Roberta, but ..."

"It's all right. Go ahead," I soothed, my hands shaking.

"Early in the night, right after dark, I think, I must have dozed off, but I awakened as my hand flopped out of the plastic sheeting over me, and ..."

"Yeah, yeah, go on."

"... Oh, it can't be true. But it fell into the mouth of a bear! Honest. I felt the inside of its mouth very clearly. My fingers even curled around a tooth!"

I had told Dina on the way down about my experience the previous night. She was stunned now, mouth open, gasping.

"And you felt its tongue, the warm moistness ..."

"Yes, and fur around the outside," Chaz concluded.

"It happened, Chaz. I was awake all night with it," I told her. "It's impossible, but I know it happened. It is just too much for me to comprehend right now, but let's both agree that it took place. It had to be a thing of Power somehow. Can you go on with your quest?"

Chaz smiled. "Sure. I guess I'm in non-ordinary reality already, huh?"

"Sure, Chaz."

Dina and I returned to base camp, both rattled. Black bears are pretty easy-going, but there are accounts of deaths from close encounters each year, often unexplainable ones when the bear does not seem to have been aggravated in any way, is healthy, and has no cubs. I admire and respect bears greatly. We are very careful in bear country to demonstrate our respect at all times. I know enough about bears from personal camping and questing experience to know that their main drive in the fall, as it was then, is food. Bears are omnivorous, but prefer vegetable and fruit matter to meat. Long ago, I tested this by placing bacon and grapes side by side on a tree stump, and bears took the grapes, leaving the bacon for the maggots and birds. They do not regard humans as a preferred food source. However, any bear who might be snuffling around a person's body out of curiosity, and has a hand drop into its mouth, would be likely to bite down.

Was it a real, physical bear? Yes. Was it a Power vision? Yes. Was it a spirit bear? Yes. What happened out there? As I always remind our questers, I do not spy on them when they are "out there," but I do experience what they do, and in that way I can do my best to keep them safe. I believe the incident happened, that I co-experienced it and jumped into protective mode, preventing injury. I also believe that Chaz and I shared a shamanic reality that night. To this day, years later, I can still clearly feel the experience and consider it to be one of the most powerful of my life, one which cannot be refuted or explained away.

Rationality

The doctor came to me as a referral from another doctor I know. I liked Jacob a lot. One of the nice things about him was that he volunteered annually to fly to Israel and work *gratis* to heal and help the poor. But he was becoming unable to perform such work due to hip pain which seemed to escape any kind of allopathic—and even alternative—intervention. He had trouble sitting and moving his body in the way he required in order to do his work properly. Jacob was overtly skeptical, but his friend had recommended he see me—and what did he have to lose?

I performed some extensive physical work on him and suggested he follow this with saunas, since he was not interested in the Sweat Lodge. I urged that during these steam sessions, he pray—not just for healing, but in ritual ways of his ancestry. I suggested that he incorporate salt from the Dead Sea into this activity—rubbing some on his body, tasting it, dissolving it in water, and pouring that over him. He thought the idea had merit and did as I instructed. He would be leaving for Israel in a few weeks, but would come for a session once he returned.

A couple of months later, I participated in a weekend workshop involving rattles and meditation, some journey work. During one of the sets, I had a profound journey involving Grandmother Rattlesnake. I used to have an embarrassing phobia about snakes, although I always went out of my way to never harm them and conversely do all I can to rescue them—at the farthest end of a long stick. Yet, here was Grandmother in my journey, rising up high before me, staring deep into my eyes as we became united. I realized that She would be a healing power animal for me. Rattlesnake does not see with Her eyes but hunts and tries to live peacefully through vibration. Her entire life is spent within or closely upon Mother Earth, so She knows the Mother's every heartbeat. I would find that Her vibratory talents would hold me in good stead many, many times in the future. (And now, living out on the land where rattlesnakes are abundant, I have found myself rescuing and relocating them upon our land often.)

During the second half of this journey, Grandmother Rattlesnake and I found ourselves on a powdery dirt road which went through some citrus groves. It was sunset. A man was walking toward us. Jacob! As he came to us, I held Rattlesnake and danced about him. Suddenly, Grandmother struck out at Jacob, sinking her fangs into his hip once—she let me know that that was for anesthesia—and then again—this time, her poison would heal the hip. I saw Jacob reel, his face distorted in pain, and then begin to dance with us. Soon, the rattles called Grandmother and me back to Tucson, and the last I saw of Jacob was that he was walking on through the grove—with no limp.

That evening, just north of Tucson, at our sunset, I was out in the desert with some students for a Pipe Ceremony over an area that had been a prehistoric village and was now a series of holes from illegal pot hunters. As we walked back to the car, I detoured to smell some blossoms on an ironwood tree.

"Stop!" In the Southwest, that can only mean one thing. I stopped in mid-stride.

"Where is it?" I asked, urgently.

"Step to your right ... no, left ... oh damn, I keep getting my directions mixed up," Chris said.

Oh god, this was not the time for a geographically challenged woman to be directing my footsteps. I could not see the snake at all.

"Roberta," came a calm voice behind me. Sharin. "Move to your left, preferably eleven o'clock."

"I'm doing this on utter faith," I muttered.

After I got out of the way, I came around again and saw the snake. It was almost a lavender color in the dusky light and had remained in a passive position although my footprint was immediately next to it. The others said that my right foot had actually dragged across the snake. We left her to hunt in the cool desert night.

As we continued to the car, Larry was ahead of us. I called out to him to be careful, that I could feel another rattler beneath our car.

"You have snake on the brain," he snapped. During those days, my phobia irritated him.

As he opened the trunk of the car to get to the ice chest, the snake sounded out its rattle, directly beneath the trunk. It was frightened and striking blindly around. We got quiet and all stopped walking until it was able to move away.

I was getting the point.

Some time later, I met with Jacob. He brought me a gift of Dead Sea salt which he had gathered for me when he swam there. He was walking smoothly and reported that he had had no pain at all ever since an odd incident when he was walking back to his rooms from work one evening at …

"Sunset," I said.

"Yes."

"You were met by me and a rattlesnake, and we danced," I supplied.

"Yes, but that is not all. The snake bit me!" he chuckled.

"Twice," I said.

"Yes, and it hurt badly at first, and then there was no more pain. I danced with you both for joy, and then you faded away."

"And you thought you were very tired?" I asked.

"No, young lady, I knew a miracle had happened for me. I do not believe in miracles, but this is a true one."

"I'm really glad you're able to walk without pain and can do your work. Never harm a rattlesnake. Oh, and by tradition, it's best not to discuss this work with other people or to think about it too much. It takes away the power of trust and magic," I admonished.

Weeks later, I was in to see his doctor friend and asked about him.

"He's limping again. Bad pain," Tom said.

"Why on Earth?"

"He met a friend downtown one day," he said, "and the friend commented on his being able to walk freely. Jacob joined him for coffee and told him about what happened with you."

Uh-oh. "And ...?"

"The friend insisted to him that it was either the work of a devil or that it wasn't real. Jacob bought into that and is back where he started. He came to me about the pain, and I went through the whole thing with him, but he's stuck in it must be evil because there was a snake involved and you don't look exactly angelic. Therefore it must not be. I told him you had given him the choice to be crippled or whole and that it was up to him. I guess you know what he chose."

How is that for sad?

Rational is safe. Power is irrational. Now, that is not to say that all irrationality is powerful. Please. But everything the shaman does is irrational. None of this is to suggest that we all behave irrationally, or that we accept everything at face value. I am a pretty healthy skeptic. I keep in constant touch with my reality checks. Let's not be too woo-woo about this rationality and illusion stuff.

"Irrational"?

As we were about to sit down to a feast (potluck dinner) one evening, the couple I had asked to do this was preparing the "spirit plate," which is placed outside containing a morsel from each dish and is for the spirits who eat with us in a sacred way. Seems right to me.

"What are you doing?" asked Ian, who was with us for the first time. Ian is proud of his intellect and seems to believe that one cannot be intelligent and shamanic simultaneously. He finds many things we do to be comical.

"Putting out the spirit plate," I answered. I already knew what he was going to say here.

"You don't really expect some non-physical spirits to come into the backyard and eat the food on that plate, do you? More likely, it will be birds and ants."

"Exactly," I replied.

"And how does that jibe with your spirit thing?" he scoffed.

"The ants eat it for the spirits, maybe," I said. "I don't know. I don't have to know everything."

"This is a silly thing to do," he was actually irritated.

"So what? Let us enjoy our little peccadilloes with the spirits," chimed in Pat.

Of course, it is irrational to set food out for the spirits to eat with us— but humans have been doing this since pre-history! All cultures place food out for dead relatives and spirits to come. It's an act of hospitality. When students wish to contact ancestors or spirit guides, one of the first things I suggest is that they put out food on a table for them.

Irrational? I guess. I've never seen the food disappear bite-by-bite before my very eyes. I do know that I have experienced someone there, however. Let's face it, it is graceful and courteous.

The Sweat Lodge—a thing all cultures all over this world have used in various forms since humans approached a spiritual life. It is not rational. I have been present when people used it in rational ways, such as cleaning out pores, cleansing pollution, and so forth, and that's okay, but these people just aren't getting it in so far as spiritual growth cleansing. For that, it must be used in an irrational way.

We had a sweat ceremony going one evening outside Tucson, and as usual, Virginia was there—and it was her turn to pray as we suffered in the heat. It went very much like this, although I have shortened it somewhat.

"Great Mystery, here I am again, in this lodge, suffering with these brothers and sisters, and I keep saying I will never return, but I do again and again. I do not know why. It hurts so much. But every time I come into this lodge, in a humble spirit, something truly wonderful happens to me.

"I don't understand it. These are just sticks in the frame of the lodge, and it is covered by ugly blankets—the throwaways of us all. It is beautiful, Great Mystery.

"The fire is just a fire, made from old trash wood that we collect. Not aesthetic, but it just sort of comes together. The rocks are just plain old lava rocks; when cooled, they are gray and black and dead-looking. The water is not special, but just tap water. It makes this wonderful steam which hurts us as it brings us life-giving oxygen.

"And our prayers are not poems or songs, merely the humble questing of our small hearts, and sometimes I can hardly understand the words of these people as they pray aloud to You. But, Great Mystery, I hear their words deep in my heart and I know those hearts, and we share it all in this little lodge.

"The Pipe we smoked before entering this lodge is just a pipe, and the tobacco a nice herbal mix, but it does open me to all this in a powerful way and calms my heart and brings out my deepest feelings.

"Great Mystery, none of this makes any sense in our world. But I am filled with joy and connectedness in this sacred Womb of the Mother. We have turned all these common things into the Womb of Mother Earth by our prayers and needs and our consent to suffer with Her and together. The Pipe is magic, Great Mystery, because of the way and for the reasons we smoke.

"Thank you, Great Mystery, for Power which is not rational or reasonable."

It's just electricity—my son, who does not want to work within this discipline, had a face-to-face with the irrationality of Power one day. He had just dropped me off at the airport in Detroit after a brief visit with him on my way to work in Virginia. It was nearly sunrise. We don't get to see much of each other, and it's always a wrench when we do and then part. Perhaps it is a little more uncomfortable because I'm no longer a normal mom, fighting to keep my job in the lawyer's office and prepare for retirement, but smoke a pipe and wave a feather and go out in Nature and sit and fast for long periods. Not many kids can love a parent like that in this day and age.

Burton was driving to work after leaving me at the airport, and as he approached some high wire power lines, he recalled that I refer to them as Kachinas and have suggested to him to stop and pray and listen to them and feel them dance. You see how eccentric I am? He pulled over.

Burton got out of his car and walked beneath the Kachinas, smoking a cigarette in the sacred way I have shown him to do in prayer, teary-eyed for his mom, trying to figure it all out. He phoned me that night in Virginia.

"For the first time in years, I heard the birds in the early morning. They have just been pests that mess up my house until today. But here were all these birds, singing, glad to be alive—and maybe singing for me. Mom, I felt those Kachinas, like you say. The ground does tremble as they dance. And I think I could hear them speak to me, but I don't understand what they say yet. Then I looked up and saw an airplane fly up into the sunrise. I wonder if it was yours.

"I was out there for a while, just thinking and wondering, and maybe even comprehending a little what you do and why you allow it. Then, I had to get back to work.

"Back at the car, I was still in this kind of ecstasy and prayed for something that would prove to me this had happened and had meaning for me. Just then, I dropped my cigarette and looked down to pick it up. It had broken into three parts and formed a triangle!"

Dear Reader, my son went on then to rationalize Power to me: "it's electricity, mom." Well, of course it is. But what does Power use it for? And why? He wanted me to lecture and explain it in those terms. No, already too many people are doing that. Explanations simply piss the Power away from things. Irrationality is what counts. Irrationality is for the courageous; wienies cling to the rational, the explainable and control. Let go of the life raft and swim into Power.

Roberta scouting a potential visionquest site.

Chapter 4
Healing

"... You must understand that when anybody, *bruja* or *curandera*, priest or sinner, tampers with the fate of a man that sometimes a chain of events is set into motion over which no one will have ultimate control. You must be willing to accept this responsibility."
Bless Me, Ultima, by Rudolfo A. Anaya
(TQS Publications, Berkeley, CA, 1972)

A large part of the shaman's life is spent healing people: physically, mentally, emotionally, and spiritually. In ancient days, the shaman was called in last when there was sickness or hurt.

Two Winds cut his foot badly with a hoe in the gardens. He was brought to the center of the village, since all are affected by any one person's harm. The bonesetter was called first and examined the wound, cleaned it, and placed cobwebs in it to stop the bleeding. Then came the herbalist who brought medicines for infection and to promote good healing. He or she then probably stitched up the wound.

*Someone was sent for the shaman (who knew about the accident already, of course) and he came that night to the patient, who was lying near the communal fire, surrounded by the villagers. The shaman's role in all this was to **reweave the fabric** of the patient and the tribe* *and to place a special blessing upon the other healers, since they were affected in a profound way.*

That is what I do best. Reweaving. I perform fewer physical healings these days, often referring clients to other alternative and shamanic practitioners whom I know and trust. During healings which I perform, it becomes complex in that we will always enter a much deeper level, locating the source. This is not always necessary, and that is when I refer. Should a client come to me to alleviate asthmatic symptoms, for example, I will now alleviate those, but I may also refer them to my kinesiologist friend, Tom Maday, for a long-term solution. On the other hand, should the asthma relate to a deeper problem, I will then go into that space. There are so many wonderful ways in which to heal with or without medication. And I am fortunate enough to know many such healers. Even allopathic medicine has its important place in this structure. I would *never* suggest to someone to cease following his doctor's orders. That is dangerous and contrary to integrity. In fact, I enjoy the few opportunities I get to work with allopathic physicians, as well as with alternative practitioners. It seems to me the best of all worlds, and certainly the client is the one who benefits in these cases.

Healing is a profound two-way cooperative effort. Not that I am one of those who insists it is the fault of the patient if a cure does not take place. That is nonsense. Nature teaches us that illness and death occur—and must occur—for the balance of life. Humans take adversity and pain a little too personally. Contemplation of any animal or plant will teach us that life, sickness, adversity of all kinds, and death happen, and not because anyone *deserves* it for, if you believe that, then you must also believe that animals and trees sin and deserve pain, sickness, and death. The healer must be a part of that All Life wisdom. The idea that a person will be hale and hearty when he or she "gives up" being sick is sickness itself. I do realize that some people hold onto old concepts, habits, and lifestyles which cause sickness. But these are exceptions. Here we will address the commonplace. If a person has cancer, why should he or she suffer not only from the disease, but societal shame for it? "You can be well if you want to be." Balderdash.

Let us take a look at the role of healer in the cooperative healing structure. The healer needs the integrity to provide healing in *whatever form it manifests*. Often a healing comes to us in an unfamiliar guise—something foreign to our perceptions. Both healer and patient must have the humility to accept what is provided—and to recognize it for what it is.

All too often, healing is rejected because it is not in a form acceptable to the intellect or not arriving in the manner one wishes it. Some of the most arrogant healers and patients are found in the field of alternative medicine. They often refuse allopathic medicine, even when it might prove to be the only relief. Of course, the converse is also true. We seldom see an allopathic physician in the herbalist's office. This is too bad. I have heard, "I would do anything to be relieved of this pain." However, upon recommendation of chemical medication, for example, the patient refuses flatly. "I don't like to take pills." Who does?

There are all too many sad and sick people who journey from physician to practitioner to healer and back again, looking for a way to feel better in the way they *want*. These folks are also the sort who look for the fortune-teller who will tell them what they want to hear, not the truth. Window shoppers. Looking for the easiest way, perhaps the most dramatic spirituality, the magic herb. On the other hand, I am aware of how easy it is for the healer to discount information he receives for a patient which does not jibe with his belief system. Some of the healing sessions I have had have stretched my ideations to the limits. In fact, if I sit and *think* about most of what I do, I balk at it all.

Here are some examples of healing work I have encountered over these years of shamanic practice.

Broken Woman: A Physical Healing

I was working in Southern California, and as is my custom, the first evening was composed of a lecture and demonstration, using someone from the audience to receive a shamanic healing. Most of the people in this group knew each other, and they asked me to use Daisy for the demo.

As I stood facing Daisy, I began checking her from head to toe. Less than halfway through, I stopped, nonplussed.

"You feel as if you are broken everywhere," I said. "I'm not sure where to begin."

The group chuckled. Daisy let me in on the secret.

"Seven years ago, I was in a car accident. It killed my husband and left me with just about every bone in my body broken. In fact, the reason I am here is that my spine fused itself and it's not straight. I have to turn my entire body when I look to one side or the other, I cannot garden well, I can't dance, and I cannot even get my hair washed at the salon because we can't get my neck over the sink! For some reason, this bothers me more than anything else, I think."

Overwhelmed, I assured her that I could help her one way or another. "You realize that what we do tonight may simply help you live a fuller life with the challenges you have?"

"Yes. But let's try to heal my body. If not, I am sure that I will receive what's best for me. I have some faith." She was in tears now.

I moved through her body, resetting this and that, realigning her physical and etheric bodies so that they matched up. Then I had her lie down on a table on her back. I gave my assistant an eagle bone whistle, and I took up another, motioning to her to stand at Daisy's feet and blow toward me at her head.

The piercing scream cut through the room and Daisy's body. We blew these whistles for some time, then taking up heavy rattles, followed with that. A rattle can alter a person's molecular structure. I concluded by smoothing her with a turkey wing.

The week in California went on, several classes and private sessions. The last evening there as people were filling up the room, a woman entered, came up before me and began gyrating and dancing. I looked about for my assistant to help me with this loony. Some other people were chuckling and watching my reaction.

"You don't recognize me?" the woman asked.

"I'm sorry, I don't."

"I'm Daisy. I was here the first night. You worked on me. I'm the one all broken up. The fused spine."

The dawn came. "Oh, right. How are you?"

"I'm coming loose all up and down my spine! Remember, I couldn't move my back before."

"Right. Oh. The dancing. You're not loony!" I am not always supremely tactful.

At this point, all the folks in the room had gathered around. People who had been there the first night were explaining to those who weren't, and applause was beginning. "I've been gardening today," Daisy went on. "I'm not completely loose yet, but it's happening, vertebra by vertebra. A kind of ripping sound and ... free! I got my hair done, and ..."

I wanted out of the room by now. People were wanting me to do all sorts of magical things. My assistant got me into another room for a rest while she settled the crowd down. I felt like crying. Was that exhaustion, tension, or elation? Probably the latter. It was very good to see Daisy so happy.

The next time I went to that city, Daisy asked me to stay at her place. I did and enjoyed her company immensely. Her spine was fully free by then and her garden was lovely. She was dating, too. What a high.

Physical and Mental

I worked Oklahoma City before and following the bombing in 1995, so I had a couple clients who were victims of that terrorism. One woman, Jean, just didn't seem to be able to shake off her experience and found herself having serious difficulty working in the building adjacent to the federal building.

"I try, but everytime I even hear a door slam, I freak out," she told me. "I don't sleep well. My body goes into a rigor frequently. I'm about to lose my job. They were sympathetic at first, but now ..."

Yeah, compassionate employers. "Jean, what do you want me to do?" I asked.

"Please help me enough that I can function again normally. I know it's time I got back to normal. Other people are. What's the matter with me?"

We all heal at our own rates, and we all have our individual responses to trauma. But the world prefers to blame people when they're sick or hurt. I know healers who tell patients, "when you're tired of being sick, you'll get well," or "you'll be fine once you learn what you need to from this." It's cruelty on top of pain and sickness. It's being sick and in pain and feeling guilty for it. How badly we treat one another!

I journeyed for Jean. We did some physical adjusting, aligning her etheric and physical. Traumas tend to dislodge our bodies.

Then I saw it. Up in her back, between her shoulder blades—the sound of the bomb blast! It was stuck in her physical body. Well, of course. I suggested to her to work with a massage therapist I knew there. And I called the therapist and told her of my findings.

Two months later, I learned that Jean was quitting her job. What had gone wrong? She was scheduled for a private session.

"Look at the newest student at the Unitarian seminary!" she crowed.

"What on earth?"

"I decided, with my new body and outlook on things, to apply to seminary, and I have been accepted. Quit my job, and I start in two weeks."

It just gets better and better.

Denise was bleeding. A lot. She would have one menstrual period and begin her next the following day. The doctors were talking in terms of hysterectomy, which she felt was not an option. She was in her thirties, attractive, and very active in her life. There was also pain and discomfort, often blocking her from her active life. Adding insult to injury was massive bodily swelling. Denise was one unhappy woman.

Journeying, I found that she needed to come into balance with her beliefs about women and goddess, which she was keeping hidden, since they were unpopular at the time and in her area, which is deep in the Bible Belt.

"Even you are not sure if these beliefs are all right to have," I suggested to her at the conclusion of the journey. "We can do quite a bit for you, and I believe we can end your massive symptoms, but you will have to help."

"Anything," she said, earnestly.

"Don't promise yet," I warned her. "I'm going to recommend some things that will sound pretty weird to you."

The swelling was caused by the suppression of her beliefs, while simultaneously, her body was releasing in the only way it knew how at the time. Swelling caused by suppression, bleeding was release. Pain was punishment.

"You've hit the nail on the head about how I feel and my beliefs," she admitted. "I just have a hard time believing that my body is punishing me."

"Oh no, you are punishing yourself. Denise, you are a very strong-willed woman with a profound sense of justice. When you are wrong about something, no one can beat on you as well as you do. Right?"

"Yeah, you're right. I just have a hard time ... one reason I came to you is that you mentioned in your lecture that you dislike healers who blame their patients for the patients' illnesses. I've had enough of that."

"Absolutely. And do I think you are to blame? No, not at all. What I see here is an incredibly strong person, with strong beliefs which are a little out of the ordinary for this part of the country. Right so far?"

"Yes."

"It may help you to relax to know that I agree with your belief system. I have a deep connection to the goddess, whom I find in Mother Earth. This belief for me is a passion for All Life. Does that help?"

Her body visibly relaxed and her face lost its tense lines. "Thank you. I feel more open now."

"Let me go on. You feel passionately about these things also, but you are afraid to feel them, and you are in a position where you cannot express them outwardly. And, Denise, you are correct. You cannot be a flagrant goddess worshipper in this city."

"Right." From all four of the women in the room.

Anything we feel so intensely and are unable to express will have a profound effect upon our bodies. It *has* to come out somehow, you know. Add to all this the guilt you feel toward the goddess and of course you will cause yourself pain—or better yet, *allow* yourself to hurt. The pain is caused by the excess bleeding and swelling, but you permit this as a way of expiating your "sin" against Her. "She's the Mother of all, but you, you worm, cannot even find the courage to admit her reality. Does that sound like your internal monologue?"

"You've got it exactly."

"Well, you also do not *think* the goddess, being the loving mother she is, wants you to suffer, but thinking a thing is far less powerful than belief. And there's your conundrum. Shall we fix it?"

"Yes and yes."

"Well, we have to do this in a way that will not cause another area of your body to work in this manner to 'help' you suppress and punish. So let's be very careful ..."

I re-entered the OtherWorld for Denise and found a way that her soul could accept this healing without further harm. It would be a way that would appease her past lives, her ancestral memories, and her modern psyche. Damn, I'm good.

"Denise, prepare an altar to the goddess and those who serve her in your back yard. Use all natural objects. Understand?"

"Yes, I can do that."

"Make this in such a way that if your mother should come over to visit you would not have to tear it down."

She blushed. "How did you know what I was thinking?"

"Right. You're paying me a fee big enough to choke a unicorn and you are surprised about this? I guess you're working to get half of this back or something?" I like to joke with tense clients. We get further with healing when they can laugh with me.

"Set up this altar that you will not have to destroy until you move or until you erect another one. And for the next four nights, take out some nice cake or pie and a cup, not glass, of wine, and leave that for the spirits, for the Faire Folke, the fairies. Okay?"

"Got it."

"You have to pay. And they like shiny objects. Get some costume jewelry. You don't have to spend a lot, but it should be something you think is nice, too. Then give it to them, to Her. Leave it out with the pastries and wine for the three nights, then bury it at the base of the tree you are thinking of as the back of your altar."

"What will I use for this?"

"You can decide. It's not an urgent matter, but must be done with respect and a sense of gift-giving. Think of the queen of fairies finding it, putting it on and dancing an Equinox celebration with it."

"Yes. I've got it."

"Do this, and the bleeding, swelling, and pain will cease at once. Guaranteed."

She did and so it was. And she returned several times to tell me how fine life was again. She used that altar to honor Mother Earth often, and finally had a few women join her in those ceremonies. Perhaps they were waiting for her.

Shamanic Neurosurgery

The first few times I tramped about in someone's brain, I was nervous. Now I enjoy it, since it so often gets right to the root of the problem. The brain, as mysterious as it seems to us all, is still but an organ which is used by the mind. When someone who is terribly brain-damaged dies, it frees that mind to perform well. That must be why so many brain-damaged people enter a coma for, at that time, their minds are free. I am able to communicate well with brain-damaged and profoundly mentally retarded people by entering a mediumistic state, as if they are dead. Those present are able to witness the client's body responding as we communicate in this way. The freedom and sheer relief of being heard by someone else and that information passed on to their caretakers and families is wondrous to see. I have also found that playing a low drumbeat near the comatose allows them to enter deeper ease. It seems that those portions of their DNA and ancestral memories awaken and become active during such a primal sound. In other words we are by-passing the damaged organ and going directly to the living mind. They all appear to be uncomfortable with loud music or sounds, so the drumbeat must be low. The random movements and abreactions of the comatose quickly become more organized, and often the patient gradually stills and becomes attentive. I believe that, at this time, family members and caretakers may then communicate directly with the patient, provided that they do so in a quiet and calm manner.

But to surgery ...

Ron presented himself to me in California as having acute problems with mood swings, terrifying nightmares, suicidal episodes, and bouts of rage. His wife was present and supported this. Cheryl is a surgical nurse, and real sharp. She pointed out that while Ron is a Vietnam vet and has been treated (and treated and treated) for post-traumatic syndrome, he has not improved, and the various medications have done little more than upset his chemistry. Ron was careful to neither drink nor do any illicit drugs.

"Do you have headaches?" I asked.

"Yes, awful headaches," he replied. "The doctors insist that I do not, and I seem to have no pathological cause for them, but they drive me crazy. It's getting harder to hold down a job."

That was my "in." I journeyed into the OtherWorld for Ron.

"I'm supposed to operate on your brain," I told him when I returned.

"Uh-huh," he said.

Well, that's a common-sense response, I thought.

"No, really. I'm supposed to enter your brain and remove an 'intrusion' of some kind which you received in 'Nam. It appears to me in the form of a long, thin thorn. That's just a concept, I think," I added.

"Well, I trust you. I've seen you work all week and, so far, no one has been hurt and they all seem better once you get through. That's better than what I've been getting at the VA Hospital," he said.

Cheryl was cautious. "Just how do you propose to do this?"

"Well, I suggest we clear the floor right here. I need a glass bowl with water and sea salt in it. I have the rest. We'll just have Ron lie down and my apprentice will be on my left with the covered bowl, and Cheryl, if you would, I'd like you to hold Ron's head and hand to keep him still and grounded. Okay?"

It was and we got busy. Taking my knife, I "cut" into Ron's lower right skull.

And Cheryl fell over! Once we got her up and out in the night air, she admitted that she had almost fainted.

"I'm an O.R. nurse," she moaned, embarrassed. "But I saw his skull beneath your knife."

"Yes, I'm really operating," I said. It's psychic surgery, but some people can see what I'm doing in the etheric body."

"It's real."

"Yes, just because there's no blood, doesn't mean it's not real," I said. "Psychic surgeons in other less sophisticated regions of the world may actually secrete chicken blood and guts to show to the patient during the procedure, but if I did that here, you would not only disbelieve my work, but such deception would likely negate the work I'm going to do here. Can you go on?"

"Sure. Maybe I just won't look," Cheryl laughed.

I re-entered the space I had previously set up with Ron's body and began again. We had a low drumbeat going, which helped us all. The light was very low in the room. Our ancient memories were all being awakened. There, now I was in his brain. Moving through the tissue, I felt the "thorn," and began edging it carefully toward the surface. Then, I motioned to Xavier to place the bowl of salt water near me, uncover it, and hand me my bamboo tube which I used for sucking healings.

I do not like to perform sucking healing because it requires that I retch up the energy of the item I've removed into my mouth. I find doing such a thing in public embarrassing and am just uncomfortable about it. But there are times that it is the best way to effect healing. This was one of them. As soon as I had the intrusion sucked and retched, we covered the bowl and asked Ron what he felt.

"I could feel it moving out of my head," he reported. "Now, I feel ... well, I'm not sure. I can tell you what I am seeing internally and hearing," he said.

"Great. Do that before I close up," I asked him.

Cheryl put in, "I saw it come up to the surface of his brain. I saw his brain and something small coming out of it."

"Yeah, that's what we were doing, all right," I said.

"I see green everywhere," Ron said. "It's hilly and some forests, and there are these big hut-like buildings, and there are some people moving around. They're dressed in real olden clothing, lots of furs and leather. It's a village, I think. I began seeing this as the thorn thing was exiting. I could feel that very clearly."

"Okay. You said you heard something. What was that?"

"Flutes, I think, and drums and something that sounds like small cymbals. I can now smell and taste things from there, also. It's very pleasant to me."

"I'm going to close up, Ron," I said. "You seem okay. First, I'll put something back in the space where the 'thorn' was. I'm packing some green moss in there, and you should know that it's saturated with healing substances. Okay?"

"Sure," he said, dreamily, "feels good."

I finished, and took the bowl of water outside, returning it to Mother Earth with a prayer of thanksgiving—very carefully so that no one else would get the 'thorn.' People can actually sense the energy in the salt water following a sucking healing, and become reluctant to even be around it.

We tidied up the room while Ron sat on a sofa and relaxed. Cheryl went over to him, sat down, and they held hands.

"Did you really see it, hon?" he asked.

"You bet I did," she said. "It was weird, but not scary. And no blood, like we have in the O.R. No bone being sawed open or stuff like that. I just got funny at the beginning because I didn't expect to see it."

"Not everyone does," I said. "And many people don't even feel being operated on. But most do experience the subtle alterations within the brain. And many have even more changes during the days following such a procedure. I want to hear from both of you over the next week while I'm in town,"

"I'm already experiencing a lot," Ron said. "My form of thinking has altered. And I keep going back to that village place. I'm of German ancestry, and that looked a lot like Germany. I wonder ..."

"I don't know what to tell you, Ron. It's not unusual for people during the drumbeat to return to ancestral memories which are locked safely in our DNA. You know, in the old days, when we were not so distracted by technology, we were able to tap into our ancestral memories far more easily. Just think of the information available to us, if we could just get in touch with the experiences of our ancestors. Think of the vast numbers of ancestors we each have!" I responded.

I continued, "One of the things I wish we could do is to follow those memory lines back far enough to get in touch with the physical fact that we are all related and all come from the first mother of humanity. I believe that we would probably walk upon this planet in a far more sacred way."

I heard from Ron and Cheryl during the following week and when I returned to their city later on, and by letter every so often since. He has returned to writing poetry. In a subsequent session with Ron, we visited his German ancestry and found that he had a real affinity with the ancient spirituality there. He began incorporating this into his daily life, creating chants and poetry which has a real primal and holy sound.

Everyone whose brain I have stomped around in reports experiencing the activity and reports major changes in their lives and dreamtimes afterward. I have acquired a "helper" since those early days, and students can tell when I am about to perform brain surgery when they see me shape shift into an old, old man who is black and has a monkey-like face, surrounded by what appears to be a lion's mane. We "go" to a high plateau in Central America, to a temple. The client is placed upon an altar there, in the moonlight, where I operate on the brain. It is faster this way, and I like it better when I do not have to suck things out of people's heads. The client still feels it and experiences alterations, but I no longer have to crouch on the floor and retch.

Vietnam

The black snake rose higher than the man, weaving back and forth, between him and the door of the bunker ...

My client, sitting in Tucson, Arizona, safe and snug in a chair in my office, was in a medium hypnotic state.

He screamed.

"Well, Bob, what was that about?" I asked him after he had calmed.

"Oh, not much. It just startled me. It was while I was in Vietnam, and ..."

"Just hold on, Bob," I said. "You were in Vietnam? We've been working together for over a year and I'm just now finding out you were in 'Nam?"

"Yeah, well, I did my thing there, came home, got married and went to work ..."

"And have been suffering nightmares about some sort of black monster, been afraid of the dark, your physical health is shot for some 'mysterious reason,' and we're just now looking at one of the most singular events in a person's life?"

"Uh, well, yeah."

We took a potty break. When all else fails ...

I had been working with Bob for over a year, both with the shamanism and as a certified hypnotherapist. He had been referred by his doctor, and we were all working together to see if we couldn't get his health normalized. Bob was a great person. No one could help but like him. It was a puzzle, however, that no matter what we did, his physical health would crash again. It was, pardon me, like trying to hold up a large snake—you get one end up, and another falls down, then the middle, then ... you get the picture. This seemed like a big breakthrough to me.

Bob recounted the incident with the cobra for me. He was in artillery, firing a really big gun and sleeping near it in the bunker. One day, as he was getting up to start his shift, he went for the door and was halted by a black cobra, rising up to his height, keeping him captive in a very small, cramped room—and no one else nearby. He felt that if someone were to come in behind the snake, it might cause it to strike him. Someone did come but was quick enough to take in the situation. The snake was killed, Bob was saved, and he went on his shift and the gun continued firing. Since that day, he had been troubled by dreams that would turn to black, bit by bit. We addressed that and took care of it simply.

However ...

As we know from my experiences working with survivors of the Oklahoma City bombing, noises are contained within the cells of our bodies. It can take quite a combined effort to rid ourselves of these noises. Certainly, Bob was holding sound. For over a year, he fired these monstrous guns, ate with them booming, and slept with them. He went in for some massage to remove the sound, but soon found that he required rolfing to dig out the deepest noise. Combined with the work we were doing together and his chiropractor, we were moving on this.

Ah, but were we out of the jungle, so to speak? Nooo. I have worked with quite a few Vietnam veterans, and there is one commonality: they were young American men, with little experience in things alien to

Mom's apple pie. In short, we sent a lot of youngsters who were very innocent—and arrogant—over to a place which has not one thing in common with this country or anything anyone experiences here. These kids were not in any way prepared for such contact. Now, we combine that open lack of experience with being in such a dangerous situation (this places us in a profound state of hypnosis immediately) and perhaps throw in some drugs and/or alcohol to make them even more vulnerable, and ... you have it.

The spirits of that land, of the people, the food, the water, trees, in the air—everywhere—are radically different from those on this continent, and even more alien to the American culture—no matter what part of the culture one grows up in. I have uncovered the strangest objects and entities in these men that I have ever run into—and I can unequivocally state that I have run into some really bizarre stuff. These entities are quite similar to the ones I find in the OtherWorld. Not one of those young men had any ability to deal with those creatures. The entities entered the bodies and minds of our soldiers. They came home with them. They exacerbated whatever the men endured—in Vietnam, upon return to the United States, and today.

In the old way, people (I apologize to all the women who served in Vietnam—you were attacked also and continue to suffer as result of the entities who followed you home, too) who had been to war were healed upon return, however the tribal ways dictated. There was a cleansing of the experience, of being in such close contact with violence and the worst aspects of sudden death—and of being the survivors. Following such cleansing and healing, the warriors were able to reintegrate back into the tribe fully, being as free as possible from the worst aspects of war. And being cleared of whatever entities had entered them while they were distracted with the business of survival and being there for their fellows.

The men and women who went to Vietnam get group counseling. Well, there's nothing wrong with that—as far as it goes. Most of us can benefit from a shared experience, or a place we can go where we will be comprehended and not violated. That's a fine way to re-socialize. What about the spiritual aspects? What about those alien entities? I have talked with a few Native American medicine men and women, and many of the tribes have provided counseling from those spiritual leaders, combined with traditional sweat lodges. Powerful work has been offered to those men and women.

What about John Doe, the kid from Wisconsin, who had just graduated from high school, drunk his third six-pack of beer, been in the back seat of his old Ford with a girl once, played a little basketball, went to church on Easter, and gritted his teeth and rolled his eyes to the sky when his mom and dad lectured him on right and wrong? He was taught to shoot and knife and bomb, and how to avoid being shot, knifed, and bombed—but was he in any way at all prepared to deal with the alien spirituality, the foreign devils, which dwell in that foreign land? Not on your life.

The same thing happened to our forces in Korea (an active shamanic country). And in World War II. Not so much in the European Theatre but in the Pacific. Some of the spirits in Guam, New Guinea, and the Philippines are pretty primitive and impossible for the average United States citizen to defend himself or herself from.

What to do? It's a little late in the game, isn't it? Well, yes and no. With the few Vietnam veterans I work on these days, I have found the entities pretty firmly entrenched. They have affected person and events during the intervening years so deeply that one cannot alter what is remaining. However, I can, and do, remove what is left there. Life can still improve with these removals (see "Vietnam" in "Chapter 6: Soul Retrievals"). One of the things I have noticed is how much the lives of the families around people I heal are altered as well. It appears that when demons from long ago are exorcised today, there is some alteration which takes place in the interim time. That surely would affect the families. Another reason to effect these healings after such a long period of time is to allow the client to leave this life free of that baggage. Thus, it would be advantageous to clear and heal someone even on his or her deathbed.

In terms of veterans returning from the Gulf War, there are some pretty unusual spirits out there! Effrits flying around the place with long talons on their hands and feet. They may sing and appear to be friendly—but we know things are not always what they seem to be. Conditions such as jungles and forests, places which are dense and close, offer us demons greater in numbers and stronger, more "cloying." Desert conditions are drier and the air cleaner—that would give one a better chance to avoid takeover. I am uncomfortable in the southeastern part of this country. It's close, and the air itself seems filled with ghosts. I seem to breathe them in with the water particles. Humidity holds in entities and memories of violence there. Yet, having lived in the desert most of my life now, I would never presume to underestimate the spirits of the desert places. We have troubled Desert Storm veterans. They are receiving, yes, group therapy and probably Prozac. They need a shaman as well.

Exorcisms

Jim was one of the first exorcisms I performed. He came to me via one of my students, Fred, who was very active in the Alcoholics Anonymous movement throughout the country. I had removed a lot of stuff from Fred over a five-month period, and he had now come to a point where he just had to begin forgiving in order to move forward, to release his karma. But he continued to study with me, and he had finally gotten Jim to come to Tucson to meet with me.

Jim was an alcoholic, drug addict, and sex addict. A lot of bad stuff going on there. I have found that a large percentage of people who are addicted are also "occupied" by some entity. When we are drunk or drugged or even completely wrapped up in sex to the point where we are way off guard, we are wide open to becoming host for one or more entities of various kinds. Jim had been working the Twelve Steps diligently; he had been in and out of several rehabilitation centers; he was in therapy with a specialist; he was desperate to live a sober life—but he just could not seem to make it.

I have noticed that a large number of really fine people who are recovering from addictions are being run by some outside force. Once they begin working at being sober and happy, the entities become angry and get more insistent. After all, they chose this body because it did drink, etc. They want to enjoy vicariously a life of dissipation. The last thing they want is sobriety and a useful life. They get mean. Let's be straight about this, however, the entity likely didn't start the addiction, but joined in. Regardless of whether or not a recovering addict has had an exorcism, he or she must still work like the (pardon me) devil to recover. It's just a bit easier to do that when one is alone, rather than filled with outside interference.

Jim was enslaved, no doubt about it. We first met in my workroom, across a table I had set up so that there would be something between the two of us. Fred sat with us. It was a small table and came to seem even smaller. We chatted for a bit, the weather differences between Tucson and Minnesota, for example. That's always a topic. Jim was a young good-looking man, pretty successful in his engineering career—enough so that he was able to take off frequently to dry out and still be welcomed back. He was, of course, quite charismatic.

Suddenly, it came to me. "Who is that black man?"

Someone in Jim's body came across that little table at me like a train! I had just time for the thought that I was now history. But Fred was prepared for this, since we had discussed possibilities. Thank you, Fred.

He grabbed "Jim" and pulled him back, and the eyes changed. Mild-mannered nice guy Jim again. I asked him what he was feeling.

"I don't know. I feel like I usually do, I guess." His eyes kept shifting back and forth, and his body was shouting "Liar."

"Well, what do you think about this black guy living inside you?"

"I don't know. Guess I don't believe that."

"Who is that talking?"

Anger. Then stillness. "I don't know what you're talking about."

"Right, asshole."

Rage. A move in my direction, halted by Fred. I laughed.

"You're not even good at this. You're going to be verrry easy to dislodge. Better get ready, because I'm coming for you. Are you strong? No. What a wuss. Jim, Fred, this is going to be the easiest exorcism I've ever done. It will go into *The Guinness Book of World Records* as so easy and the fastest."

I went on in this vein some, just to aggravate the mystery guest into making some mistakes. The best way to handle incorporeal baddies is to make fun of them. Or ignore them. I would do that next.

I set up a schedule for Jim and Fred, including a sweat ceremony the next evening at our place, walks in the desert, staying away from people and noise. Just relaxing. We scheduled the work for Sunday evening.

Placing Jim in a light trance so that he would be aware of what we were doing, but relaxed about it, I began picking at the mystery man. He was pretty good, didn't get too vexed until I attacked his mama. Should have known. Mom was a hooker, but she loved and cared for him.

Once I got him enraged, it was easy. I dragged him out of Jim, explained his two choices: come with me to the appropriate place or become nothing. He went along quietly. Okay, he cursed the entire time, but he came along.

The entity was Paul. He'd been a porno actor in Los Angeles, on some pretty good drugs (his judgment) but was killed by a car several years back. He wasn't sure why he chose Jim, but he did admire that Jim enjoyed his films. Hmmm.

Paul is part of the Source now.

I did a little reweaving on Jim then, and brought him back to us feeling no pain. And the story came out.

As a youngster, Jim was often invited to a neighbor's house, a friend of the family. But the friend had this collection of porno movies and a penchant for young boys. Thus, Jim "met" Paul, who appeared in many of these movies. The years went on, and I see no need to trouble you with the details of Jim's growing sexuality. It was heterosexual, but free from any constraints—seemingly. It is also of interest to note that Jim had begun to acquire a collection of Paul's movies and tapes as he grew up, and had just recently acquired the last tape. It had been difficult to do because the man was dead.

Apparently, Jim's sexual vagaries were completely hedonistic, but he paid for each and every act. Jim was, indeed, overly moral. So moral that whenever he participated in sexual "immorality," he paid for it greatly, causing him to drink or drug in order to live as the evil man he felt he was. A completely vicious cycle.

Jim felt better, different—well, odd, actually. I explained to him and Fred that it would be unusual, indeed, if he didn't feel "odd." I had removed a portion of him that had been with him for many years. It would get better and more comfortable being alone. I counseled him to get to his therapist and set up extra appointments for the next few months; they would be rough. I also urged him to retackle the Twelve Step work he had been struggling with, and I spoke with his therapist, bringing him up to date.

How did Jim become possessed through a film strip? I was puzzled by this at first. But as we become experienced in working with time and space, illusion and reality, it is a bit more comprehensible. It seems to me that the more modern we become, the more gadgets we bring into our lives, especially electronic (remember, the soul, spirit, life essence is comprised of electricity), the more open we are to these phenomena. I think that the connection was all on Jim's part at first. When "Paul" died and was disenfranchised and looking for a new vehicle, he was drawn toward Jim because of Jim's obsession with him, as well as his obsessive sexual and chemical life. We already know that dead people are drawn back to us by our thoughts and mental calls.

A Jump

His mother brought Roger to me while I was working in Southern California. She had spoken to me about him earlier and wanted me to "fix" him, but didn't know how to get him to agree. We set it up that he would accompany her to a small workshop I had scheduled at the home of a friend of hers. He was familiar with some of the people who would be present. Roger was seventeen. He was a mess. Suddenly, about a year previously, he changed radically. His personality seemed to be someone else (not too alarming on its own, especially in an adolescent), but even more alarming were his sudden physical changes. Roger had overnight acquired a dark five-o'clock shadow, a much deeper voice, gravelly and older, and a change in skin tone; he who had despised smoking was now chain-smoking; and he was doing cocaine, she believed. Not a lot, just enough to keep him stimulated constantly. Always up. He seldom slept, except in the daytime.

Taken piecemeal, this could be the behavior of any adolescent—except the instant beard and voice change. Roger's voice had undergone the normal change years previously. He also had become an inveterate newspaper reader, especially articles involving crimes, and even more specifically, crimes involving drugs. He just wasn't Sabrina's son Roger any longer.

At Ray's that night, a small group had collected, most of whom were health care givers of one kind or another, and counselors or psychologists, and a couple who were healers. We were going to discuss emotional anomalies as they pertained to shamanic healing work. This would fit in nicely, I thought. And if we did not address the topics I had planned for the evening, we would make that up later. Roger was at ease with this group of people; he knew most of them and they had always been nice to him. The group had also become aware of the radical changes in Roger and had been concerned. This was the perfect venue.

I started out by doing some other work and discussion, but kept an eye on Roger as he sat next to his mother's legs, on the floor across from me. As I lectured, he became relaxed and lethargic. Good. I began addressing him, or "them."

"I know you are in there. Why have you chosen Roger? What is it you want of him?" Along those lines. I would address that, and then change and continue the evening's lesson. Finally, I got a response.

"Look, bitch, I know what you're up to." I wonder why it is that most of the possessors I've met are so verbally abusive? Even some of the nicer ones.

"Well, that's good. No secrets here. What are you up to?"

"Leave us alone or I'll take out the kid. I can, you know. Just a little suicide ..."

"Suicide is right out. Then you would be homeless again. Correct?"

"Okay. But I can remove him from the loving arms of his family. And you all would be interested in some of the things that go on over there ..."

"No. This is about you. You are our star tonight. Let's get on with this. Are you going to help? Or shall I not even bother with trying to treat you with respect or courtesy?"

"Look, I'm a cop, does that answer your questions? Bitch?"

"Well, I like some cops, too, but I don't like being called bitch by anyone, living or dead. Even by my friends, which you are not."

"Fuck you."

This was not productive, except that I had him admitting to his existence, which was a plus. So I cut to the chase.

"Why are you in Roger? And how did you get there?"

"Fuck you."

Sigh. "Okay, we're your captive audience. We have a lot of professional health givers here, and we're all fascinated with your story and how you accomplished this feat. You must be pretty damn good to move in on this kid."

Voila.

"Well, it was chance, mostly. He came upon this bad accident, and I had just been thrown from my body and was interested in acquiring another right away ..."

I was there. In "Bill's" body and mind at the time of the accident. He was a vice detective, assigned to narcotics. He'd been very busy. He had pulled a double shift, and he was on his way home to his wife and kids when he dozed off and slammed into the rear of a tractor-trailer on the highway. It was rainy to top things off, making it pretty slick.

In shamanic reality myself, I relived his death. It's typical of traumatic death to experience an intense desire to remain alive: he desperately leapt back into his body, which was so terribly damaged that he was catapulted back out again just as quickly. Screaming. But not aloud, because his body was already dead, remember? These are the most difficult deaths to relive (or re-die), the hardest for me to endure. It's not so much the physical pain, but the emotional torment. That's terrible. The intense desire, *need* to get back into that body, to make everything all right again, up against a body that is incapable of containing life. In this case, Bill's body was beyond any life—he had been nearly decapitated from below the neck. Part of his shoulder was with the head. Well, you probably get the idea. The remainder of his body was crushed between the steering wheel and seat, which was crushed between the trailer and the trunk of his car. Bill owned up to using a "little" cocaine just to keep going on long shifts. "Like No-Doz." He was also a chain smoker. "The kid doesn't buy my brand, no matter what I do. We have to smoke his mom's brand," he complained. And during life he had had to shave twice daily.

Roger had passed the accident scene, slowing down due to the traffic mess. He seemed open and defenseless, so ... well as a result of that coincidence, now Roger had an additional facet to his personality.

Naturally, I explained who I was and what I intended for Bill. And naturally, he rejected my plan. Equally, of course, he rejected the idea of a shaman. Well, I gotta give them a choice.

"Okay, Bill, I'm going to get a nice drumbeat going, and I'll be in there with you shortly. Be sure to pack up your stuff, because we're going traveling, guy." I entered Roger's body and found Bill throughout him. Since he wasn't getting his stuff "packed" quickly enough for me, I helped out. It wasn't neat. He complained, and I treated him as if he lived with me. 'Dammit! Get this mess cleaned up.'

Then we came out together. Bill attempted re-entry, but I grabbed his shirtsleeve and we head across my little magic river, he resisting all the way. Bill's belief system was pretty much nothing, but he'd had some sort of generic Christian belief on the back burner, "just in case." I used that and got him baptized and over in a trice. He was still angry, but his emotions became less defined as we went. This is typical. I turned him over to a "security" type person over there to be rehabilitated. I last saw

Bill entering this wonderful Light, still feebly jerking his arm from the hold on it and grousing. I assume the Light shut him up.

Back to Roger. He woke a bit, smiled vaguely, crawled up onto the couch next to his mother, and fell back into a deep sleep with his head on her lap. During the following hour or so of work we did, we were able to observe the beard disappearing, Roger's face becoming seventeen once again, and quite a number of subtle physical changes. The only word I can think of to describe this process is "sweet."

The next evening, Roger returned to the house where we were meeting. This time, he drove himself. This time, we were meeting with an adolescent young man who had an open face and a shy enthusiasm.

He was happy to process with us. Yes, he had been by a really nasty auto accident on that highway a year or so ago—just before Christmas. He recounted the details, and had even brought with him the newspaper account of the wreck, involving a detective with the county, who was assigned to Narcotics at the time of his death, and who left a wife and two children. Yes, he had been on his way home from a long shift at work, a big drug bust, which had kept him late with paperwork.

Roger said he didn't think too much of the incident, except that it was upsetting to see the body before they had covered him, and that he was concerned because his girlfriend was with him and could see it. He could not recall why he felt it necessary to clip the news item about it, but now he understood that. He could also understand now about being so inordinately interested in crime reporting. The beard had him horrified and fascinated.

"You mean I was shaving his beard? This dead guy's beard?"

I can see how that would be disconcerting, and what answer could I have for that? He was also angry about the cocaine, which he still had in his body. And the cigarettes, which he was still somewhat addicted to. And just exactly who was dancing with his girl at the prom ... and kissing her? I deferred his queries by explaining that dwelling on details would piddle away the power of the healing. In essence, it would be mind-fucking and possibly create doubts. But later on, out of Roger's presence, this offered us some interesting riddles. The fact is, I have learned from some of the exorcisms I've performed that our bodies do respond to the possessor's mind. Thus, if you become possessed by a smoker, you become addicted to the nicotine. This is an area which can be mind-boggling. I further believe a certain number of people are committing suicide because of the severe depression brought on by a possession. Are some possessing entities addicted to dying? Why not? It could be a high for them.

There are a growing number of psychologists and psychiatrists who specialize in exorcisms—or depossessions. If you think about it, such intrusions are likely rampant these days. When I consider that, I become tired and my body responds with anxiety, as it reacts to all the work in this area. Beware the practitioner who does not "heal" the dead person, for that is just placing him or her out there to do it again. Any real healer must take the possessing spirit somewhere best for it, then heal the possessed. It's also about maintaining sacred balance.

Hallucinations

Pete had been to a Halloween party, in the high desert of Southern California. There was alcohol, some marijuana, cocaine, and some LSD. Oops. Pete partook of the acid, became uncomfortable with the trip he was experiencing, and decided to walk home. Never mind that he was close to twenty miles from home. And it was Halloween. Halloween, or Samhain in the old Religion, is a New Year and the sacred time wherein the curtain between life and death is at its sheerest.

As he walked through the desert that night, he found that he had become a wolf and began creeping on all fours. After a time, he realized that he was a werewolf and continued to creep, but on his feet and hands, rather than knees—it may have saved his ability to walk thereafter. He made it home the following morning. After getting to a rural home and becoming more himself, he was able to phone his mother to come pick him up. She brought him to me when I hit town again.

What a mess. Pete had continued to behave strangely—even *he* found himself strange. This was not Pete's first experience with LSD, not by a longshot, but it was the most physically harmful and had the most residual problems.

As I journeyed for him, I found him in the desert, creeping along through the night—in the form of a large, black wolf with a humanoid face. After observing this for a time, to gain information (I always do this—for the client and for other similar situations in the future), I met with Pete's soul and spirit helpers. They were quiet and appeared depressed, even confused. Well, to a lesser degree, so was I. The werewolf experience had actually occurred.

I then went to my teachers and sources of information, where I was informed that *whenever we hallucinate, it becomes real.* Any hallucinogenic experience morphs into psychological, emotional, spiritual, and physical reality. What can change that? Certainly, psychotherapy can cover it up some, but it continues to exist, this reality—if nowhere else, in the body, in that physical memory. *Nothing we experience is ever lost or removed. Whether it is real in terms of ordinary reality does not matter. It finds its place in our cellular makeup. It remains our reality—even into death.*

There is a reason to think it over prior to ingesting hallucinatory drugs, or even alcohol. It is ironic that a generation which is so wrapped up in control and controlling its environment and individuality is also so quick to ingest LSD or marijuana, so taken with cocaine and alcohol—each such instance bringing with it the possibility of a complete altering of reality, even to leaving this spatial reality altogether. And, thinking about it, look at the humans who have done so. The streets are filled with them, as are our mental hospitals. The street people we fear because they are so "out there" are in their own reality—likely brought upon by being flung into it by a specific "trip."

So what can we do about it, once it has occurred? I entered Pete's past and helped him come to terms with the werewolf who had controlled him that night. It's still there, and always will be, but he has controlled the situation, much as anyone who has experienced a serious trauma does. Once any of us controls and consciously rearranges a past trauma, we have healed it. It is still there, we will always suffer some pain, fear, whatever, but we are no longer victims of the action.

Changing History

Joyce had been coming to all of the workshops I had offered in Honolulu during two of my trips. She was now before me for a session. We talked for some time. She hoped to be relieved of persistent migraine attacks. They started when she was in her early twenties, shortly following the birth of her daughter. She had been to every doctor possible and was currently seeing a psychologist who specialized in chronic pain.

I journeyed for Joyce and her soul showed me clearly that the root of her pain and other problems was the rape of her by a friend's grandfather when she was about seven years old. I told her this. And she wept, shaking all over, all these years afterward.

"Yes, my psychologist and I have been working on that for over a year, but we seem to get nowhere with it. I'm desperate. It seems that that old man continues to rape me, even now."

"I suggest that I combine hypnosis and shamanism and see if we can't just alter what has happened to you," I said. "Would you feel more comfortable with a friend present, or your psychologist?"

"Yes, I think I would. Can we schedule for tomorrow night?"

We did. There were two friends and the psychologist, a man who made it clear that he was not only a skeptic, but he expected to have a boring evening, watching me make a fool of myself.

"Well," I said, "at least with you present, we can be assured that I will do no harm. I assume that if I get close to harming your patient you will step in?"

"You bet I will. I just don't believe that you can do anything, much less harm her. This is ..."

"Bullshit?"

"Crudely put."

"Shamans have never been prized for their finesse," I said.

I placed Joyce into a light to medium hypnotic trance and tried to get her to "find" the day that her problem began. She kept coming up with little traumas of her childhood and teen years. I nicknamed them "cookies" and dumped each one as she brought it up. Finally, she got around to the day of the rape. I glanced at the shrink, who made a big deal out of yawning.

"We've already been here," he said.

"I know. She told me. Be patient," I said.

"Joyce, let's relive the day," I suggested.

"Don't want to."

"Do you want your headaches to continue?" I asked.

"No."

"Then, let's get on with this. Enough fooling around," I said, getting stern.

We went back to the day. I had Joyce describe it first from the point of view of herself at that time, then as she was today.

Gramps took the two little girls to a park, sent his grandchild on an errand and raped Joyce in the backseat of his car. When I hypnotize people, I am able to see what is going on. This can be a real advantage ... as well as ugly.

As Joyce's sobs subsided, I suggested to her that she return to that scene as the woman she is today. I would accompany her. Okay? We went back there. We both described what was taking place. There was the old man. Ugly old thing. The brown sedan. The other little girl went off on her errand. Joyce began abreacting, so I reminded her that this time I was there with her, and she was now a powerful woman who could save the little girl that she once was. She calmed.

The old man had little Joyce in the backseat and was pulling off her panties.

"Now, Joyce, let's go," I said. "We are dragging that old s.o.b. off her. Let's throw him into the gutter. Good. Now, you pick up the little girl. Take her in your arms, brush her hair back from her face. Good. Let's take her up this little hill under that tree."

We placed little Joyce in the shade of a tree with a Raggedy Ann doll. We both assured her that she was safe and that big Joyce would be right back and would take care of her. And then we returned to the old man.

"Okay, Joyce, what shall we do with him?" I asked.

"I don't know. Can he go away?" she said.

"Joyce, you're a very nice lady," I said. "But this is the time to be nasty. This man rapes little girls. What should be done with him?"

"Well, he should be hung," she said.

"Okay. Get his attention, first," I said. "Call him some names."

"Hey, nasty old man," she said.

"No, Joyce, call him what you really think of him as."

"You son-of-a-bitch," she shouted.

"Is that the best you can do?" I asked. "This man is the scum of the earth. He does not deserve to breathe. He ... rapes ... little ... girls! I hate the motherfucker!"

"I do, too," she said, stronger. "You filthy bastard!" She began to shout, now. "You child-raping fucker, you cock-sucking son-of-a-bitch!

You deserve the worst possible death. You aren't fit to be on this earth ..."

The psychologist looked shocked.

As Joyce began to run out of steam, I suggested that we kill the man. "Want to?" I asked.

"Oh yes," Joyce breathed. "I hate him so much. But how can I ..."

"Well, how would you kill him?"

"I'd castrate him, and I'd stuff them in his nasty mouth," she snarled.

"Do it."

And she did.

I described it as it took place, to strengthen the memory within her. "You are virtually tearing him limb from limb, Joyce. There is blood everywhere. He cries piteously, but you have no pity. There, he's lying in his own blood on the backseat where he would have raped you."

Joyce was panting from effort.

"Joyce, we can't leave him there. We gotta get rid of him."

"How?"

"Well, let's let time take care of it," I suggested. "Watch him decompose, now. And crumble. The car is rusted, the tires flat, the springs sticking out of the seats. Now, the car is actually caving in, there is little left of his skeleton. Now, there are only a few pieces left of the car. Shall we have some kids steal those?"

"Yes."

"There is only a little spot left on the pavement," I noted.

"He's gone," she breathed.

"Hey, Joyce, we have to take care of the little girl," I said.

"Did she see this?"

"No, she was playing there with her doll all this time. But you promised to take care of her," I said.

We went back to the child and Joyce took her in her arms and walked away from the park with her.

"What shall I do with her," she asked?

"Hand her to me," I said, "and return here to this room in this time."

In a few moments, I brought up the misty blue light in the palm of my hand which was the essence of that little girl, her soul, if you will.

"Joyce, image your life today, the best parts—your husband and kids, your home, your abilities, your strength, the power you feel from killing that old man's memory."

As she did so, I "blew" the essence over to Joyce and it entered her body. She just glowed as she was reunited with herself.

I do not believe in inner-child psycho-babble, but this may be similar to that, albeit far more tangible. As we discussed what took place, I urged Joyce to work with child Joyce, to have a room, read books, to discuss with her on a daily basis her strengths and self-power. But I cautioned her to help young Joyce grow up healthy and quickly. In short, to reintegrate.

The psychologist was upset because he felt that this work encourages people to deny what occurs. And I have heard that all too frequently. I believe that we are altering the past by changing how we feel about it, our reality. Just as hallucinations become our reality, so can this sort of experience. Joyce still recalls the rape. But she also recalls how she trashed the rapist and disallowed it to happen.

Whatever the case, her migraines ceased.

In these cases, I am careful to replace the space left by the intrusion. If not, then the client is wide open for someone or something else. Any empty space is filled quickly.

The floor of the Cosmos is filled with countless cracks through which all sorts of things can and do fall. It is up to us to ensure, as best we can, that nothing we work upon does so.

Chapter 5
The Dead and Dying

The couple had invited me and a few other people to their apartment to see if I could help them with some unusual events they'd been living with.

"Nothing evil or even tiresome," said Sheryl, "but we've come to believe something kind should be done for this, if possible, and everyone we've talked to has mentioned you."

"Thanks," I said. "What seems to be going on? And ... I know some of these people, but who are we all?"

We were all introduced around. Some of those present had been involved in what I called at that time my Tupperware seances. I'd been doing these for people who got a group of no more than ten or twelve together; we'd meet and I would go about the circle and bring in dead folks for those present. Some amazing stuff had been happening, too. But this work had been helping me to increase my mediumship and to control it better; my skills had grown considerably performing like this with like-minded people.

As we sat down in this lovely apartment, I asked Sheryl if she could describe some of the activity there which seemed out of place. She took her husband's hand and together they told me of childlike whimpers, scents, and even touches.

"Especially on Sundays, huh?"

"Exactly. You got it. It's like living with a toddler. We both experience the same sorts of things, so it's not just my imagination. Sure, I want to get pregnant soon, and I think baby thoughts all the time, but that's not what's going on."

Pete chimed in, "We decided to get help with this because it seems cruel to have this baby here, when it seems to want love so much. Just not right. We have a lot of love to give a baby, but this one isn't ... real, I guess."

"Oh, it's real, but not easily hugged," I noted. "Let's get busy."

I began my pacing as I started to "go fishing." The apartment was quite spacious and well-lit from skylights, a very clean and well-kept two-story. It's often easier to work in a clean space than a cluttered, badly kept one—it seems that mess distracts the work somehow. I went upstairs and simply walked about, feeling the rooms, walls, ceilings, as I opened myself for contact with the baby.

"Oh, the poor baby!" I cried out. The child flooded into my body and mind ... and heart. "He is about a year-and-a-half old and is being terribly abused and neglected. Both. I can't stand this!"

I stopped, calming myself but still keeping the boy with me.

"I can smell the filth, and ..."

"This place had to be completely redone inside," Pete told us. "The folks before us had trashed it big time. I understand there were feces on the walls, rotten food and, well, you get the idea. Holes in the walls, carpet ruined, broken windows. Amazing for an apartment of this type."

"The baby has infected sores all over him, and he's so very thin ... the odor is horrific, and he wants so much to be held. He's been cold all his little life. Wants to be held. Wants to be held." I was beginning to cry as my arms ached to hold the toddler.

"You've heard him, and it comes from his room and sometimes even the kitchen, where he's hoping to find some food or crumbs on the floor. And he comes to your room and pulls at the blankets on your bed to get your attention. That's what you've noticed so much. And it's so very sad in here. I noticed that when I entered the apartment. The deep sadness."

Others in the room nodded to that. Some were weeping and sniffling. We passed around the tissues. Spirit rescue is always very emotional, but a baby ...!

I took a sip of my drink and rejoined the little one, lifting him onto my lap despite the stench, which now all were noticing. His little hands clutched at me, both outside and inside. So afraid. "Baby, I won't let you be alone ever again," I murmured, holding him even closer. "We're going to fix you up and get you some good munchies and you'll never be lonely or cold or hungry again."

I carried the baby into my meadow and down to the stream, as he dangled his hand in the tall grasses we passed through and made child sounds. At the stream, I sat in the water with him on my lap and bathed him in the healing waters there. As I did so, I kept everyone present by verbally describing what we were doing. It is a lovely thing that, whenever I do this type of work, the living who are helping me also experience the emotion of the thing. All have reported to me that, even slightly before I verbalized what was going on, they knew it and had vivid pictures of the action.

Soon, I picked him up and crossed the stream to the Land of the Dead. What to do? I can't just drop this baby off and assume someone will take him under their wing. I looked about, and for the first time, met the Illusion (?) I've worked with so often now. Is it an illusion or a reality? I think now that it is both: perhaps an illusion which is real. So much of what I do is like that. Just doesn't bear any kind of human explanation. What I do know is that it is completely real to me and the dead I'm healing. And it works.

Just before us, I spied a small garden/magic forest with a clearing in the center. As we moved closer, this lovely smelling child with bright alert eyes and busy fingers and I, we saw a lovely woman all in blue and a handsome prince in the clearing, seated upon a throne. There were bunnies, fawns, and all sorts of small animals about, romping together. All stopped and gazed at us as we approached the garden.

The woman looks like the fairy godmother in Pinocchio! The prince is handsome, young, and well, charming. I walked into the magic garden and the woman reached up for the baby boy, who immediately went to her. I was almost sorry to have to relinquish him. The prince bent over him and spoke softly. The baby sat on her lap and played with her earrings as she smiled with her incredibly loving and gentle face.

"I am leaving the garden. Looking back, I see the baby on her lap with a little brown bunny, his fingers moving through its soft fur with such glee. He doesn't even see me anymore. As I move back toward this apartment, the prince smiles to me once and then returns to the baby. I'm back," I announce.

As I opened my eyes, looking about me through my tears, I saw that all were crying and smiling. The room was filled with the scent of baby powder.

The dead and living are separated by a layer of near nothingness—it is rather dark, much as a flight at night. Crossing this non-barrier takes perseverance and desire, for one is discouraged from being in the required state, seemingly weakened, helpless—an uncomfortable situation for both living and dead. To talk with the dead, both parties must be willing to enter this "no-man's land" and to cross it. Not just willing, but to have that perseverance, a certain sort of strength to endure the apparent nothingness. I suspect that many dead cannot hold the purpose to follow through. This meeting must be the result of *two* people moving toward a mutual goal. The medium cannot do this alone, as cannot the dead ... although either one might instigate the meeting and be the stronger of the two involved. It is a matter of *two decisive wills*.

Thus, the appearance of a "ghost"—a dead who intrudes upon the living without invitation—must be extremely emotional, neurotic, or even psychopathic in order to effect the intrusion, resulting in an off-balance contact. What a superhuman effort it must take. A "spirit" is different from the ghost phenomena in that it is dead (well usually—we have all met up with living spirits, but I will not include those here) yet does not seem to be disturbed. Communication is still a struggle for both but seems smoother. This may be the dead person who has a specific message or desire to communicate with a loved one. Or—and this is most usual—the living asks me to contact the spirit, commonly for reassurance of his/her continuance and well-being. However, to return to ghosts, this is not the same as the "ghost" or ghostly activity which repeats itself over and over. That would be within the realm of unconscious memory, a non-intelligent repetition of events imprinted on the very environment, such as in the case of Justus, below.

A determined medium may enter into that scenario/memory to effect a "rescue," putting to an end the memory, healing the aberration, or at least beginning the healing and leading the "ghost" to the appropriate "space" for such healing. The environment then experiences an immediate and dramatic cessation of activity, also "healed."

Perhaps the medium finds it easier to enter such a situation if she is in a state of mental illness herself at that time. Again, emotion is essential in order to cross that span of darkness to meet. Apparent mental illness is certainly emotional. This is where being Shaman is useful, in that shamans are irrational beings, dwelling in irrationality at all times while dwelling within the rational world that is expected.

I have heard horror stories all my life about people living in houses built over old Indian burial grounds. Ooooh. Well, get a grip. There are a lot of dead out there, and most of their bodies are in the ground, somewhere, and the likelihood of one or more being beneath you is quite good. In this country, it's likely to be Native Americans, since they lived and died here a lot. And let's not forget the pioneers who died, and ... well, just everybody who died over the past several hundred years.

But still, those Indian burial ground stories ... Nope. I have met very, very few ghosts from shamanic cultures. There was always a shaman to take the spirit over to the proper place, you see. Then Christianity came along, and ministers declared that if a person "believed" their way, then they would automatically go to the right place for them. Personally, I have met up with only two Native American ghosts.

One is an Apache medicine man who remains for a specific reason: to protect a certain parcel of land in southeastern Arizona. He wears deer antlers and carries an odd-sounding rattle. Once he realized why I was in his area, he and I got along well. He is protective and demands respect for this parcel which has great meaning for his people. Since he is working, I do not consider him to be a ghost but instead an energy which has purpose. After interacting with him for a few years, I got him in touch with an Apache woman and my work in the area was over.

The other Native American ghost—well that is another story. The call came from a couple who owned a big home up in the Catalina Foothills of Tucson. Nice place, nice homes, nice view. They were trying to sell their house, but no one would buy it. It was haunted. They had tried exorcists and a priest, and now they were ready to try me. Once at the house, I initially found the essence of the woman's father, who moved through the place smoking his pipe, trailing a nice smell of good tobacco behind him. But a ghost? No, I wouldn't call him that—just a fond memory, an essence, non-intrusive. We walked outside to the patio. Hello. Here it is.

Walking back and forth rapidly to bring up my energy to match that of the ghost, I brought the dead man in. To my surprise, he was Native American. He was confused and unhappy, but glad to be recognized at last. Recently, he had been invited in by people placing salt about the place, in the windows and such. Salt is a cross-cultural gift of the highest order, but for some odd reason it is used by bumbling exorcists and parapsychologists to banish ghosts. What an odd notion. Then the same person ordered him out. What do they want?

His tribe was one of the tribes which had settled along the Santa Cruz River that runs through Tucson. At one time, the river was a large, constant-flowing watercourse. Near that river, his tribe flourished, and close to that was the entrance to the UnderWorld, a *sipapu*. By the way, this *sipapu* still exists; it was found near the place shown to me in this work, and proposed construction in that area has been stopped because of its presence.

This man was a tool and weapon maker of some renown. He had been married and fathered two babies. Then, one day, while he was out seeking stone to work with, he was taken by a warlike band of other native people. They knew of him and desired his power of tool making, which is highly valued always. They felt that the best way to obtain that power was to slowly kill the owner of it, trapping his soul and taking the power, ingesting it, so to speak. This they did. The man was placed into a trunk-sized box after being slashed by knives. He lived for days and days in that box, as the maggots ate him through those cuts. His lasting fears and concerns were for his wife and children and the fact that he would never find rest or join them in the UnderWorld because he was kept away from the *sipapu*.

He drifted in that area for many, many years. Then people came and began digging in the earth there. They dug a deep hole at this house, just a few feet from his death site, and filled it with water. A *sipapu* by a river! He had been there ever since, becoming more and more insistent that he be allowed entrance to the UnderWorld so that he might find and be reunited with his family and tribe.

I showed the man who I am and told him I would take him back to the village and the *sipapu* where his family and clan exited this world. He wept for joy. We flew across Tucson that night, and as I went, I collected bones from trash cans. Once at the site of his village, by the river, which is now dry except during the rainy seasons, I formed an outline of his body in the sand of the wash; he reclined into it and gently sank into Mother Earth.

While this was going on, the family cat jumped into my lap, and I absently stroked him as I finished with my spirit rescue. Upon returning fully, I found the couple staring at the cat and me with amazement. He had not let a human touch him in months. They were convinced. They also had witnessed the cat follow the dead man with its eyes. And they had all been aware of the presence and highly charged emotion of this action. The house still did not sell because they decided to stay.

This was a rare case of a Native American who had not had the services of a shaman at death. I am unsure why the tribal shaman did not take him over *in absentia*. But there it is.

Belief Systems

Religion fears death and the dead. I cannot count the times I have had quoted to me, "Let the dead bury the dead." Now, I take that to refer to the living dead, of which there are many. Religion tells its followers to come to the church for comfort when things are bad. When they do, after death, frightened and lost, they are told to get out. Where is the comfort? Where is the love of God? Compassion? Further, we have many dead people who don't like that condition, and so they take over or partially inhabit living people. Even though they have not behaved well, they should be healed by taking them to the appropriate space/place for their situation and belief system. Exorcism and every "ghost-busting" should be performed in a healing mode.

Can I heal every lost dead person existing? Absolutely not! I have taken over large groups, thousands at a time. Even so, I would have no time for anything else. How very many humans have lived on this planet!

There are also the gray/beige people. That is what I call the souls who hang around, whining for help. They are needy in the psychological sense. And in that sense, they will not help themselves and, often when helped, return for more sympathy and attention. I have had to heal living people who were being drained by these dead gray/beige people. They seem to be attracted to colorful, talented, and charismatic people. I have no patience with them.

There are the dead people who believe in Purgatory or the like. It is their belief; therefore, they go there and are "punished" for their sins. What a waste, since such a space exists only for those who feel they require such treatment. We must take these folks into their belief system. That is ultra-important. One is not likely to get anywhere when one begins arguing religion with a dead person! One man I accompanied over believed in nothing. And that's where I ended up with him—in nothingness. Indescribable and most difficult to escape. Blah.

As usual, a word of caution about dealing with the dead. I am afraid of ghosts. Really afraid. At least when I'm not working with them. I am cautious about teaching people to work with ghosts. Yes, we must have compassion. However, we forget that ghosts are just dead people, and people come in all kinds. As I have said, most ghosts have mental problems, and I'm uncomfortable with living psychopaths, much less an incorporeal one which has fewer limits to govern behavior.

Further, we must not allow our compassion to overcome our practical natures. A woman who studied with me for years became obsessive about "saving" ghosts. Her home was opened to them, her husband and children harassed by the dead. I was there often to clear the home. Her response to me when I remonstrated with her was that it was her Christian duty to help those poor souls. It was tantamount to giving away food her children needed to eat.

If you want to work with the dearly departed on a grand scale, re-read "Chapter 8: Danger, Judgment, and Protection." Then read it again. Do not call me in the middle of the night when you're in over your head. Heh, heh.

Again, most of a shaman's work is with the dead. This is not out of a sense of morbidity but of naturalness. We meet things through a different doorway than most humans—neither better nor worse, just different. The dead are people, just incorporeal. I enjoyed working briefly with law enforcement to find lost people and dead people. It's satisfying to help in such helpless situations. However, the foolish opposition I have run into in law enforcement makes it impossible for me to, in short, waste my time with them. I have worked a little with private investigators, but I have not pursued this avenue out of a lack of mobility and time. Let's face it: most investigators will not come to the mountain.

Another "death" area which is interesting to an unattached shaman is that of haunted houses or people. There are many psychotherapists now who can capably exorcize patients, and that's great. But few people truly treat possessed buildings. Here's a church I removed a dozen lost and disenfranchised beings from.

Hauntings

We drove into the darkened parking lot early for our appointment there. This church was on the edge of town, amid the beautiful desert foliage, high enough to look down on the city lights. I had been contacted not by the pastor himself but through one of the board members, who also requested that this be kept very secret.

The church buildings and grounds were all haunted. Some felt it was one being; others thought it might be more than one, perhaps two or three. This was going to be fun. I also looked forward to working with an open-minded pastor. Hopefully, this one would not ask me to leave his church.

When we had all gathered, there was the pastor, the board member and his wife, the business manager/accountant, my apprentice, and myself. We entered the church at the vestibule, and stood talking while trying to warm ourselves from the cold desert winter night. The talk was stilted, since all but two of us were pretty uncomfortable with the very idea of tonight's work.

We got down to business.

"This must be kept confidential," the pastor commented, "not only from the parishioners, but it must not get back to the bishop. I have gone to him for help regarding at least one of these disturbances, requesting a church exorcism, but he has ordered that I put a hold on that until we pray and do all we can. He will be here next month to make the final decision."

"How do you feel about that?" I asked, sensing that he was unhappy about the way his concerns were being treated.

"Not good. I have read over the church exorcism ritual, and it seems adversarial to me. I believe these phenomena to be cries for help. I do not feel that they are evil demons."

Good. "We are in agreement, then," I smiled. "What about the rest of you? Where do you stand on this? I just want to know who I am working with here, and what sort of attitude you are laying onto the space here."

The board member was all right. He had heard of my work previously and knew that it would not be anything overly dramatic and that I have a reputation for respect. The accountant seemed to be harrumphing in his mind, but he was honest.

"I don't see that you can do anything about this. I mean, why should you be able to? You're not a priest, or even a member of the church. Why should these spirits listen to you? But I am working on keeping an open mind. Truth is I hope you succeed. You seem very likeable, and the bishop isn't. I also do not approve of his attitude and agree with our pastor that the church's official approach will be hostile. I just do not see that that is necessary here."

"Sounds good," I said. "Okay, first of all, the entire place is active. But one would expect that of a church. The church tells people to come here when they are troubled, so I am sure that many are here, but they are incorporeal. Most are not terribly upset, however, just probably enjoying the good "vibes" they find here. Not pests, just here. Since we have only one lifetime, as well as one night, let's leave them alone, okay?"

Agreement all around.

"How about a tour? We'll go fishing."

The pastor turned and took us into the sanctuary. It was modern and simple and lovely, big windows bringing nature into worship. I went immediately to one window, where I could plainly see the dusty imprint of a small owl which had crashed into it. We looked, but it had apparently been able to fly off afterward. Glass windows are treacherous for birds day and night.

I sat down in the middle of a pew toward the back. The lights were off, except the small sanctuary lamp and the outside lights, making it seem even more as if we were outside. But there was someone in here.

"Father Don, please tell me what goes on during services. Apparently, they are being disrupted? And even when not disrupted, you and others are often distracted by the appearance of something in here?"

"Exactly," Father Don answered. "Very good, it appears most often at eleven o'clock services ... oh, and at evening services when we have them. How much shall I tell you?"

"Not much. I think I have her. It's a woman. And I bet you suspect you know who it is, right?"

"That's right," Father said. "I just have not discussed her with you because you told George that it was best if you came in cold, right?"

"Yes. But I have her now. And we can now communicate freely ... as freely as you wish. I don't want you to 'give' it all away, since this first one is somewhat of a test for you all to judge me. She died in a hospital but not of sickness. Oh, oh. She committed suicide. Depressed woman. Chronically. Many doctors, many attempts to cure her. Three youngish children, impatient husband." I had my head down in my hands. I turned to the pastor, "You were impatient."

"Yes," he conceded. "I tried not to be, but I'm not very good at working with depressed women. My honest response is to shake them a bit and tell them to wake up. And I realize that is not what is needed. My mind tells me that it is a physical problem, chemical disorder, a real disease, but my male reactions are poor for this sort of thing."

He's honest! "Have you considered putting together a group of parishioners who would specialize at counseling and supporting chronically depressed people? Perhaps those who are dealing successfully with it will help."

"A great idea." He chuckled. "Probably another secret to keep from the bishop."

I knelt. Well, I think she knelt and my body did the same. She was in my body, after all. She was weeping.

"She walks back and forth throughout the sanctuary during parts of the services, crying. Can you ever hear it? And she moves like this, which is what you can see."

I paced around the room, swinging my arms from time to time, holding my hands to my head and to my chest. It was a very distinctive set of movements.

"Yes, that's it!" Father Don nearly shouted.

The board member was astonished, for he soon admitted that he had been aware of the "air around the room" doing that sometimes. It was such that he had thought he was hallucinating or his eyes were tired. His wife, however, said she had seen it all many times and had even heard the faint weeping sounds.

I was on a roll. "And a faraway voice calling out names you could not make out?"

"Yes!" she exclaimed. "I would even come in here when I was present for meetings to see if I could re-experience it. It is the saddest thing I have ever heard."

I agreed. "It is sad. She killed herself but was not wholly responsible, since she was quite ill, and I judge that she could not know exactly what she was doing or what it would mean afterward. I can guarantee you, Father that this woman wanted back into that body the same instant she left it. If she had been able to under any circumstance, she would have re-entered, even if it meant being a vegetable the remainder of her days."

Father Don smiled sadly, "I thought so, and that is why I gave her conditional absolution and buried her in consecrated ground. The bishop and I ..."

"I know. That man has to stick to canon law, doesn't he?" I said sympathetically. This man has a hard row to hoe in his parish. "Let me explain what has happened here, and if you will, I would like you to work with me to help rescue this poor woman. There is definitely help waiting for her, and we can heal her. But I think that the two of us, working together, will be best for her."

"Absolutely," Father Don nodded. "Shall I get my scapular?"

I nodded. "Please do so quickly, if you can I don't want to lose her."

While Father was gone, I communicated further with the woman, soothing her and promising her that help and healing were there for her tonight. No more lonely grief and guilt.

Father returned, placed his scapular about his neck and sat on the pew, fully attentive.

"I'll do this aloud so that we can all participate. If any of the rest of you wish to pray or even adopt the attitude of prayer, please do. She will appreciate it."

"Oh, and what's her name?"

"Patricia Ma- ..."

"Just the first name please, Patricia? Yes, she's here and close. In fact, she's hovering over my apprentice, Sorba. I believe she may enter you, Sor."

"Yes, she is; I can feel her etheric—cool and misty and part of it is in here. Oh, oh. So is her memory. Poor, poor woman."

I would now address Patricia in Sorba. "Patricia, the church promised to always be here for you, right?"

Sorba's head nodded.

"But you have come over and over, begging for help and they have not noticed, right?"

"I even came with my husband and children to worship, but no one noticed. They would not speak with me." Sorba's voice, Patricia's delivery. It was soft, hesitant, and seemed to expect to be turned out once again.

"Patricia, they noticed, but they did not understand your situation. They care, but they did not know how to help you. Father Don is here to help you, now. And he's sorry it has taken so long."

"That's right, Patricia," Father's voice startled me. "I am here to give you whatever help you need to find peace."

Couldn't have said it better myself. "Patricia, do you understand that you are dead?"

"I think so. It's very confusing. Yes, I remember ... oh, no, I killed myself! I shall go to hell!"

"No, no, Pat." Father Don was rising from the pew. "You are buried in consecrated ground and receive masses every week for the delivery of your soul. Please. Wait and hear what this woman has to tell you. We will work it out, I promise."

What a nice minister to people.

"Patricia, you were very, very sick when you died. What took your life does not matter now because you were not responsible for your actions. It was an accident, a terrible one. People miss your presence. But we all pray for you to be able to go on to someplace better. Father Don is here to provide you the healing and the forgiveness you crave so that you can be free. Be at ease. Let us help you. You are worth it."

It became calm in the sanctuary. Sorba murmured to me that it was gentler within her also.

"Patricia, let Father speak with you at last. He didn't see you before, but he can now. He just needed a little help."

Father Don asked, "Patricia, do you know that you received Extreme Unction and conditional Forgiveness?"

She did not.

"You did, my dear. Your children and Pete are beginning to move on, to rebuild their lives, and I know they would want you to do the same. They miss you and speak of you often, but they would want you to be free of your suffering."

"Father," Sorba said lowly, "she is ready to go, now. She accepts your words as truth. Oh, one last question ... will I be accepted in Heaven?"

"Yes, yes, child. Heaven awaits you. Go with this woman here. I shall meet you when it is my turn to join you there."

Sorba and I took Patricia down to the river, bathed her clear of her "sins" and feelings of unworthiness. She emerged radiant, looking ahead. Since she was Christian, we had the Blessed Mother and Her Son waiting to receive her there. I let go of her hands as she moved toward her new existence. Safe and sound. In the right place. Forgiven and worthy to go.

I turned and saw that all three men were teary-eyed. It is a very emotional experience to witness this sort of work, spirit rescue. That says it all.

Soon, we entered the vestibule once again, just to talk. This rescue was the main agenda as far as Father was concerned. His sanctuary was peaceful and still again. But as we talked, I felt something coming in through another door. I turned to the accountant at my right and asked if it made him uncomfortable.

"Yes, I don't know why, but I feel afraid," he admitted.

I placed my medicine blanket around his shoulders. "There, that should stop it," I told him.

He told me later that that was the moment he knew I was legitimate, because the "touching and poking" and hair-raising fear left immediately. It was something tangible that he could use as confirmation.

"Father," I caught his attention. "We have more here, at least two in here and a nasty one outside."

We proceeded with the work. The first was a woman—a sister from the convent about a half mile from the church. It was a tooth-cruncher. She had not been a sister long. In fact, she had not considered the religious life until her father raped and impregnated her. She miscarried late in the pregnancy, and her father placed her into the convent, informing her that she had to enter there since there was no life outside for such a bad girl. She died not long afterward during a cholera epidemic. But why was she still here?

Upon death, she began her trek over to the other side, but she saw her father's spirit there awaiting her. He had died during the epidemic, just prior to her death. Seeing him waiting there, she feared crossing over. He was still watching her with a purely evil intent! She stayed here. Many people had reported seeing this woman's shade alongside the busy street which passed by this convent.

Seeing this filthy human being waiting for his daughter, I rushed across the stream, grabbed him, and trashed his spirit. All my outrage exploded against this horror. Not only had he tortured his daughter in life, but here he was, waiting to torture her even more! This was true evil. Once daddy dearest was gone, I found the image of Our Lady and brought the little sister to Her. As I returned to this life, she was being bathed in roses and embraced in holy love.

The other was a man who had died when this was all desert, probably also of cholera. He died without benefit of the church and craved to be shriven. Father Don, his scapular still over his shoulders, seated himself, the ghost kneeling before him, and forgave him all his sins in God's name. Poof! Another dead person healed and gone.

Outside, I learned that two of the men present had heard gravel-crunching footsteps following them to their cars following a nighttime meeting on several occasions. This one was not a human ghost. We walked around, looking for a focal point from which to begin our work on this one.

It was a circle of benches around a giant saguaro cactus—a place for kids to have bonfires and meetings, a place where people renewed their marriage vows sometimes. Mass had even been said here. But this Thing liked it here, too ... evil is always attracted to power of any kind.

We entered the circle and sat on the benches. The Thing came from very long ago. I stood and began walking quickly counterclockwise around the circle. Upon the third lap, the wind suddenly came up. By the eighth lap, it was howling, the saguaro actually weaving above us in the wind. I went back in time in this manner and contacted the entity. It was just something that did not belong here, in this time. It had little consciousness. Almost an elemental, and I warned everyone that this one could be troublesome. It would still be safe, but they must all be alert and on their toes. If they didn't feel they could do this, then please step out of the circle. Two did.

I took the entity back to its time. Walking counterclockwise in the circle, reversing time, I created the "door" to its previous home. As I collected it from 1994, it became "hostile" and the wind howled. Father Don's scapular flew from his shoulders, high into the air, but the others outside the circle were able to catch it because it was so long. They also reported to us that it was merely breezy where they were, only feet from us. Father's hair was blowing and we had the sand from underfoot stinging our legs.

Finally, I got the entity in through the portal—all of it—and shut the "door." The wind ceased immediately. It did not lessen first; it ceased. I turned, asked the others inside the circle to do the same, and paced clockwise around the circle twelve times to bring everything back to the present, including ourselves. It was quite peaceful.

We celebrated a good night's work by meeting at a nearby restaurant for pie and ice cream.

Medium Pizza

The Medium Pizza group met twice a month on Sunday evenings to evolve our abilities to work with the dead. We worked, then had pizza delivered in. The name also helped us to keep perspective. I balance serious work with silliness. We had some very interesting times.

Larry told me of a place he was working on in South Tucson, close to the Veteran's Administration Hospital, in which he could not work after dark. He was watched in the house, and felt very uncomfortable. How about Medium Pizza looking into it? We met there one Sunday evening. It was a nice little house, built prior to World War II, and although it had been added onto randomly, it still had charm found with old southwestern homes. We decided to do a run-through as soon as we got there and then meet back in the little room off the front.

Nothing obvious. Larry was in the midst of fixing up and repainting the place so that it could be rented out. New carpeting was rolled up, waiting to be laid when he was through with his work. That sort of thing. The kitchen yanked my psychic chain. Outside the back door got all of us, although we processed later that most of the energy we were dealing with had to do with drug use and family fights subsequent to why we were there. It isn't easy to tune. Each house, or even piece of land, holds memories of what has transpired there—the medium has to sift through to the pertinent part and time.

Returning to the front room, we all sat around the room on the floor. Speaking quietly, we exchanged our findings. Most of us agreed on what we experienced in there. We were "spiraling" in on the "haunt," when all of a sudden, I began choking.

It got worse. I felt the cord about my throat. I was being hung! Strangled! I pantomimed frantically as the group began guessing what was going on. I have found that the best approach for me with hauntings is to relive the death until someone present recognizes it and the dead person. That is what most dead people are seeking—recognition and validation.

Finally, as I was turning blue and could no longer keep my tongue in my mouth, Lorie shouted, "He was hung! He hung himself!"

I began breathing again. In a gravelly voice, I described the man's death.

"He did it in the kitchen, with an electrical wire. Cloth-covered, old fashioned. Ah, he was so sick. And he was addicted to ... morphine. He was a vet from the war. Oh, that's why he lived here—close to the VA. What's wrong? He only had one leg. He's Mexican-American. Wife left him. He's a nice guy, but feels unmanly, can't get a real job. The pain and the morphine combine to make him temperamental. He did this on a warm summer evening. In 1947, I think."

We joined together to take the man over safely. The men in the group were especially helpful in this case. They imaged and told him how they respected his life and what he did for his country. One of the women spoke in Spanish. We explained that these many years he had been here were Purgatory. That hooked him. It was certainly believable. All the things that man must have witnessed in his house during the interim—it must have seemed like Purgatory.

Finally, we took him to the Stream, bathed him, and I brought in the Blessed Virgin, in the form of Our Lady of Guadalupe, to come for him. Her radiance was warming; he floated up to her in a state of bliss, no longer even aware of us. And then he was gone. The house was empty of his sorrow and confusion.

We cleansed the placed with my Medicine Pipe, to soothe the energies there from its history. We picked up a pizza on our way to our meeting place, and had a ball.

I had bruises on my neck and throat, and my voice did not fully return for several days. Larry returned to finish work on the house, reporting that it was finished and actually visually lighter, as if the windows had been cleaned.

The Brothers

This story is hard because it does not have a happy ending as do most of my dead stories. Sam called one evening to see if I would contact a family member who had died very recently. I explained that I preferred not to contact dead people until they have had time to acclimate, but that I would consider it and call him back.

After contemplating the situation, I determined that it would be best to see Sam right away. Whomever he wanted to contact was anxious, and Sam sounded suicidal to me on the phone. I called and we set the appointment for the following evening. Sam was only eighteen years old.

As we chatted, preparatory to working, I told him I knew it was his brother he wanted to contact, that it was not a "normal" death, and that his brother was just a little older than he. Right on all counts, we began.

"Oh my god, my head," I nearly shouted. I traced a line from my left lower jaw line through my mouth, through the right eye and out the top of my head.

"He lost five teeth. You have four of them," I told Sam.

"Yes, I can't find the fifth," he was sobbing.

"It's inside his cranial cavity, in his brain, although the medical examiner has probably extracted it by now. Let it go," I advised, "it will be buried with him."

David had shot himself.

"My religion teaches that there is no life after death," Sammy told me. "I can't stand it if Davy doesn't still live somewhere!"

By now, I was clawing my arms frantically. It was awful. Later, I would find that both arms were bleeding from my scratching.

"What is this about? Why was he clawing at his arms?" I asked.

"Cocaine," Sam said. "He was on coke and it made him do that when he had too much. It's him, isn't it?"

"He's terribly tired. Awfully tired," I murmured. "Why is he so damn sleepy? Why don't you just sleep, David?"

"He had been awake for three days when he killed himself," Sam said. "It was the coke."

"He didn't die immediately," I said. "His heart and lungs continued until ... at the hospital."

"Yes, he was pronounced dead at the hospital, but he was brain dead before they got him there."

"There is a baby ... no, babies." I said, a little puzzled. "They feel like one baby."

"His wife is expecting twins in less than a month," he clarified for me.

By this time, Sam had proof that we were communicating with his brother. We moved onto some questions he had, but this part was unsatisfactory.

I explained: "Sam, your brother has only been dead for a few days. He needs time to collect himself and adjust to his new situation. We cannot expect him to be fully coherent tonight. In fact, this is why I seldom will make contact this soon. I only did it for you because I was concerned that you were suicidal."

"Well, you were right about that," Sam told me. "But I do feel better now that I am sure Davy still exists. A lot better."

"Good. Then I suggest you go and put your life together; help your sister-in-law and those babies which are a part of him. By the way, they are a boy and girl, and will have some real troubles they'll need a strong uncle for," I reminded him.

I saw Sam off, still clawing at my arms. When I entered the main part of the house, Larry took one look at me and said, "You were working with a coke head, huh?"

"He was. How do you know?"

"Clawing at your arms—a common symptom of overdose and last stages. I bet he died coked up."

"He did. How do I stop this?"

We sat quietly while Larry talked me down from the contact. We soothed my arms with aloe and they were fine in a few days.

Sam came back weeks later, following the birth of his niece and nephew. The family was not doing well; many of them were doing some drugs, including "legal" ones ingested by the mother. I met Shirley, David's wife; she was a mess, just not coping well, and expecting everyone around her to cope for her.

A year or so later, I got a call from Sam for another appointment. Something in his voice warned me off.

"I'm on cocaine," he confessed.

"I won't see you until you're through a rehab program, you know," I told him. "I have some numbers of people who can help ..."

"Nah, I feel closer to Davy when I'm tooted up," he said. "But I respect that you won't work with me like this."

Sam was living with his brother's widow, and wanted to marry her. He was wearing his brother's clothing. Living his life.

I said, "That's just a bit obsessive, Sam."

"I know, but I like it. I thought you would understand."

"Oh, I understand; I just don't think you should be behaving this way. Sam, it's time to get on with living," I pressed.

"Fuck it. I am living, and it's just the way I want to."

He called back a couple days later in a more amenable mood.

"If I go through rehab, will you see me again?"

"Of course, but don't do it just for that. You don't need me to live well," I said.

"Just hearing your voice, even on the answering machine, helps me feel closer to Davy and better."

"That is not a reason to call me." This was getting to me now. He was a nice guy; I really hoped he came out off this, but I felt pulled down.

"If I don't make it, I'll call you from time to time and just listen to the machine. I respect you too much to keep this up with you."

"Thank you, Sam. Good-bye, now."

There were hang-up calls, some of which I knew were him. Years later, he died. Too young, just like his brother.

A Murder

Larry was hanging up the phone as I came in from work one evening. I grabbed a soda and sat down. Judging from the look on his face, there was some trouble.

"That was my mother. Some friends of hers lost their daughter last week under odd circumstances, and ..."

"She was murdered by the guy she lived with," I rattled out. Sometimes, it just does that—catches me off guard and takes over.

"Well, that's what they fear happened. Do you want to help them?" he asked.

"Sure. If they are prepared to hear the truth," I said.

Sometimes, people think they want to know, but are not prepared, and it causes me to "choke" and temper the truth. It's a rough situation, and I have learned, the hard way, to always ask people if they are ready to hear the very worst. If so, I'll work with them—and hopefully, it is not the worst.

As it turned out, in this case, not only did Larry's mother contact them about me, but they had talked with some other people who recommended me. We did get together. There were three of them, plus my daughter, and Terrell, my hypnotist, who wanted to sit in on the session.

"He is possessive and basically a weak person, although he pretends strength. Young, I would say nineteen. She is seventeen, and is beginning to comprehend what she has gotten herself into with him. They share a small one-bedroom apartment in a cheap complex. He has been depressed, dark, always talking suicide—in fact, double suicide. But she doesn't feel that way. This has been going on for several days. I suspect he is doing some cocaine and drinking."

This much the family knows. I have asked them to tell me nothing. The deaths appear to be a double suicide, and because "they loved each other so much," according to the young man's family, they are buried side by side. I am ready to go on this.

And I am there quickly! A rush. The young woman is grateful to have her story known. As usual, whatever she "says" or shows to me, I say aloud for the family.

She finally gives in to her boyfriend and pretends to go along with the suicide one evening. She expects him to pass out or leave to get more alcohol or something before it goes very far. She's just worn down by the constant hammering she's been getting from him. But first, she tells him, she wants to get the dishes done from dinner, and the kitchen cleaned up. "She's a very neat person," I tell the family.

"Absolutely," her mother replies.

As she is in the kitchen, at the sink, the discussion—argument?—escalates. He continues to wave his .22 around and talk about dying together so that they can always be together. She half turns toward him.

"We're not going to be together at all if you don't clean up your act, get a new job, and stop this," she tells him.

She turns back to the dishes.

He walks up, puts his right arm around her, a beer can in his hand. As she tries to fend him off, he brings the .22 semi-automatic up to her head and fires it.

"He was left-handed," I say.

They agree.

He stands, looking down at her body on the floor by the sink, tries to think what to do, then drags her into the living room, where he leaves her on the floor, returning to clean up the kitchen. But he can hear her crying and moving about. She is not dead. It makes him nervous. He keeps cleaning things. He even goes outside and dumps the rags and paper towels into the dumpster. The police never even looked there!

He returns, finishes washing the dishes and leaves them to drain. She is still crying from time to time. There is not a lot of blood—it's because the bullet is lodged in her brain and has not passed through anything large. But she is trying to get back into her body. "I must get to her and explain that she cannot!" I cry. I actually experience the death of each person I contact. This is terrible.

"It causes her tremendous pain to keep crawling into that poor body," I say.

I went into the death scene and took her soul and showed her the set-up and held her and then showed her what was awaiting her "across the stream." She calmed.

"Now, he is placing her head upon a pillow—it's a pink one from the sofa. She has stopped moaning and moving, so he arranges her body as if she were sleeping. Now he sits next to her and shoots himself."

Once they had wept and settled down again, and I had pulled myself together, I asked the family if they needed more information to confirm that this was, indeed, the situation. They said no, that in fact, the bodies had been found in that condition.

"... with a pink sofa pillow beneath her head," her father said.

They did not know about the kitchen. I suggested that they have the police recheck the place. They said they would. What happened after that? I don't know. I'm not sure that it matters. The next time I was at that cemetery, I stopped by the young woman's grave—still next to his (cemetery lots are expensive and moving a grave very difficult and even more expensive)—and prayed a bit. I walked right across his grave.

Suicides

I have worked with a large number of suicides. It seems that their families come to people like me more often because suicide is such a painful thing for the survivors.

"Do they suffer for their sin?"

Sin, no, not any more than any of us suffer when we die for whatever we believe—but it also has to do with the reason for the suicide. Those who do so because of painful terminal diseases seem to do well after death. However, those who commit suicide because of financial worries or depression or "I'll show them,"—those people invariably want to undo it immediately, trying to crawl back into that dead, broken body—for they have found, in that moment, that death does not change anything.

If they were depressed enough to commit suicide, they will continue to be depressed after death. If they were worried about money, now they still worry about money, but also about their funeral expenses and the trouble they have left their loved ones with! If they want to "get even" or something on that order, they find they have not, for now they see the mess as it is, not as they had wanted to view it; and now, they feel guilty as well as all the rest. Nothing changes until we begin to change it, even after death. Only, once dead, it is even more difficult to resolve things with those we love—and have left.

Most religions insist that the ultimate evil is suicide. Thus, we are taught to despise our dear ones who do kill themselves. I hope we can let go of that kind of propaganda and feel more compassion for those who have killed themselves—and perhaps those who are contemplating suicide will stay and work things out in the physical world, rather than drag that over into their new lives.

A Ghost Story

There are so very many ways to lose one's way in death. Penny and her mom met me at a month-long seminar where I had been contracted to teach mediumship. After my lecture and demonstration, they approached me and asked if I could help their family with a problem. I spontaneously "brought in" a dead person for them.

"It has to do with someone not in your immediate family, but like an uncle. And a piece of property ... a store? In the South."

"Yes," said the mom. It concerns my husband's uncle who owned a liquor store in Alabama, and ..."

"Shall we meet tonight, after classes and dinner?" I asked.

We did so. The women came over to my motel room and I met Justus. It came fast and furious. It was even difficult to take the time to verbalize what was happening as it happened.

"I see the store. It's just off the main square of town, to the north, I think, of the court house. A side street."

"Yes."

"I'm entering the place. You have not been able to sell the store. It's been rented, but people break the lease and leave quickly," I said.

"Yes."

"Justus was murdered there. During a robbery. There were two people, a man and woman. Black. He was beaten to death ... with a pipe?"

"A pipe wrench. The man who did it is in prison. But it was only one person."

"That may be all they caught and thought it was, but there was also a woman present, and she was with the killer."

"We'll never know," she said. Yes I do.

"He's been dead, what, some seven years?" I asked.

"Nearly nine years," she said.

I was hot into it, now. "I'm entering the back part of the store, where Justus was killed," I said. "It seems to be a storage area, but smaller than I would expect, almost like a hallway."

"Yes. No matter how much we paint the walls ..."

"The blood seeps through," I finished. I could see it. No wonder they couldn't keep a tenant. Yuck.

"Okay. I see the murder. I'm in the hallway area." The assailant is smashing a middle-aged white man, somewhat overweight and balding, over the head and shoulders. He was performing a successful robbery until Justus decided to resist. Now, he is beating the store-owner to death before my eyes. I draw attention to myself.

"What are you doing here?" demands Justus.

I begin to explain my presence, but he's too impatient and anxious to care.

"Do something! The damn nigger is killing me!" he shouts. I am taken aback by his language, but I will become more surprised.

"What the fuck are you doing, lady?" Justus demands. "Can't you see the nigger's killing me? Call the police. Do something!"

"Ah, sir … Justus. He's already killed you. You're dead."

"What are you yammering about? Help me." He's fighting hard to live.

"Justus, I am a medium from 1982, you are dead. This happened almost ten years ago, and it's time you move on," I try.

"God damn woman!" He screams. "Do I look dead? Help me!"

I can no longer see the murderer. Only Justus, covered with blood and brains, and struggling alone for his life.

"Justus stop and listen to me," I say. "You were killed by that man. He's been in prison for many years, and you have been dead a long, long time."

"No I'm not. But I will be if you don't get help!"

"Justus, look." I bring his consciousness around to my side and showed him himself being murdered. Just then, his body drops to the floor. Definitely dead. Justus next to me sobbed.

"The nigger killed me," he weeps. "You didn't help me."

This simply was not the time to remonstrate about his language or ethics. I had to get this man out of here.

"Justus, you are dead and I have come to help you over to God," I say. If He'll have you, I think. "Pay attention only to me."

"Just who are you?" he asks.

"Ahm, I'm sent by God to bring you to Him," I reply.

"Shuah," he says. "You're some kind of strange angel, right? Naw, I'm not going off with some weird woman. I gotta find my pastor," he says.

I grab Justus by the right elbow and moved him to the meadow by the "stream" through which most people expect to pass into their "eternal reward" or whatever. Good. I get him there. I placed him on his back into the water, bathing the blood and stuff from him and, as I did so, his appearance begins to alter, clearing, even his clothing looking clean and pressed. Almost home free.

But instead of crossing immediately, we return to the meadow. I show him his people who have come to greet him from the "other side." They are holding out their hands to him, calling and greeting him in joy. He is ready to go, his attention solely on those folks.

All of a sudden, he stops.

"Bubba, what are you doing here?" he demands in a loud voice. He is addressing a rather young man, who was encouraging him.

I had never heard this word before. "What's a bubba?" I asked the two women.

"That means brother in the south," said the mother.

"Who over there would call him that?" I asked. "He's stopped and won't move. He's staring at that man and asking what he's doing there."

"Why, that must be his younger brother who died last year," she said.

Bingo. Of course he didn't know his brother was dead. Damn.

"Don't worry about that, Justus," I say to him. "Let's just go over there, and I'm sure the family will explain it all to you."

"But that's ..."

"I know. Honestly, it's okay. Look, he's happy to see you. Let's go."

"Okay." And over we go, Justus straight into the arms of his family. As they all walk in a group up toward the Light, Justus looks back. "Thank you, whoever you are."

Nice.

The women had questions. What had happened? Why didn't Justus know he was dead? Why was he still in that store?

"Well, there are lots of cracks in the Universe," I said. "In this case, I believe Justus was so involved in his fight to live that he simply stayed there, in time, in that same physical position, warding off the pipe wrench. And that's why the place has been haunted. He was still in his last struggle there," I explained.

"How terrible," she said. "To be stuck in time for so many years! That would be a lot of suffering."

"Well, not for him," I said. "No time had passed for Justus. It remained that moment for him."

Later on, I did a great deal of thinking about Justus meeting up with his younger brother and the ramifications of that meeting. It could have queered the whole thing, that moment. I would have to be more careful and prepared for that sort of thing from now on. I'm always learning.

Dying

Slipping through the gateways of hundreds of deaths, I am awed by its simplicity. It is only in my times of rational thought that I find it so difficult to believe that I still hold onto corporeal life.

A student brought this woman to me to contact her dead mother. Not unusual. As we went along, the mother came in to me; I gave proof of her presence, and asked if my client had any questions of her mother. Is that why she had come?

"This cannot be my mother," she said.

She's angry. Why?

"I thought I had given you enough proof of her identity," I said. "You agreed to that."

"But my mother suffered terribly during her death, and this spirit seems at peace."

"Well, she seems to be fine," I said. "Isn't that what you would want for her? I guess I don't understand even why you have come to me."

"My mother died of starvation," she snapped. "That's an awful way to die. She had cancer and just stopped eating during her final days. She wasted away before our eyes."

"But that's the normal way for the dying to go," I said. "Why would they eat?"

"I can't stand the idea of her starving to death."

"Was food withheld?" I asked. I dumbfounded.

"No, of course not," she snapped. "I begged her to eat. I fixed her her favorite meals, to no avail. She simply would not eat. She starved to death."

"Well, frankly, that sounds like your problem, not hers," I said as softly as I could.

"Starvation is suffering!"

I decided to turn to the dead mom. As we reunited in her past, I found her leaving her body frequently in the process of dying. She was comfortable. It was as fine a death as I have seen. She had plenty of time to transition, and in fact, was not in the shock I have often witnessed by people who have just died, for she had "practiced" so often during the process.

I described this for my client. And, indeed, we went over this for more than two hours until I was so exhausted that I terminated the session. The woman simply would not accept that "starvation" was a normal part of a normal old-age deathing.

"I suppose you expect me to pay your fee," she snapped.

"No, pay nothing. You have my address. If, later on, you decide what we did her tonight was valid, you can send all or part of the money then," I sighed. I was shaking from exhaustion. I wondered how tired her mother was from this evening's work.

She sent me half my fee some weeks later. But I have never believed that she came to the conclusion that her mother didn't suffer from that starvation. How sad.

As a school child, I learned from the teachers of how horribly the native peoples would treat their elderly—leaving them to die when they moved the village, or taking them away from the village, erecting a hut or lean-to, leaving water, and returning weeks later to their bodies. "How cruel," our teachers moaned to us.

Or was it? The more we return to the naturalness of deathing, the more we realize—and even doctors are agreeing with this—that the dying process is a shutting-down of our requirements of living. That is to say, our organs slowly cease to function, we no longer require food or drink, and, finally, we slip away. This is very different from withholding food and drink from healthy bodies. The dying body actually rejects food and water. I have witnessed that several times.

As my mother lay dying, in my loving ignorance, I urged drink on her. I was thirsty; Wasn't she? No. But she drank some—for me. Out of kindness for me. She would smile and sip. Finally, the last day and night, she could no longer do so out of kindness. And I watched the Foley bag as her kidneys ceased functioning. It was then that I came to comprehend the sweetness of this kind of natural deathing. So simple—just slipping out of that old useless body. There was no pain or discomfort. Ceasing.

Our ancestors honored their old people by allowing them this gentle slipping away. They even gave them privacy. No bustling, noisy hospital setting for them. Just a return to nature.

Imagine spending your last days, hours, and moments in a beautiful setting, perhaps in the trees at the edge of a lovely meadow, hearing birdsong, seeing butterflies, the clouds, the stars at night. No hollering children from next door, no light bulbs suddenly coming on as someone checks your vital signs, no rousing, even by loved ones. What a wonderful way to exit this earthly life!

Virginia and I have named this the "last visionquest," since we have both fasted in nature often. It can be sublime. We have both stated that if we were in a situation where it was possible, for our last days, we would go into a "last visionquest," drive into a favorite place in nature and leave our bodies there. Of course, we would ensure that our families could find us after several days, so that strangers would not have to come upon our decomposing bodies. I am certain that our families would find us peacefully dead with no trace of suffering on our faces.

This being an unlikely scenario today, I hope that, alternatively, I am allowed to die in the privacy and comfort of my home, surrounded by my few earthly treasures that I can look upon. Since I live in the forests of southeastern Arizona, I will be accompanied to death by birdsong, stars, and butterflies—as well as my cats, the braying of the burros, and clucking hens. I can only hope that I will be granted a conscious death-ing.

We have all heard people insist there is no such thing as dead. Well, they should work in a mortuary for a few days. People die. Their bodies fall down, rot, and stink. Their spirits leave those rotten bodies. That is dead. People need help to die well, and even more, need help after death to attain their proper space. As I have often stated, "the floor of the Cosmos is filled with countless cracks through which all sorts of things fall."

Shamans are called to help people die—certainly an important phase of healing. Let us be clear about one thing: this chapter does not follow the one on healing implying that we have failed to heal. When my mother lay dying, I asked her doctor if there was anything else we should do. He flippantly replied that we could call upon a shaman. Mother warned me with her eyes, but I blundered ahead anyway.

"She has one."

"Oh, really? I know a few from the reservation. Who?"

"You know medicine people. I am a shaman."

"Heh, heh," he said, patronizingly, "then why don't you heal your mother?"

"I am. I am helping her into death." So there, smarty.

It is exciting work, similar in so many ways to birthing. That is why the work is called "midwifing death." And that is precisely how it seems. We are busy, working with the dying person, the family and friends, and bringing it all together so that the experience can be the best possible for all concerned.

One should never be flippant about death. I hear many taking it very lightly. That's probably because they have never been that close to it. I have been pronounced dead three times in hospitals, and I can tell you that as I get closer to going, I draw back out of fear of the mystery of it. I have read the works of Tibetan masters, of all kinds of very spiritual people who know as well as anyone can what death is all about, and most have that last-moment dread of encountering the mystery. That is human nature. People who take it lightly are fools and lie to themselves.

Each person I have helped to die has had something, usually in their heart chakra, holding them back. For many, it is simply the habit of survival. Sometimes, I find that at the last minute, even. For Neal, it was that he truly believed he was evil and was terrified of what awaited him. Telling someone in that condition that he's a good person and will not be judged, or that he will be accepted with open arms falls on deaf ears … no words will alter that belief. What to do? In this case, I had to wait until he was so close to death that he was semi-comatose; then I began speaking to him as if he were very young, taking him back prior to even being able to be evil. I then promised him over and over that we would "walk out of this hospital together," meaning that I would not leave him alone before or after death. He eased immediately and was dead in about ten minutes. I was there then, and I was there to ensure that he was in a place and space which was not cruel and in which he could be safe.

A dying person does not necessarily want to hear, "Go ahead, you can go. Everything is all right, we'll do fine." Wouldn't you rather hear, "Dear one, I'm going to miss you terribly. Nothing will be the same. You are a light going out in my life. But it hurts me to see you in this condition even more. Go with my blessing. We will be together one day." It's just common sense. The shaman who attends preparations for death is a go-between among the family and patient, an interpreter. The shaman clears the patient, can even forgive the sins. The shaman can advise the patient with authority what will take place shortly, once the soul is freed of the body, because the shaman has been there many times.

The shaman rehearses the patient over and over, practicing the actual act itself so that the death is eased and the fear lessened. Performed with a loved one present, that person can continue the rehearsal, and it helps him or her to deal with the natural grief as well. Shamans know what the dying person is experiencing at all times, can communicate that to others. The patient actually may rejoice that someone recognizes his role in all this. In fact, the shaman knows what each person in the act is experiencing, so can be of great support to all.

A conscious death? Aware, rather than drugged against pain; in my bed, rather than on some awful life-prolonging machine or with various tubes in my nostrils, down my throat, or inserted into my veins. I am poor, so I am more likely to be granted that desire than a rich man; it is the wealthy who seem most to be tortured by life-prolonging instruments.

With hypnosis, one can be pretty well assured of a conscious deathing—barring trauma. I have assisted many clients in overcoming their fear of dying, and a similar program is used in helping the dying client "practice" dying until they just slip over quickly and quietly—to the appropriate space. That's the shamanic part. These techniques can be taught to the family who will then assist the dying person, thereby increasing their healing participation in this exciting experience. Such a holistic approach eases possible guilt feelings (a part of grief), stress, and exhaustion since all are involved in the healing.

When my mother was dying, we began practicing her transition. I had promised her that my dad would return for her when it was time. She even complained in the days prior to her death that he wasn't there yet. I continued that promise. Hours before her death, all present saw his hand on her left arm. She smiled. We continued to practice. Each time I took her over the "stream" into the land of the dead and left her there, she was smiling and at total peace. As she would slowly return, her frown also returned and she would whimper quietly. I took her back. As her soul convulsed from that hardy body, I held her in my arms and repeated the journey over. She was gone. It was like a swift breeze. The room was empty. The hand removed from her arm. I imagined my folks dancing the fox trot in the ether.

This is the way of the Old Ones, and it is not necessarily in any opposition to our technological way of life today. All over this country, we are turning away from the nasty habit of tucking our dying into frightening, impersonal hospitals. If one cannot die at home, there are now wonderful hospices where a more natural setting is prepared for the dying and family members. How different from when my dad died alone in the hospital. I was there when Mother received the phone call. A phone call! "Your husband just died." Doesn't get much colder than that. Because of the societal times, they were not even able to discuss his death with each other. They had to pretend he was going to be fine and home in just a matter of days or weeks. Being there and witnessing that was one of the saddest things in my life. These two people loved each other very much, and they were not able to share this amazing event in their lives. Today, they would have. It was an honor and privilege for me to share her death. When will we cease thinking of death as the worst thing and, rather, participate in it in a natural way, as great a part of life as birthing?

That is why shamans are often referred to as midwives of death. Since humans walked upright, we have been helping people through the door and along the journey to that place for them we cannot see with our physical eyes.

The energy in a room with a dying person residing is very similar to that of a maternity ward. The metaphors between dying and birthing are almost identical—the dark tunnel of transition, the light, the new life, the fear, the pain and flexing of the body.

The first deathing I assisted at was that of my uncle, Howard. I wish I'd had the experience I've had by now for it took him years to die. I went to Phoenix to help him, I took a medicine woman to help—nothing seemed to get him out of that miserable body. My aunt was exhausted. Howard wanted desperately to be free.

"I get to the little wooden bridge and begin to cross it, and almost to the other side, I am stopped," he panted to me. Howard was Native American and had worked often with the Taos Pueblo people. He was imbued with the naturalness of dying. Why wasn't it working?

Finally, my aunt moved to Tucson and Howard was placed into a nursing home near her. Time after time, the staff would telephone her to tell her that Howard was dying, in convulsions. Should they hospitalize him? Would she come? She always did go.

One Christmas Eve, she called me late at night. The nursing home had called again. What should she do? She just couldn't think anymore. We went to the home together.

Howard was holding his owl feather and alternately convulsing and resting when we got there. I urged my aunt not to hospitalize him because it would only be painful and harsh for Howard. He nodded. I began working on him, massaging his limbs. I noticed that his soul seemed "stuck" in his feet, and massaged the bottoms of his feet. Over the next few hours, his soul struggled to leave that body, only to return. My aunt was at his side, holding his hand, encouraging Howard in his struggle.

"It's fine, Howard darling, go. Let go and leave. I love you," she crooned.

After he was settled again, still within that poor body, my aunt and I drove home.

"Next time this happens," I said, don't go there."

"What? That would be cruel," she said.

"No. He can't leave with you there. He's too proud to show that total vulnerability. He was raised to never be weak before a woman," I said. "Right?"

"God, you're right. That's one reason he's so hated being dependent upon me these last years. It's going to be hard, but that's what I'll do. Please support me in this."

I promised she could call me next time she got telephoned by the nursing home and we would wait it out together. The next time, she was visiting friends in Phoenix and could not be reached until the day after Howard died.

Traumatic Deathing and Ethos

Traumatic deathing is different, although when my dear friend, Bud, was dying, he seemed to "know" it. He said many things during his last couple days. I even asked him if he "knew something," and he simply chuckled and said no. Yet, all during his last twenty-four hours, he told me many deeply intimate things which enabled me to continue my own life. I am convinced that very often people know they are about to die, but just do not realize it. We have all heard of situations where the person who would be shot the next day almost seemed to predict that act in detail. Even with animals, I have observed that for several days preceding their death they seem to become a little remote, as if looking into a space we cannot see.

However, there may be no or little time to transition. That is why we should all prepare ourselves ahead of time. Not just with clean underwear and baths, but with attitudinal shifts which prepare us to transit to a situation compatible with ourselves. The Land of the Dead is diverse—far more so than this land. Many souls who enter there are so unprepared that they become insane. I suspect that is what our basic fear of death is. Our ancient memories must retain the sense of that possibility. Without a shaman to walk over with the dead soul, our ancestors were sure to be lost in that sheer vastness of space and time and possibilities.

Monotheistic teachings are the only ones I have found which do not provide us with a way in which to deal with what transpires following death. They seem to say, "Believe the way we tell you to and everything will be okay." That is not even rational. One of the most haunting movies I have seen is "What Dreams May Come." In this film, the two children of a loving couple die; a few years later, the father is killed in a car accident. He stays near his grieving wife, but gradually moves forward and locates the spirits of his children. Then he gets the news: his wife has committed suicide. He sets off to find her and rescue her from the hell he is told suicides condemn themselves into. The scenes are insane and nightmarish. No, they are not exactly what I have found there, but they are representative enough to be uncomfortable for me to view.

I have found souls performing seemingly aimless acts over and over; some souls are dancing, perhaps because their bodies were crippled in life; some are frantically trying to find St. Peter's Gate and they cry out to me that things are not what they thought they would be; some actually enter a hellish type of scenario, perhaps in order to expiate what they deem to have been a sinful life—I found a "purgatory," but also found that those souls were free to leave anytime that they realized that they were not required to be there! When I have to go over to the Land of the Dead (a spacial concept), I find it frightening, disorienting, and many of the people there pathetic. These are other examples of ethos running our show.

The greatest stumbling block I have discovered regarding what I term self-determined deathing is societal and religious ethos. Ethos makes me anxious since it accounts for most of what will take place following death. Am I to be a prisoner of how society believes? No matter what our personal belief system becomes, ethos is stronger and can regulate where we end following death. One's personal system must be constantly strengthened in order to override ethos. We may enter death via ethos but, if our personal system is strong enough, we can move through the ethos-after-death state into our own reality. Preparation is essential for this. Unfortunately, death usually comes upon us when we are too weak to deal with the power of ethos.

My friend's father was close to death. It had begun with some health problems which led to extreme pain and surgery. The pain-killers and anesthesias weakened him and, most importantly, his ability to remain in self-determined consciousness.

"Frank, you're so strong in the beliefs you've built during these past forty years," I spoke softly to him. "You were born and raised Catholic and led a good Christian life. Then, as you began looking deeper into life, you left Catholicism and recreated your belief system."

Faintly, "Yes, but I've failed."

"Well, it's pretty close and scary, but remember my promises to you that I will take care of you at death. Of course, I know you'd rather see this through yourself, but just to remind you that you will not be tortured by being out of control at this time ..." I began.

He interrupted. "It's torturing me now."

"I know," I touched his arm. "But let's talk about it and see if we can help here. Kathy will do whatever she can to coach you when I'm not here. You're not alone. I need you to know that. Hmm?"

He nodded and his face relaxed somewhat.

"In the midst of all this physical torture, you suddenly reverted to Catholicism, didn't you?"

"Yes, it was just terrible," he whispered.

"Okay. Inquisition time, hmm? Did they appear to you in red robes?"

"Actually, yes," he said.

"I know. I'm in your memory. You're wide open. I don't mean to intrude."

"Roberta, we've known each other too long and too well ... You can't intrude on me because I'm open to you at all times."

"Good. Well, it feels to me that the Inquisition is torturing you just as they did in your past lifetime in Europe, right?"

"Yes."

"Let's see what we can do. First of all, Frank, it's not your fault. You're weak now, and your mind is not yours to control at this point. You're also helping me immensely by sharing this with me. I can use this for many others. Okay, if that matters in the state you're in today," I chuckled. And he joined me in a moment of humor.

"You know, all I believe you need is to maintain daily contact with Kathy. She can remind you of your belief system that you've fought so hard to live ... and, well, to die within. I'll also make a tape recording of some of what I know about your beliefs and you can review that frequently. We will see you through this. You do not have to die Catholic. That's the belief system of other people."

"Roberta, it's not confined to Catholicism. In this weird fog I'm in, I wake in a real fundamentalist Christian mode. You know, I'm really afraid. Very afraid," Frank began to cry.

Later on, I began "taking" Frank on imagery trips through his beliefs of life and death. "You will not get stuck in the deaths of strangers," I assured him over and over.

Frank survived this time; his thinking is still foggy and unformed, but he and Kathy continue to work on his preparation. Still, this is torture of the religious sort. And it angers me and causes real sorrow. It is a violent attack upon us in our weakest time. Of course, Frank is afraid to die, even though he holds onto my promises and those of Kathy.

What might happen if he were to die in a typical American Christian ethos? He certainly would not be in the space he belongs in. There would be intense fear and sense of being lost in the deepest jungle of terrors. His emotions would be torn to pieces. No matter what your belief system is, imagine for me how you would feel if you were forced to live within the ethos of, say, what most of us consider to be a brutish, evil system. No way out.

Yes, over time, we might move free of that slavery but, until then, we are being brutalized in very real ways. I wonder what would occur if one re-entered corporeal life still within that reality. Bad tasting food for thought.

The souls who are focused at the time of death do well. They remain focused, while being slightly aware of the horror involving the others. Many choose to continue "working" on their "life's work." But what is your life's work? Do you really want to spend life after life working out mathematical problems? Accounting? Selling insurance? Politicizing? One woman I went over for for a client was still seeking "the truth" in religion. Her family confirmed to me that she spent her life going from one sect to another, including some pretty far-out cults. She continues to do so. I even tried to intervene with her, to no avail. Her focus was firm upon her search—sure to find the "right answer" to all questions and needs.

An aunt of mine died in rage at her husband. And years later, she continued to be enraged. That was all I was able to get from her—rage and more rage. She was unaware of her surroundings or potential. As I have demonstrated within this chapter, some people who die in trauma remain there, stuck in time, as ghosts, in the act of dying. These people are unaware of anything, simply frozen in time.

If you believe in reincarnation, perhaps you can see the problems arising from an unprepared deathing. If, for example, one remains in a fundamentalist radical religion when one dies, one will likely be reborn into that kind of situation over and over until freed of it by determination and focus. This is why suicide seldom improves our lot. If one commits suicide out of depression, chances are good that one will be rebirthed into a depressive body and brain.

What hope have we if we are not prepared? A personal example is my first husband, Ken, who committed suicide in 1969. At first, his soul was a mess. People would not enter our home. The kids and I existed in a state of fear and stress from what this poor disorganized soul manifested. As with most suicides, Ken realized at the moment of death that he had made a serious mistake, that death would not solve his problems. He tried to return to the dead body and could not. But he returned to us. Parts of his etheric body flew across the rooms, furniture and books and pots and pans crashed around our ears, friends fled the house. This went on for months, despite the fact that we moved from that city.

I tried to help Ken, as inexperienced as I was then, but part of my reaction to all this was that he had hated my psychic side, had called me names and insisted that I "just stop it." Now it was all I had. Would he be angrier with me if I used it to help him? My confusion increased when I opened myself to his spirit and my body would levitate and my hair was pulled and I was touched by burning fingers. I know now that it was simply his eagerness to communicate and disorganization which caused this. There were times when his communications were sweet. He often tugged at my pillowcase by my eyes at night. I could see the case wrinkle and curve and feel the tug. Some of his touches were gentle. But when I opened so that it was more direct, the reactions became inept and clumsy and violent.

I talked with him. After my initial disorganized grief and reactions, I was able to do so calmly and lovingly, with some objectivity and desire to see him advance, even if it meant our separation. The result was that he began to "study" and learn and grow, just as he would have in physical life. He "looked over the shoulder" of students of various spiritualities and often brought the results back to me in the form of concepts. He began looking out after our children, actually physically intervening and saving our son's life (witnessed by those present) as he fell from a rock face. He appeared to us all on certain occasions and we could observe his growth and depersonalization as time went by. He worked with me as I accepted my life's work. People have often described him in a room as I communicated with the dead for a client. He was especially helpful with those poor souls who had committed suicide.

A woman came to me following the suicide of her teenaged son. I connected with him and we had a three-way conversation going, when suddenly, she stopped.

"This is not my son standing here. He has dark hair, a white shirt, and dark pants. It is a ghost, and I have never seen a ghost before!"

"It's all right," I soothed. "His shirt is rolled up to the elbows, right?"

"Yes."

"This is someone who often helps me with suicides. He cares very much." In fact, Ken told me what the boy was doing and how he (Ken) would help guide him to some "people" who can help him grow. I relayed this to the grieving mother, who was grateful.

There are many religions which teach that suicides are hopeless. Not so. Some New Age junk tells us that suicides remain on "lower levels" and must work their way up. No. As with all traumatic deaths, it depends upon the focus and the hold our social/religious ethos has on them at the time of death. It can also depend upon whom they meet in the Land of the Dead, or loved ones who can communicate with them, or mediumistic intervention. In all cases, it must be done with love and kindness and hope.

As with any sort of journey, a major portion of it is the preparation. Actually, I enjoy looking at the road maps and making lists of what we'll pack and daydreaming over what we'll be doing and seeing. Preparation should be fun—you can make it fun. As the sages all agree: it is the journey, not the destination. In this case, the journey determines the destination. What if you were to die today? What would be your reality? As I contemplate people about me today, I realize that most would end up in insanity, since so many are unfocused and inattentive to what is around them now, let alone following death. The sages also instruct us to be aware at all times. Being unaware today is the most common cause of traumatic death. And that will continue following the transition.

A deer (Cute'Ems) that Roberta watched grow up.

Cute'Ems with bigger antlers, at about 2 years of age.

Chapter 6
Soul Retrievals

Soul retrieval is an integral part of the shaman's life work. Originally, I was prejudiced against this phase of my work because it seemed too much like inner child silliness. I have found three basic retrieval actions: 1) the common ones wherein a person experienced an unbearable trauma earlier and part of his soul fled for safety; 2) the past-life retrievals in which a part of the client's soul has remained at death previously, rather than come forward, perhaps even as a ghost; 3) and the kidnapping part of one's soul by OtherWorld inhabitants or even so-called UFOs.

A Physical Healing and Soul Retrieval

As I scanned this Juliette from the OtherWorld, I found a "thing" in her belly. Yuck. This is her problem. Jeez, I hate to have to return from a journey and tell someone she has yuck in her body. Let me find the nicer words.

"Juliette, I found the problem," I say. "There is something in your center, beneath your solar plexus, which doesn't belong there. Well, that's hard to say, too. It's not unnatural, but I think that at this time, it should go."

Not out of the woods yet. "What is this thing?" Juliette asks.

Drat. "Well, when your mother was expecting you, she was initially expecting twins, right?"

"How did you know?" she asks. "Oh, yeah."

"It's what you're paying me for, right? To amaze you?" I laughed. Stalling. "Okay. What I find here is that as you and your—ah—your brother began to grow from cells into fetuses, you consumed him. That's pretty common in twins."

"Yes, I know." Juliette smiles.

"Well, in this case, well—ah—your brother is still here, inside you. Some of him. Physically. No personality and not quite his soul, but some of your soul is in there, you know, in his, ah, body." I'm doing this sooo well.

"Yuck," she says.

"Exactly," I say. "Well, it's all natural, you know, so don't get upset …"

"Upset? Why should I be upset?" She is upset. "You tell me that my baby brother is living inside me and that part of my soul is stuck inside his little body, and …"

My apprentices are edging toward the door.

"Juliette, it's not cut and dried like that," I say diplomatically. "Your 'brother' is not human, he is not exactly in human form."

"Not exactly?"

Got to get out of this. "Look, why don't we just take care of it and worry about the rest later, if you're still interested? Okay? Just give me a minute; I think my apprentices have to go to the bathroom."

When I go back inside Juliette, there is this thing—it's made up of gristle and flesh and skin and hair. Small, but I can see the head and hands and butt. It's a three-month fetus, but petrified. Stephen King stuff here. And—guess what—some of him is still in here; no, attached—comes and goes—not really consciousness, but near-consciousness. What to do?

I contact him gently as his soul seems to breathe in and out. And I take him into my arms in a soft blanket. He's out! I carry him over the river into the Land of the Dead and find the Lady who cares for children for me. She is ready and knows what to do. I feel tears in my eyes; it's always so sweet to see her take the babies. I know he's safe and at home now.

Back to Juliette's innards. The body is still here. And still yuck. How do I get this out?

"Juliette, when does your moon cycle, your bleeding time, come?" I ask.

"I'm cramping already," she said. "Any minute. Probably by morning."

God, I'm living right. I gently and slowly move the fetus down into her womb. It's the size of half my thumb or smaller, and so petrified that it cannot be revived into soft flesh. I'm okay with this. Juliette notes aloud that she is feeling intensified uterine cramps and doubles over. There! That's it. All done there. Now, her soul.

I scan the fetus for her. And I don't find her there! Juliette has reported a feeling of weakness since I took her "brother" over. My apprentices report that she is pale and almost transparent in her chest. Oops.

Back to the Land of the Dead and my Lady. She's waiting.

"Did you forget something, Shaman?" she asks. "I think that only part of this belongs here."

She's right. I've taken the boy's soul and a small portion of Juliette's—entangled a bit with his. I bow to the souls and extract Juliette's wee soul, scooping her up in a ball and return.

"Juliette," I say aloud, "I have a small portion of your soul which was interwoven with your brother's. Will you receive it back?"

"Oh yes," she breathes.

I bring up the energy of her soul part enough so that all present can see it and float it into her chest. She can feel it and we can all see how much more solid she looks.

I go through a little more physical work, closing her up against intrusions since she is so vulnerable right now, and we proceed.

"Juliette," I instruct her, "when you begin bleeding, you will clot more than usual. Please don't worry about it. It's normal for this time only. Ignore it. Okay?"

"Roberta, is my brother's body in there?" she asks.

"Well ... you may be curious, but please, please, curb it and let it go."

"You're right."

"And, Juliette? Please call me before I leave town and tell me how it's going," I request.

Juliette had come to me with sick headaches that were not migraines, but they were still devastating. She had also reported nightmares with monsters in them. I expect that they will be bothering her no more.

The last I heard, they do not.

The **common retrieval** is pretty easy, and it can be accomplished by anyone practiced in shamanic journeying, such as a tutored shamanic practitioner. It is almost psychological in nature.

Pat came to me because she was experiencing intermittent depression, a sense of being lost, and a lack of wholeness. This usually indicates the need for a soul retrieval, but not always. Prior to engaging in retrieval work, I always spirit journey to confirm this.

As I did so for Pat, I described to her a house in which she lived when she was seven to nine years of age. She had a strong memory of her years there. I described her bedroom as she was awaiting sleep. I found her there, frightened into paralysis, waiting for the dark man to come to her and touch her and cause pain.

She nodded. Pat had "worked through" all this molestation and incest by her father with a psychologist several years previously. I was telling her nothing new. Good. I then described how it was that when he left her, she would creep outside her room onto the landing of the stairs and into a dirty clothes hamper there and hide.

Pat gasped. She had forgotten that part until now.

"Part of little Pat's soul is there, to hide permanently, to preserve your sanity," I told her. So this does call for a soul retrieval. It will be a comparatively easy one, since she has been waiting for this. "It is up to you, however, to make within yourself an environment where the child soul part can come to feel safe and secure. And it will require that you welcome her freely."

"No problem," murmured Pat. "What do I need to do?"

I explained that when I brought back the soul, she would see it in my right hand. It would appear as a ball of soft light, probably misty. When it had gained its integrity, I would release it and it would float toward her chest, entering mid-chest. She would feel it clearly.

When that happened, she must breathe deeply and calmly, "breathing" it into each particle of her body and demonstrating internal joy at the soul's return. As I journeyed for the soul, I asked Pat to begin imagining her life as it was today, strong, independent, and safe for the child part. She agreed. I journeyed.

I found little Pat after a short search. She was using some great metaphors, hiding beneath a hydrangea bush (which Pat recognized from her early home). I went to her slowly, showing her why I had come, allowing her to pet the mountain lion accompanying me. I sat near her, and she gradually overcame her suspicion and sat on my lap. I brushed her hair from her face. Magically, she had a fresh new dress on and pretty curls in her hair. That sure impressed the girl.

I explained what had happened through imagery. I showed her the grown up Pat, and she was in awe of her. I "negotiated" her return.

Grown up Pat would keep her safe. Yes, she would buy her burgers and she had two dogs and they were going to go on a trip in a van and she could have ice cream and ... She agreed to return.

Back in the room from my journey, Pat could readily view the ball of mist forming in my right hand. It became the size of a softball and intensified until she could not see through it. Then, I held it up and blew gently on it. It floated across the space between us, entering Pat's chest. On cue, she breathed deeply and gently; I could hear her crying softly as they reunited. I then healed an energy "hole" I located in her back and we were through.

Pat was very pleased. She felt different. She was leaving in a couple days for an extended trip through the northwestern United States.

"Please send me a postcard and let me know how it goes," I requested.

I got two cards describing how things seemed so different, being whole. She was having a good time. A few years later, she sent a letter telling me she had rejoined the church and was living as a lay person at a monastery. She was whole and happy.

Past-Life Soul Retrievals

The second type of retrieval is for a "ghost" from a **past lifetime**. This is especially interesting when the client does not believe in past lives but is faced with this reality and cannot deny it. I am cautious with it because of that fact. However, we often discover this anomaly during a regression, as in this example.

Jessie came for a hypnotic regression, thinking that it might help explain her lifelong menstrual problems. She had tried a little of everything, it seemed, to correct the problem, but as one problem was isolated and dealt with, another cropped up in its place. What about finding the source of this trouble in a past life?

She regressed to a time in medieval Europe. We both reckoned later that it was in northern Germany or Switzerland or Austria. It was cold and gray most of the time, although that might have been due to how she perceived life at the time. I had asked her for the country while regressed, but she did not know, since she had never left the convent ... except once.

Laid upon the front step shortly after birth, she was brought into the convent, raised there, and generally used as a servant. Being a teaching order, she was educated enough to teach some courses, which is where we found her. She had never been outside the convent walls, but she could hear the sounds of the town outside, learning from them something of life. When there had been a victory (there seemed to be a lot of war), she could hear the excited sounds from the people and the parades of the victors. When it was spring, she heard the sounds of renewed life. And so forth. She asked to go out, but she was always denied.

"You cannot, for you come from bad blood, probably an adulterous union, and would surely fall there," her superiors always replied.

She continued to be curious. Finally, one day when she could hear a great celebration going on, she crept outside from the convent. Once out, she was terrified—of the noise, the rush of bodies, the faces ... everything was overwhelming to her. She could not get back into the convent, so she hid deeply in the nearest alleyway. And there she remained for just over twenty-four hours, until she was found by the nuns asked to search.

Dragged in disgrace back to the convent she had so ardently wished to re-enter, she was cleaned up, then brought before the entire order, accused of terrible things, most of which she did not comprehend, and beaten severely. She was also ordered to the worst work: to assist in the dungeons where men and women were being horribly tortured for various crimes. Nights, she could return via the dark underground passageway and sleep in an alcove off the kitchen, as far away from the other sisters as possible.

There were more beatings, one finally causing her back to hunch and apparently rupturing her womb and/or ovaries. She was just over twenty years of age but appeared to be in her eighties. The pain was relentless, but she went about her work in the dungeons, cleaning up blood and feces, doing whatever chores those in the convent didn't want to do, eating little.

I brought Jessie to the day of the little sister's death. She was on her pallet on the floor of the alcove, all alone. But Jessie did not go into the death and freeing of the soul. We sat there. I suggested she go forward, but nothing happened. I entered the scene with her, using a shamanic reality. The poor woman was dead but left where she lay. I could see no soul rising from her body. I perceived Jessie nearby, looking at her and waiting … I moved forward in time. There she was—a ghost in the convent!

Calmly, I explained to a lightly entranced Jessie what I had found. I asked if she would like to assist me in rescuing her ancient soul part and freeing it to be reunited with her today. This would be a soul retrieval and spirit rescue. Jessie was amenable. We got busy.

I went back to the death scene and explained to the sister what had happened. She did not understand, nor could she believe me since it went against her church teachings. I took on the appearance of the Virgin and approached her again. A response. Shame. The "Virgin" held out her hands, forgave her sins, and "told" her that she was there to take the sister to her Lord. The soul came to me from that poor body. Still as the "Virgin," I helped her to find freedom from that body and lifetime.

With Jessie accompanying us, we took the little sister over, purifying her in the stream between life and death, and into the Light, the Source there. Since Jessie was there also, I brought her into the Source for a healing, and we left.

A few days later, I had Jessie return. I found the little sister, who was light and healed. I explained to her what had happened and that she "belonged" with the rest of her soul in Jessie. She agreed to take the long journey to reunite.

Jessie gradually became much better. It was gradual because her soul had to follow her through the intervening lifetimes. This is tricky, and I have always felt concern, because such a retrieval alters everything, albeit in subtle ways. Once we tinker with time, especially past time, we cannot be sure of the outcome, for each of the intervening lives has been altered somewhat. How does that affect today's life? I am not sure. It even affects the lives of subsequent children. So far, it seems to have worked out all right. I have performed this sort of soul retrieval many, many times, and the feedback has always been positive.

Why so many? I believe that this has gone on since humans became complicated—a very long time. At this time in our species, this special time, souls are longing to be whole to participate. Soul retrieval is something I was opposed to doing for years, but as I came to understand its importance today, I embraced it.

Another example was when Sammie came to me complaining of nightmares and phobias. She was claustrophobic and extremely afraid of the dark, and she felt vague much of the time. Memory problems, trouble focusing, and those dreams … she could not speak of them. She had read my brochure and felt she needed a soul retrieval.

I journeyed through her and had to agree with her self-diagnosis, although I don't always.

"Your nightmares—I'm sorry to upset you—involve being locked into dungeons, buried alive, crushed by stones—that sort of thing," I said.

She broke down into tears. Her husband was angry that I had upset her so.

"Sometimes we have to be upset to become open to healing," I told him. "I can't do much for anyone if they sit before me, arms crossed, in complete control."

I entered the OtherWorld and found Sammie's soul.

"Found you," I said. "You're a real Anglophile, aren't you?"

"Yes," she said. Her husband laughed and agreed.

"Your soul part is left in London," I murmured, seeing what was before me there.

She began to cry again.

As I saw the following, I related it aloud.

Sammie is a young girl, carrying a little stuffed toy of some kind, wearing a woolen coat and hat, holding the hand of her "mummie," and entering a bomb shelter in London during the blitz. I see now from her eyes and hear from her ears—the people, all around us, the light from the lantern becoming dimmer, the smells of the people, her mum's hand holding hers, the feel of mummie's coat against her cheek. The sirens outside, the gruff voice of the warden in charge of the shelter, and now the bombs being dropped above.

A bomb hits square on the shelter and kills nearly everyone. Some are dug out, but Sammie's mother is dead and on top of her. Sammie lives for quite some time—seems like days. She tries to call out but is never heard; there are too many shelters and too many bodies to exhume. She finally suffocates beneath her mother—and in some ways, she not only accepts this fate but welcomes it since she cannot imagine life without her mummie.

She is still there.

I find this in many "buried alive" situations: that the soul seems to have difficulty in getting out. Perhaps this is not rational, but that is still what I have often discovered.

I enter the tomb and find two "guards" by her. Damn, I'm in the OtherWorld deeper than I thought. I've gone over into the dangerous part.

"They" are here. And I'm bent over. That's a pretty vulnerable position. I'll try sucking them in with my "poor little old lady" routine. It works. They attack me and I "get" them. It's a nasty but brief fight, and they no longer exist. I'll be more careful.

I find the child's memory, body, and soul. She doesn't want to leave her mother, but I "show" her that life has gone on, that even the tomb and her real body no longer exist. I show her who the rest of her soul has become.

"Sammie, I need you to let pictures of your life as it is today pass through your mind right now," I say quickly.

Back to work. I take up the little soul, and we go to the stream where I bathe her in consciousness. She sees her mother's "ghost" on the other side, smiling and waving to her in an encouraging way, and we return into this reality together. After Sammie's soul parts were reunited, we discussed the retrieval. Her husband was quiet, after reporting that he could see the soul in my hand and as it floated into his wife's body. He saw her looking more solid and "different" now. He telephoned me a few days later to report that Sammie seems somehow more alive and whole, and that those "thrashing and yelling" nightmares have ceased.

Sammie reported that she was still an Anglophile, but perhaps more so now, since she wanted to visit her grave in London.

"Sammie, your grave, and your mum's, is paved over by streets now," I told her. "I don't believe they were ever able to excavate that shelter. I can't be sure. But it seems to me that it received more than one direct hit—perhaps some following that night. The main thing is how you feel now, that your phobias lose their hold and that you can live a full life at one with yourself."

A letter some months later indicated that she was doing well in all respects and that she and her husband were planning a vacation—in England. Oh, she wrote that they were taking SCUBA diving together—a proof that her problems with claustrophobia were at an end.

Kidnapping

The third type of soul retrieval has to do with **kidnapping**. This will be the test of your trust in the author and my ability to find some words in our limited language to describe it. There are beings I have described in "Chapter 11: UFOs and the Faire Folke," which "kidnap" soul parts to use, such as we use rats in laboratories, to educate and form for cooperative work, out of curiosity, and just because. We find these situations among people who have had UFO contact. I do not mean UFO in the sense of extraterrestrials, but as it reads: unidentified flying objects. And many people who come to me for various sorts of healings have been profoundly affected by contact with UFOs.

It is not my place, nor do I condone—ever—forcing or supplying memories for people. If a memory is suppressed, then it is for good reason, likely to preserve the person from it. There is no reason for the client to know details unless he or she wishes. And when given the choice, most turn it down. We are interested in being healthy and happy and whole, not knowing things which could drive us into insanity. The "intruders" or "kidnappers" do not block our memories—we do that out of a sense of self-preservation. Once I understand a client's belief system, I proceed within that, using it to explain only what must be explained.

Kirk expressed some of the usual difficulties, but little in the way of physical symptoms. I decided to do what I call an "exploratory" journey. Immediately into his OtherWorld, I found some threatening non-humans. Aha.

"Kirk, are you afraid of the dark?" I asked.

He paused very briefly. "Well, actually, yes. It's embarrassing, but I am. Always have been. No reason, really."

"Oh, I think you probably have plenty of reason to fear the dark, Kirk. Don't be embarrassed in here," I assured him.

I then asked him a series of questions, observing his physical reactions closely. These questions have nothing to do, really, with the results of his physical reactions. It's just a way I have of accessing. And it always works. It did this time, and we soon ascertained that Kirk had been the victim of "abduction" as a child and at least a few times since.

"Kirk, I find that you have had some pretty frightening experiences in your dreamtime, particularly as a child, say, about nine or ten?"

He went tense. "I don't like to think about that time. I was having a lot of trouble. But, okay, yes, it was very bad when I was nine and ten years old. Ah, do you have to do this?"

"Kirk, it's causing you tremendous trouble in all ways. I think we should proceed. But let me assure you that I will not bring up stuff that will upset you tonight, nor will I open any memory that will cause you distress. I can promise that. On the other hand, with this in mind, you've got to agree that while you may ask questions, I may not answer them. Okay?"

He readily agreed and seemed to relax somewhat. My assistant knew what was going on; we had done a lot of this together. She would only verbalize things in a way that would not upset him too much, and she was aware that I was going into *that* place again tonight.

"One final thing before I get busy here, Kirk," I said. "I'm going to be going into a place that is life-threatening for me. You will hear Chaz verbalizing things she sees around us, and I ask you to do the same. Some of it may sound scary, but just let it roll and it won't stick to you. The more you participate in this, the more profound the healing work will be. Okay?"

"Ah, yeah."

The drumbeat began and I prepared to enter the World of Illusion to search for the nastiest of the nasties to fight with them over a fragment of soul. What a crazy job I have.

I found them quickly; they weren't hiding. They had been messing with Kirk pretty consistently since he was nine. The soul part was a connection so that they could easily harass him at whim. I watched them for a few moments, checking out the lay of the land, so to speak. I am careful not to look directly at these beings, but I am able to see them and see *into* them. They are indescribable in any known language. They cannot be identified as "bad" or "good" or in between by appearances, or even by behaviors; I have to go on some kind of instinct which has come with experience. These were real nasty guys.

All telepathic: "I have come for the soul of this man here"—do not give names, they hold power over a person—"Give it up quickly, for I am impatient."

"Ah, Shaman, good to see you. We are bored and look forward to an interesting time with you. As you can see, we have his soul over there with blah-blah. Look." All this followed by some "saber-rattling."

As they babble at me, I am checking things over to see if this is real or not. If it seems too easy, I'm extra cautious. But sometimes it is very easy. Sure would be nice if there were recognizable laws in this place. I am careful to look elsewhere than the place or being who is trying to gain my attention. And, of course, there's always my back to tend to. I look through them, through the façade they present. Real or not real? Test. Taste.

"I say you lie," I shout.

Nice test. They begin a frantic defense of their position here, sort of like Keystone Kops in the OtherWorld. And that confirms that they're not what they are pretending to be. I turn away in contempt and continue my careful journey, deeper into the World of Illusion. There, a group of beings is at one o'clock, across a "meadow" from me, with a "forest" behind them. They "sit" around a heavy wooden slab, which seems to be a table, and they are "feasting" there. Yes, I sense Kirk's soul clearly now. I move near them.

Pretending at first not to be aware of me, they behave as if they are the Mad Hatter's Tea Party. It's meant to distract me (if this were a movie, I would be laughing uncontrollably). I locate the "leader" and address it.

"Give me the soul."

"Why should we?"

Now I am absolutely certain that I am in the correct place. This is going to be a fine meeting, for it is complex in every way. These entities are not bad—they just have their own agenda, which is positive for the planet, but sometimes costly for the individual.

"Ah, Ancient One, it is I, Nightwing the Shaman, who addresses you. I have (image) Lord Elf with me and we are one. May I converse with you at ease?"

A nod of the head and grudging respect. My name is known to these people, and the presence of the one I have imaged is held in high esteem. I approach the table and continue the "conversation." It seems that Kirk was selected to work with these Faire Folke as a child, and they took what they believed was theirs to take, to train and prepare.

"This man is unable to work with you. He has not the resilience to withstand your presence and never will have. He cannot become willing and cooperative. Give back the soul."

There is some, well, not exactly discussion, but a bit like that, among them. The leader spoke. "We cannot give it back, as you know, Shaman. We have put much effort into teaching the little soul, and some of us have become attached to it."

I knew that. Even the best of them will not willingly return soul parts. I imaged to them what I must do, and they accepted that, although the leader knew they would lose. But that was fair, you see, since it must be done that way.

I killed them all. Nothing but little shreds remained around the table. Only once was I able to do this without mayhem—once I was invited to sit and eat with them, and I did. They didn't think I would, nor if I did that I would survive. A test. But I won that soul without killing. I doubt that test will ever be repeated. As I took up the soul part and prepared to return, I wondered if these creatures regenerated, if I killed the same ones over and over. Something to contemplate later, at leisure.

The soul was a little resistant at first, until I began imaging to it, taking its memory back to the night it was taken and the boy it left. I did this as I began my return journey, one still filled with danger. As I dodged and moved back toward my starting place, I imaged to the soul the man that boy had become. The re-attachment was beginning.

I returned the soul to Kirk as I always do, and he was able to experience it fully while there. According to his follow-up call, the reunion continued for weeks. He also slept deeply, dreaming well, and his fear of the dark was easing up gradually. He no longer had the feeling that someone was following him. It was a successful soul retrieval in all ways.

Vietnam

Gordon, author of the foreword of this book, has known me and my work for nearly fifteen years at this writing; we have enjoyed a relationship of walking very similar paths, but each in an equally different manner. We often disagree with the how-to, if not the reason. But recently, he became "ready" for a soul retrieval which I'd sensed necessary for some time, and he was invited to my cabin one evening for some serious work toward that. So far, we have accomplished one retrieval of the three I believe are ultimately required. This one was so exotic, complex, and interesting to me that I decided, with his permission, to include it here.

What I knew of Gordon which is pertinent was fairly simple: he had served in Vietnam (I had done some work on that, but he'd only allowed the most superficial healing). I knew also that he continued to battle demons from that period of his life, along with some nasties from his childhood. However, I (as I usually do) held myself utterly aloof from his personal life that he did not wish to share.

So here we were, facing one another in my cabin in the mountains, both a bit edgy within our own spaces. I journeyed first as I always do, obtaining information from Gordon's soul pertinent to the retrieval.

"Gordon, what was your nickname in the service?"

"I don't think I had one; nothing comes to mind."

"Hmm, I get that it's an important part of this. Oh well, I've been wrong once or twice."

So, I find that the largest 'piece' of soul missing comes from his Vietnam days. Recall that I have often ranted about how our young—and even mature—men and women who served in foreign lands were never prepared to co-exist with the spirits there, the cultures, the spirituality. Full of mom's apple pie, a sense that Americans can do no wrong and are invincible and righteous in all ways, a sense that they were in personal contact with the only god, and so forth, our young people go into an alien land and existence. They enter constant fear of annihilation and a life of constant overwhelming noises and, in many cases, drugs. This is the perfect state for deep hypnosis, which results in a completely open psyche waiting only to be filled with whatever is proffered there.

"So, Gordon, you lost a large part of your soul there, particularly in a situation of extreme emotional violence, the memory of which continues to shatter you. I fear for that soul part, for I sense that it is not simply hiding, but is being manipulated at best, tortured at worst."

Quiet in the chair across from me.

"Gordon, do you want to proceed with this?"

We took a break.

Back in our seats, Gordon said, "I must. Let's do it."

"Okay. Here's how it works. I will go over there, locate your soul, negotiate its return, do battle, whatever it takes, and bring it back, probably heal it, and return it. Likely, it will return through your mid-chest, but I'll be talking you through it. Once you experience that soul part entering your body, draw it all through you, be joyous, even though you might feel a bit off balance. Demonstrate to it your current powers and abilities to keep it safe. Again, I'll help you through it as best I can," I instructed.

Drumbeat going, darkness all about us, I began the hunt. Gordon had been reminded to stay present in all ways and to assist me by stating aloud what he felt, experienced, and saw. He was a good subject, and I seldom had to prompt him.

Going to a specific direction in my work space, I "looked" over into the OtherWorld for clues. Lots of those. I spent time checking many out, not to overlook any possibilities, and found most of that information to be not only false but outright lies to distract me from my hunt. The thought of his nickname hovered about me, and I was about to open my mouth to ask Gordon about it again when he spoke.

"Brad. My god, I'd forgotten completely. My nickname in the service was Brad." I almost came back to this world. The name Brad was so incongruous. Of course many things going on in our twenties were incongruous, huh?

"Great, Gordon. Now I'm truly ready."

Returning my full attention to where my shaman part awaited my full attention, I proceeded with the hunt. I've worked for so many years that I can actually be in both worlds simultaneously, however costly that is to body, mind, and soul. It's a wonderful plus for me. And things moved with startling rapidity. The following all happened simultaneously and is impossible to fully describe. The reader must try to put all layers into one.

"Gordon, it's your name! I've found it in ..."

"Watch out for the old ..."

"... an ancient cemetery."

"... cemetery."

I was definitely on my toes. There was almost too much at one time. I needed help, but Lord Elf wasn't there, and I was on my own. As I have taught so very often, when things come down to the real nitty-gritty, all we have is us.

So "us" went further. "I've got to retrieve your name. No, your soul. No, both are the same. Oh, damn it. Nevermind. I'll explain later. Just go with me. Are you okay?"

"Yes. I do trust you completely. So don't worry. And I will behave appropriately. Promise."

"Your soul and name have been kidnapped by something most ancient, a spirit, if you will, of the land there. But also an old ... priest? Yeah, I think so. Like that. There are others here, some killing? I'm seeing the history of this place all at one time and am working to sort the time thing out."

Gordon. "There was killing going on all around me in real time there. It was terrible and my worst memory now."

"Your mind almost broke into shards, I think. The mental pressure is overwhelming. Animals being tortured, too. I want out of this. Gotta find your name."

I search, even entering an old ruin of some kind. And at last, while fighting off the uglies there who want desperately to send me into oblivion, I find it! I tuck it into my body and begin my return, being sure to keep anything from following.

"Gordon, we're back. I'm going to heal Brad in the sacred water and we'll be there very soon with you. Begin preparations for yourself."

I took the young soul to the water, bathed him, healing him. "Gordon, he's been tortured constantly since the kidnapping."

"Why?"

"Because they could. Likely great entertainment. But we're getting that cleared away. I'm being sure that you won't have to deal with that part of yourself. Gordon, you do not have to go back to those memories and re-deal with them. It's past for all of you. Believe that. It's important that you do. No dwelling on what else you could've done, blah, blah, blah. Promise me now!"

"Not sure. I've always been told not to hide from the past, but to deal with it."

"Yeah, and I'm sure that's helped some. But enough now. Okay?"

"You bet."

So I finished up healing, not taking too much time because I don't want the soul part to become distracted and lose focus. We returned to this reality, Brad still in my body as I resumed full occupation of my chair. Then I began "draining" him from my heart/chest down my right shoulder, arm, and into my hand.

"Gordon, do you see the ball of mist?"

"It's very vague."

"Well, let me know when it's really strong. I have to focus on giving it more integrity. As soon as I do that, I'll tell you it's on its way."

Soon, the ball of mist was so solid that it could not be seen through. I "blew" it gently across the space, and it began to enter Gordon's left side, just under his arm. He experienced it and focused on my earlier instructions while I encouraged him and smoothed things. When all was still, I healed over the opening beneath Gordon's arm and began to tend to myself, stretching, checking about to see that all was well. It was.

Gordon was crying very quietly, but smoothly. I let him go on for a time. Then, "How is it going?"

"Everything is changing. A lot. I can't describe it all. But I notice that things look differently to me than they did an hour ago."

"That's to be expected. You are seeing through two experiences," I explained. "Now, don't expect it to be all at once, nor try to make that be. Just allow it to occur in its own time. It may take weeks to integrate this newness."

"I think I like it. It's just very new."

I laughed. "Well, I guess so! Now, we must eat something fun and then off to bed."

Gordon, like most people, demurred that he wasn't hungry. I bullied him. "I'm the witch doctor, you know. Do what I say."

We ate, and after some desultory chat and exchange of experiences Gordon went to his camp-bed outside under the amazing stars. I dropped half dead into my bed. He was up and left so early in the morning that we didn't talk, so I didn't get to warn him about his altered eyesight and possible discomfort at being in a car, driving through our wonderful desert back to Tucson. But I heard about it that night from Val, his wife.

Over the next couple weeks, I received calls from both Val and Gordon about his progress. He had had problems with his left side for many years, much numbness, to the point of inability to control that side. Since the soul had re-entered through there and apparently "took up residence" there, Gordon first experienced some real pain (waking up pain?) and finally normalcy. I urged work with his nephew, a massage therapist, to help integrate and smooth things more completely.

A few days ago, Gordon and I spoke on the phone. He's coming out in a couple more weeks to do retrieval segundo. And we hope that his nephew will come along.

Are You Prepared To Die For It?

During one of my earlier soul retrievals, I learned about fear and these creatures of Illusion I work with so often now. Fran asked me to journey for her since she had been feeling seriously depressed, which was not normal for her usual ebullient self. We had just finished some work together, and I was "warmed up," so I performed what I expected to be a brief, simple journey. It would change my work.

Immediately into the journey, I found Fran held hostage by some pretty ugly looking non-humans. Respectfully, I bowed toward them and asked what they were doing to her? Their response was sheer insanity, a rush of foul images, incomprehensible. By then, I realized who the leader of these creatures was and directed my questions to it/her.

"We are killing her, of course," or something like that.

"You can't do that," I replied in my most ingenuous fashion.

"Why not? Who will stop us?"

"I will."

Much laughter, hooting, and rolling about.

Following some more threats and counter-threats, I wrapped all my power about me and revealed myself to them. The leader responded.

"Oh, it is you, Shaman. How we will feast tonight!"

"No feasting, except by me. I have come for (image) her. I will take her from you."

"Are you prepared to die for it?" the leader asked slyly.

A deep breath. "Yes."

They were as nearly startled as I was.

"Then come ahead, brave one." Did I sense any respect there?

I entered their world, killed most of them and took Fran's soul from them. Now there was respect, and now there was a new body of work with new skills for me. Never let them see you sweat.

But what about soul thefts which are for the highest good of the client? That happens. And I do my best to explain this situation to the client and help them understand how to cooperate with it and that, at least for now, it is a good thing.

Nancy, who is a long time apprentice and one of the finest shamanic practitioners I have ever met, came to me shortly after we met and asked for a generalized healing. She related some information concerning a creature which had been seen by a former teacher near her and which she referred to as the "white lady." It seemed that the teacher was rather unsettled by this entity and did not comprehend it. It did not seem to be the usual "spirit guide" she was used to. I journeyed and met up with a beautiful snowy owl. This was Nancy's white lady. During the journey, I found that part of Nancy's soul had been "abducted" by the Faire Folke. We discussed this, and Nancy asked me to perform a soul retrieval, as is common among people who have been so intruded upon. I went over to the OtherWorld to do so.

What a surprise! I was met by the Snowy Owl/White Lady, and it was explained to me that, indeed, a portion of Nancy's soul was removed when she was young. However, it was done to instruct and to prepare for her future healing work. The soul looked robust and happy. I was even allowed to have a short chat with her. She understood the work she was preparing for, and had chosen to do this. In fact, the "soul-entire" had agreed to this prior to birth. She would return and reunite with Nancy before long, particularly since Nancy was well along her road to becoming a fine healer. I returned to the present space.

Nancy was content with this, albeit pretty curious, and looked forward to the return of her soul with the information it would bring with it. We discussed the possible form this might take, and I agreed to check the progress of her soul from time to time. Despite our curiosity and puny preparations, the Faire Folke and the soul had their own agenda, and Nancy has reunited, not in a dramatic way, but gradually over the years as she has moved into her Wisdom. And the Snowy Owl/White Lady is always there to oversee the work in progress.

A man who was angry with UFOs and Faire Folke demanded of me one time how I felt about being abducted. He felt outraged at the premise. I replied, as would Nancy today, that one isn't "abducted" if one is cooperative.

Power of the Name

Marcia and Gwen were telling me that they were practicing, albeit tyros, witchcraft with a man and attempting to form a new coven, since they had not found any others which seemed "just right" to them for the work they had felt drawn to. The Tucson area—I guess Arizona altogether—is a welcome home to a large population of those who hold with the Old Religion, the space here being one of tolerance, do-what-you-do-as-long-as-it-harms-none. The Sheriff's Office has a full-time deputy just for Satanism, who has not only given his stamp of approval on the local witches publicly ("They seem more harmless, more Christian, if you will, than churchgoers," he says), but often calls upon them to help him with some of his cases involving those who refer to themselves as Satanists (witches do not believe in a satan and are profoundly opposed to things like living sacrifices and causing pain or harm to anyone or anything). These two women were welcome in my home and workroom.

Both women seemed very gentle, although Marcia was the more assertive. I had noticed a lack of liveliness in Gwen as they entered. And it was for her that they had come. Marcia became the spokeswoman.

"We worked with Donald for a few months, but he seemed to be getting more and more out there as we continued to meet each month," she said.

"What were you doing most of that time?" I asked.

"Mostly, we were putting together some rituals that felt good for us—some from here, some from there—from our diverse backgrounds in working within other covens. Donald comes from Texas, Gwen from Northern California. And I have lived here most of my life. Together, we have a real varied experience," she related. "We were feeling our way, working pretty hard. We would look for others to join up with us once we got our basics down, the personality of our coven established."

"Okay, then what?" I probed.

"Well, Donald seemed to become a little possessive of us, even when we were not working together. He wanted to know what we were doing all the time. He wanted us to find a place and start communal living," she said.

"And you didn't want to?" I asked.

"No, we each wanted our independence. Witchcraft is a large part of our lives, but not all of it," she said.

"So what did he do? And let's not refer to him by name any longer," I cautioned. "I've found that it gives the person some edge. Just refer to him as him."

"Great. For some reason—probably because I'm of a more independent nature—he focused on Gwen in his campaign to control us. She and I would discuss it away from him. But soon I noticed that her energy level was 'way down and dropping', and she seemed to care less and less about anything, much less defying his insistence."

Gwen chimed in here. "We both work at the courthouse, and someone there saw how weak I was becoming and suggested that I see you. They don't know that we're witches ..."

"Don't worry, they will never find out from me," I promised. "But I wonder why they recommended me?"

"The person who seemed the most insistent about it said that she felt that Gwen's weakness was not just physical and that you were the one to take care of anything else," Marcia said.

Interesting. But here they were.

"I believe I can help. If not, I can point you toward someone who can. First, we have to find out what he's done to Gwen—and possibly even you, Marcia. I just can't believe he's attacked one of you without touching the other. It just seems like Gwen got the most overt shot of it," I said.

"Makes sense to me," Marcia said. "I'm older and have been working within the craft longer, been exposed to some of the more controlling people who seem to emerge in any sort of spiritual or religious life. I'm so involved in other aspects of life that I'm less likely to be gotten to. Gwen is far more new at this."

Gwen nodded.

I journeyed. And stopped almost immediately.

"You each have your spiritual names," I said.

"Oh yes," Marcia said. "Of course."

"He knows them, naturally," I pointed out.

"Yes."

"Gwen, he's stolen your name, and with it your essence," I said. What a swell man.

"I'm going to go back to the OtherWorld. It will be life-threatening, so I need you both to stay with me here, stay alert, and if I ask anything respond immediately and succinctly. I will not have time or the safety necessary to wait while you two ponder and hem and haw. Okay?"

They both agreed. I asked Marcia to keep an eye on Gwen and to ask her aloud several times as I worked how she was doing, to keep her "present" while I was "gone." She agreed, and I felt comfortable with her ability.

I went to the OtherWorld, through tunnels with all sorts of non-human and non-animal beings hanging about. I had to be careful to watch my front, back, top, and bottom. So much activity, so much to watch—yet not get involved with. I had to keep it all at some distance from my mind. I came upon an old stone building; it looked like an ancient monastery, crumbly but still strong, vine-covered, dank, dark, heavy doors. Not a pleasant place to enter, but enter I must. In my mind was my purpose: to locate Gwen's sacred name and bring it back to her. And I knew it would not be easy.

I looked into or "sensed" room after room. Hallway after hallway, I walked through, mentally "calling" Gwen's essence. It was something like the game I played a lot when young: "now you're warmer, now you're hotter, now you're colder." Finally, the door was before me. I could "hear" the names held in there. I opened the door. The place was filled with names. They appeared, metaphorically upon wooden slats, and they were heaped upon a large table and all over the floor, stacked up in the corners of the room—more than knee-deep. There were spirit forms in here also, likely those who were keeping the names from their rightful owners. They were something like the pictures one sees of griffins and ogres, and some resembled hateful humans.

"Gwen, fast, what's your sacred name?" I asked.

No response.

"Gwen, please!" I was in two worlds at one time, and it was beyond dangerous.

Marcia just snarled at Gwen: "She said to respond quickly. Do it!"

A soft, unintelligible voice.

"What?" I asked.

"Her name is Falcon Stoops," Marcia finally took over.

Whew. I began searching for the energy this name emits. Through all the heaps and piles and stacks, slipping and sliding on some of the names there. All these people, held captive and weakened and enslaved by having their names taken by people they probably trusted! The dust was choking me also. And I still had to keep my senses on those entities here who wanted me out of there or, best, dead.

There it was! I grabbed the wooden "sign" with Gwen's name, put it inside my shirt and began my journey back. This was early on in my work and I was still retracing my journey back. Now I move to a clear space, check things out to ensure that nothing comes along and jump back to my special starting space.

I brought Gwen's name back to a woman who was already more alert and alive than she was fifteen minutes ago. By the time we'd all had some iced tea together, she had color in her face, and Marcia agreed that she was Gwen again.

"Get away from that man," I urged.

"We already have," said Marcia. "We see him from time to time in some of the great meetings the community witches have, but as far as we know, he's practicing solo now. And we will warn others about him."

I learned later that this man left the Tucson area and went to San Francisco. He was said to have decided that Tucson was "just too provincial" for someone with his abilities. Yawn.

Most shamans won't have their pictures taken, since one can take a photograph to a *bruja* or other black arts practitioner and have a curse placed through it. I used to be very careful with my name, also. Now that I have worked for so long and been attacked so often, I have the experience I require to prevent this. I can feel the touch when someone is attempting to attack me, and I simply do what is necessary to refuse their entry. That is why should you meet a shaman, from whatever culture, you will find that they are elusive; even when they appear to be open and above-board, there is something omitted—not a lie, exactly, just some part of the shaman's presence which isn't there. One I know allows photographs to be taken, but "sends his soul" elsewhere during the taking. I did that for a time, and the pictures all look as if they are of a dead woman. Which, I suppose, they are. Nowadays, I do not need such tricks, but no one in this world sees or knows the Shaman entirely. Probably only superficially, in fact. Heh - heh.

Chapter 7

Curses

Curses are an integral part of Southwestern culture. I never sat and thought much about them. Actually, I held the common "civilized" attitude that I was taught in school: the person cursed causes his or her own demise. That's partly true. The other aspect of this "superior" attitude is that the cursed must believe in the curse to be affected. No. The modern attitude regarding curses and the cursed is that you must be terribly gullible to be affected. Not so. No, no. All are partly true. But none of these theories are truly applicable to real curses.

Let's break down a curse. The cursor must be aware of her power (men curse also, but we'll use feminine here since it has been viewed primarily as a female weapon). Even women who are not so aware are occasionally so taken away by the emotion of rage that the curse comes bubbling up from somewhere deep inside. I believe this place to be primordial and derived from our genetic makeup, our DNA. Our ancestors may become one with us during that sort of extreme outrage. I have not found curses to be as effective when thought out and planned. The ones which boil out are killers. Throughout the ages, people everywhere have feared above all the woman's curse. Even more fearsome is the old woman's curse. The most awful of all is the curse of a dying person. This is a power I wish we could harness. It is more awesome than any bomb or hurricane, more awesome than even the great Niagara Falls. A simple from-deep-inside curse.

Long ago, someone I was very close to caused me to perform an act which resulted in the painful deaths of three kittens and their mother. It still haunts me. Hours after the occurrence, I faced that man and heard words pouring from my mouth, words I had never thought of or heard before. I cursed him thoroughly. I recall that part of the curse was that he would never again know joy or peace. The man committed suicide less than six months later. Did my curse cause that? I don't know. I hope not. But I *do* know for certain that he was never happy or peaceful again. I have never been able to recreate that in a purposeful way. I felt that it came from some dark pool, deep, deep within my psyche. It seemed to be more powerful than I, for it was certainly contrary to my nature in those years.

There are people who make a good living cursing for hire. In the Southwest, they are called *brujos* or *brujas*. They are greatly feared, of course. But they are approached when one wants something done very badly. Here is a cautionary and true tale.

A woman I knew in El Paso was having trouble with her husband. He was away a lot and often with other women. This fine lady saw little of him, as did their young children. Sophia wanted him to work and come home. She wanted him to be a good husband and father. That's not asking a lot. She asked me to accompany her over the border into Juarez to visit a *bruja*. Thinking this would be fun and interesting, I did so.

The *bruja* was civil but distant. Sophia explained her dilemma and what she wished. The *bruja* told Sophia her price. My acquaintance did not have the full amount with her, but she promised to bring the balance in two weeks. The deal was made.

The *bruja* worked and got it together. She said that the errant husband would be home and under foot within the month, never to stray again. We returned to our homes.

It all went as planned. The husband became the world's ideal spouse and parent. He worked and spent the rest of his time at home, caressing his wife and teaching his kids. The wife became bored stiff and decided that she wanted him out, out, out. Would I return with her to Juarez?

"Sure. But have you paid the lady?" I asked.

"No. We'll take care of that today. I'm not happy with the results of her work."

I demurred. It seems pretty foolish to mess with someone who turned a Casanova into Mr. Mom. This was starting to sound like an old Vincent Price movie. But I went with her.

At the woman's door, the *bruja* smiled and held out her hand. "You're a month late in payment, but I am glad you have come to me with it now."

Sophia asked to enter. They conversed for quite a while in Spanish too rapid and involved for me to follow well. They argued. I became slightly alarmed, edging toward the door, glad we were in my car. The explosion happened. The *bruja* threw the money at my acquaintance, screaming what even I knew to be a curse at her. We left.

Less than sixty days later, the woman was dead of some minor "woman's ailment" in the hospital. None of the doctors could explain it. Her husband was devastated, as were her children who had lost their very young mother.

I believe that it was not just the money which caused the *bruja* to react in such a deadly way, but the lack of respect by my erstwhile friend. I also believe that even had Sophia shown the required respect at their last meeting, it would have been too late. These suggestions come from my experiences with those who curse and with my own work. The shaman inside *must* have a show of respect, no matter what my work—even just in passing conversation. If not, the shaman within me flies into a towering rage. It takes a special aptitude to lay down a curse. And those I have met who lay curses are as varied in their approaches as there are healers. Most seem to require a focus—perhaps an item of clothing, candles, or a photograph, something to focus the curse upon.

My first curse took a period of time to complete, being laid over and over with little obvious effect. The cursee was miserable, but that could well have been circumstantial, for he is a most miserable person. However, the curse took dramatic and immediate effect when I obtained a shirt of his and, with certain alterations, placed it where the man was sure to find it. Bada bing. Curse completed. As if an electric current connected. It seemed that he needed to know that he was a victim.

Multi-Generational Curses

The Grijalva family made an appointment with me after being referred by Tom Maday, my chiropractor friend. They were concerned that their adult son was cursed, causing him to be unusually accident prone. I saw Andres with his sister. It was to be the start of quite a relationship with a wonderful *familia*.

Let me state upfront here that I have a hard time with curses, since I don't *think* curses can affect us. I have been programmed by school and civilization. I do *believe* in them, since I have experienced them through my work and by witnessing the results. So I had to shift my thinking quite a leap to work with Andres.

"I believe someone has laid a curse on me," he said, "because no matter what I do, I get hurt." He went on to list his injuries, which were multitudinous.

"What about your home life, your job, other portions of your life?" I asked.

"No, all is well there. I have a wife I love and two children, and I am valued at my job. I am also a fairly successful artist in my spare time."

Huh. But still ...

I journeyed for Andres and found that his entire birth family was cursed by the same person.

"Andres, you were cursed when someone placed a curse upon your mother as she was carrying you. It went through her into you," I said. "In fact, your entire family has received this curse to a lesser degree because it has splashed onto everyone."

"That makes sense," he said. "My mother believes she was cursed when young, shortly after marrying my father."

His sister agreed.

"I will probably have to see everyone, but let's start here tonight and see how much we can do through you since you were the second in line," I said.

I went back to when Andres was in the womb and found the curse.

"It comes to you from a family member—she is related to your father," I said.

"Yes, that is who we think it is," both agreed.

"But the curse itself was placed by a *bruja* at the relative's order. It was bought, of course," I said.

"Yes. The relative is not able to lay a curse herself," he said.

"Well, I'm going after the *bruja* right now, and we'll take care of the rest later on," I said. "This may be complicated."

I journeyed and found the *bruja*. She had died in the interim. I had to search the Land of the Dead for her and found her hiding in a phone booth. What? But I dragged her out, identified myself, and gave her two choices.

"Remove the work you did those years ago and repent for this bad life and go to this lovely land (image). Receive forgiveness of the Virgin. Or ... (image) enter nothingness." I showed her both. She snarled like a cornered animal.

I am not as patient as I was at the beginning of this work. Once, I would have gone over and over the situation with this woman, but no more. Sure, if the dead person is in trouble, I can be charm itself, but not when she has spent her life doing bad things to people. That may be none of my business; there are too many bad people for me to concern myself with. But here she was. I had revealed to her a way into goodness and forgiveness, into healing light and One-ness—and she wasn't even polite!

Into the Void. Zoom. The room cleared and was peaceful.

Do I have the right to decide these things? Sure. Why not? People preach non-judgment, but they really want others to do the dirty work. Without courts of law and judges on the bench, our society would be in far worse disorder than it is. So I'm a judge in a blanket. And, folks, she did choose, didn't she?

I returned to Andres and performed some healing on him.

"Andres, things aren't going to be peachy keen from now on, even with this curse lifted," I admonished. "It's been there since before your birth, and has affected your body through and through. I have been able to remove it utterly from your children, however."

"Good," he breathed. "But how about me? What should I do?"

"Things will be better," I said, "but you will always have to be a bit more careful of where you place your feet and where you are than most others. You are freed from that curse, but it is as if you have had a bad disease, and the side-effects from it linger. For example, if you had had pneumonia several times as a child, you likely would always need to be careful of your lungs. You see?"

"That makes sense," he said.

"Now, I need to see your sisters and parents to clear them."

As I healed the sisters from this curse, I also found that they were pretty sensitive to things around them. One in particular, Olivia, had intense interactions with the Faire Folke all her life. As a result of our work together—and her own strong inclinations—Olivia has taken classes and is now a wonderful massage therapist, with an amazing aptitude for intuitive healing. She would be termed *curandera* in the native culture of the *Familia Grijalva*.

Back to the saga of the curse. I cleared the Grijalva mother. It was she whom the curse was first placed upon, remember? Actually, she was pretty easy to clear, after the initial work upon her children. With her came the father, whose relative paid to have the curse applied.

As I sat across from him, I explained that through him, I could heal the woman who had started all this. Would he like me to do that?

"*Si*," he replied.

"Well, there is a catch," I said. "If I heal her from her hatred and bitterness, she may die. She might react as if she had nothing left to live for."

"I know. Do it," he said.

I did so. As I returned, I explained that they should expect to notice a profound change in this woman's lifestyle and behaviors. At least, as long as she lived. And I did not know how long that would be.

Olivia has reported to me several times that the woman in question has returned to the church, received forgiveness from a priest, and even visits the Grijalva family with home-made goodies. She is also busy as a volunteer for visiting the sick and caring for children. She truly seems to be doing all possible to atone for her "sin."

Past-Life Curses

Genna came to me because she had read about soul retrievals and believed that she needed one. But during my initial journey for her, what I found was much, much worse. In an ancient Inca lifetime, she had been a healer. She was so good at it that she became renowned for her works. Naturally, that brought with it jealousy among certain colleagues, chief to our story of which was a priest who just seemed to lack any real talent. One might even suspect that he had to have had connections somewhere to have been in the position of authority. This man was bitter and nourished his feelings of resentment until they expanded into full-fledged hatred. He spent much time laying a curse on that long-ago Genna. And, folks, it followed her through the centuries into the late 1990s.

As near as I could tell, Genna's intervening lifetimes had been affected in all sorts of adverse ways by this ancient curse. And here she was, sitting in my work room with me, at her wits' end, her body broken and ill, her mind confused and her spirit just hanging on. She had been to several allopathic physicians and had worked with all sorts of alternative healing methods, to no avail. She was practicing positive thinking about her body. Still, she could hardly drag herself around. Since some of her organs had shut down, what could I do? Even if I went back in time and took out the good-for-nothing priest and his curse, how could we regenerate what is already lost?

Well, I was getting nowhere with that kind of wondering. Get on with it. I can only do what is presented before me. There is no use wishing a client had come earlier, prior to permanent and severe damage.

Returning to that time in Genna's long-ago history, I located the situation. Observing the relationship between the priest and Genna-the-healer gave me ideas of an approach. I then scanned all the possibilities which could arise from healing in this case, and moved.

Back in time, I walked toward the priest in my full shaman regalia, with my animals pacing and flying and slithering alongside me. He groveled, and that was nice but not a solution. I explained to him who I represented. That got more of his attention, and he even jerked himself upright, forgetting his fear. I suggested that he remove the curse at once.

He refused. I showed him the probability facing him if he continued to refuse. He did not believe me. Oh well.

Pow! Into the Void. And I threw the curse in after him. But as I say, curses take on their own lives after a period of time. So I followed the threads of this one back to the present time and into Genna's body and mind. Withdrawing as much of the "poison" as I could—it had integrated well into each of her cells by now—I exited Genna and proceeded with a regular physical healing.

Was her recovery a miracle for the books? Well, it was miraculous in that she regained her mental equilibrium and her soul thrived. Her body improved to the extent that it did not become more ill, and in fact, improved some. She began to respond to normal medical treatment. And that is a healing, for we remove the blocks to health and can only allow the body to do the rest.

A few months following this session, Genna returned because she was having severe nightmares which were interfering with her daytime life. She feared going to sleep and got little rest when she did sleep. I journeyed and found that the work we had accomplished previously was "crashing" through the interim lifetimes. Her present body and mind were responding to some of those experiences via dreams, since she could not consciously cope with all those memories. We agreed to leave the memories alone, since most were unpleasant. But Genna was still in a vastly improved state. We discussed her options to advance her spirituality, like joining meditation groups and learning some healing techniques such as Healing Touch.

So I would have to say that this curse-lifting was successful.

Troubled Sites and Houses

What about cursed sites? You bet. I have entered houses and left them immediately. I can tolerate haunted houses, but cursed houses are different. There seems to be no hope for them. Yes, I have worked on them a few times, but to little avail. The cursing seems to cease for a time, but then it slowly and surely begins again.

Some of this is natural in that the house is in the wrong place, since we pay so little attention to the sitting of our homes. We choose a nice spot with a view and have the house built there, ignoring whether the site or even the positioning of the house is harmonious. We have had our land witched for water recently, and one of the things he did for us was to witch the site for "bad rays," explaining that there are all sorts of natural energies which move back and forth and at odd angles, in which we do not want to have our home. We will position our permanent home in the area which is clearest, of course.

What about "sick houses?" I have been able to clear some of those, but it is so difficult that I usually suggest people move. Cancer houses. Lung disease houses. When working on such places, it seems that when one problem is removed another one crops up and so on. Perhaps it takes a year or more, but it usually does. This is quite different from a haunted house, in which the problem is identified and healed quickly.

The call came from an old friend I had worked with, a private investigator. Dan had a very interesting situation which he could not solve, no matter what he did. Was I interested? Sure. I figured it was a lost person or something. We met. No, it was a house.

"A house?" I asked. "Since when do P.I.s look for lost houses?"

"Funny. No, this man called us and said that he is being attacked by something no one can see. It bangs on walls. Well, it has escalated so much that now it is banging on the wall and shouting through his window, calling him filthy names and threatening him. We have staked the place out many times, but it never happens when we are there. And I really believe this guy. He's desperate. Nice man, religious, non-threatening. I have interviewed his neighbors, and no one hears it. But we do have recordings of the shouting and banging. We have even spent nights up on his roof!" I went to the man's home. It was smack in the center of several energy lines. His place, not his neighbor's. Very precise. The entire area is also in a strong power site, one which the native people avoided. Aerial photographs show that there was a great deal of activity in that part of southeastern Arizona in the form of villages and trails, but that specific site of perhaps two square miles was avoided. The mission was erected nearby, but not there. Trails pass around the area, not through it.

To compound the problem, the man himself was haunted as the result of a trip to Rome, Italy, during which he walked through the catacombs and picked up a restless spirit from there. He also had some problems with himself, whom he despised. This seemed to attract some of the abuse.

I did a little work there but gave it up shortly. At that time, I just was not qualified to fix things. Today, I would have tackled it a bit differently, starting with approaching the situation as one of a poltergeist (see "Chapter 9: Evil and Shadow") and work my way back. Obviously, there were multiple problems, but the focal point was the man himself, the victim. It was real. And it was a cursed mess.

There is a place in the old mining areas in the Patagonia Mountains west of here in which I and some friends used to hunt (a long time ago). It was just right for our big tent and kitchen setup for the six of us—flat and cleared of brush. But as we began to set up the tent, an argument broke out. It rapidly escalated to a fight during which two guns were drawn. I calmed people down and urged us all to relocate. We did so. And all participants once again became decent and peaceful. We talked about it around the campfire that night.

"I think it's the minerals," Bob said.

"I agree," I said. "This has been heavily mined. I wonder what minerals are most specific in that area?"

We returned the next day and took samples in to friends at the university. I do not recall what all was there, except that there was an extremely high quantity of iron. In investigating the history of the area, there was a higher than usual death rate there during the 1800s, when it was being mined. More than double. From what? Sure, the usual cholera, tuberculosis, and mining accidents, but there was a large number of murders and suicides. Hmm. Can this be interpreted as cursed land? I think so. At least for humans.

I placed a curse on a piece of land. Yes. It was a beautiful area near the border between Mexico and Arizona. When I first entered this canyon, it was breathtakingly lovely. I named it the Enchanted Canyon. Trees grew together over the ancient roadway, moss covered large areas, a stream bubbled throughout the canyon. It seemed untouched by humans. Difficult to get into because the roadway was so rough—we had to "walk" the pickup in carefully.

Two years later, some illegal woodcutters had found the place. Not only had they cut down trees to sell for firewood, but they had felled many trees in such a way that they broke down others for later. It looked as if a bomb had been dropped there. Five years later, the mosses were gone, the stream ran only occasionally, the falls had ceased, and there was little shade left.

I camped and placed a curse upon the place. One that would frighten people away. I worked and worked at the specifics, but I could not find a way to allow only "nice" people to be there. I had to curse it so that it would frighten me out, too. I did so. The last time I camped there, I was very uncomfortable. There were all sorts of scary shadows which appeared, and my dreams were not peaceful. The people who had joined me were unaware of my curse but very aware of their discomfort, although they had loved being there previously.

Someone I know drove over there not too long ago and was nice enough to let me know that it was still scary in there. There were also new trees growing and the old ones were being left alone. No tire tracks into the place, no trash. This was even during deer hunting season! There were mountain lion tracks, javelina and deer, lots of birds. I miss the place, but not enough to lift the curse that serves to protect it. The canyon is living again.

Control and Balance

Mike was an apprentice. Young, but naturally powerful. Undisciplined. He was good-natured and the idea of cursing was an uncomfortable one for him. As he came to trust me, he confided why.

"When I was a teenager, one of the guys I ran with pissed me off," he said.

"Yeah?"

"I got so mad, I pictured him dead."

Uh-oh.

"He died a few days later, drunk in a car wreck."

"And?"

"Roberta, I did it. I know I did!"

"Has this happened often?" I asked.

"Yeah. Not death. But sickness and broken arms—stuff like that. I picture it and it happens."

"I know," I said.

"Well, what do you do about it?" he asked.

"I turned it inward, on myself," I said. "I don't recommend that. It's pretty painful, and it becomes permanent."

"Yeah, I know. You talk about it. But what can we do?"

"Well, Mike, I think we have to control ourselves—to a degree. We have to be aware all the time that we could flare up. So have something innocuous prepared to fire out at them."

"It's still not a good thing to do, is it?"

"No, but it may not be only bad, either. I don't know," I said. "Look, you know that I used to think bruises on my sister's arms when I got real mad as a kid, right?"

"Yeah."

"Well, how is that different from us getting into a hair-pulling fight?"

"Hmmm. Is this justifying?"

"Damned if I know anymore. But I have learned that when people attack me, I will no longer turn my reactions inward. Remember when Jackie did that awful thing at the feast a couple months ago?"

"Oh yeah. I moved away from you. I could feel it coming."

"Well, she got the migraine. I didn't," I said. "And she deserved it for being so stupid, self-centered, and disrespectful. I really feel that way. It may not be the way for everyone to feel, but it is working for me. Today, at least."

"Okay, it makes sense. I still have qualms about it though," Mike said.

"As do I. It bothers me. I want to be a saint," I said. "I'm not, I'm just a shaman."

Mike worked with me, practicing non-invasive, non-permanent retaliation for situations where he felt attacked and vulnerable. We had discussions about when it was appropriate and when it wasn't. We prepared as best we could.

Sometime later on: "Roberta?" Mike on the phone.

"Yeah, Mike. What happened?" I asked.

"This woman at work was yammering at me the other day about torturing animals. She likes to stomp mice and put out poisons. She knows I'm vegetarian and was taunting me with how they kill meat."

"Yeah, Mike."

"I gotcha-ed her. She's at home with the flu. This is the second day. I feel bad about it."

"Good and good," I said. "The flu isn't so bad. She's basically healthy and will get over it. Clean her out some, right?"

"Still bothers me that I can do this."

"Did you ask her to stop?" I said.

"Yes. Over and over. She thought it was funny."

"You have every right to protect yourself and retaliate," I said. "At least, you didn't punch out her lights."

"Hey, you're right."

"If you feel so bad, send her some healing," I said. "You know it's the same energy."

"Guess I will. We're shorthanded with her out," he laughed.

"Way to go."

Curses are real and they are flying all over the place. Be careful of yourself. Pay attention. You can accidentally walk into the path of one. Even if you don't believe in them.

Postscript

Remember the Grijalva family? As I was in the throes of finishing this book, I received a phone message from Olivia. Her brother Andres was having some trouble; could they come out for a session? Of course. She, Andres, his wife Sophia, and Ernestina, an apprentice, arrived on a Sunday night. We had a fine visit, then Ed, a student, joined us. We began our work. First, they reported that the grandmother who had initiated the Grijalva curse had died recently.

"Do you think she could reach out from beyond and harm us?" they asked.

"Why would she do that?" I asked. "I understand that she had a complete turn-around prior to her death."

"True. I just could never find it in me to trust her," Andres said.

"Well, I'll check for sure as I work on you, but I do not feel her presence. I imagine that she's gone for good," I said. "After all, it is better 'over there' than messing with you—and me for that matter—since we've given her nothing but trouble."

Andres got right to it. "I got laid off from the mines when they began shutting down," he said.

"Good. As I recall, I wanted you out of that from the beginning. It's harmful for people to work beneath the earth," I said.

"And you were right," Sophia said. "His health is better since then, and he just seems to be more *here* now."

Olivia agreed. And I had seen the difference in his physical being from when they first arrived.

"So what is the problem?"

"Well, the mining company paid for me to go back to school, and I chose computer training," Andres said. "I thought that would give me the best possible chances of good employment."

"Sure."

"But when I got all my accreditation, I found little work. I signed up with the phone company and worked there for a while. And I partnered with a friend to do some freelance work as well. Things were pretty good at first. Then, the friend boogied, leaving me with the bills and a lease on an office downtown."

"Bummer."

"And 9/11 happened, and shortly afterward the phone company put me on stand-by for work; you know, on-call."

"Yes. Did you get called?"

"Oh yeah," said Sophia. "He gets called all the time. But not for paying work. They call to ask questions about problems. Andres solves them over the phone for them and gets nothing in return."

"That's right," said Andres. "I've had next to no work lately. And I've been putting in applications all around, but no response yet."

"Well, I'm sure things will break loose," I said. "The trouble with schools is that they set you up to believe that specific education will just automatically result in a major career for their graduates, but that's not real life. Especially these days. But I understand that things are beginning to pick up."

"Not for me. Not yet," he said.

"Okay, let's take a look," I said. "How about your dreamtime? And I know you had a problem in your home from an evil entity. Did I get that taken care of? Did it come back?"

They both agreed that since I had worked on that problem over five years previously, things had been normal and quiet. It had been a nasty job. One of their pet finches had died during that attack from an Other-World entity. And one of their sons had been "abducted" during that time. He was now an accomplished musician, had his own car, and lived the full life of a typical teenager. How time flies!

Pulling out a pipe and some tobacco, I decided to check Andres out first by smoke. This involves taking smoke into my mouth, mixing it with my breath, then blowing it at the client, from over the head to toe, front and back. If an area is negatively affected, it will "refuse" the smoke. The smoke revealed a large "hole" in Andres' energy field in the center of his back. It also demonstrated that he had no legs—he had been "cut off at the knees," as the metaphor suggests.

Since they had all studied with me, I invited Olivia, Ernestina, and Ed to journey as I did so for Andres. The drumbeat began. It was soon apparent that while Andres has virtually unlimited potential, he could not realize that in his "legless" state. As I moved onward in my journey, I found that a large portion of his soul had been stolen very early on.

Why hadn't I found that and restored it years ago? Things seem to come in their own time, not mine or ours. I believe Andres had to have layers removed before we could deal with this critical situation. Perhaps he had to have the maturity and trust and belief in order to approach this—all of which had come with our previous work together. Sometimes, it's difficult to accept the "wasted time" when these kinds of things happen, but I have to believe that in the great scheme of things for each of us, timing is not only essential but precise.

The other three sojourners had each found that Andres had more potential than any person had a right to, but that he could not realize it in his legless form. Each one of them saw him in the identical manner. They each addressed his need to meditate daily and to actively work on his self-esteem. It was impressive.

"Okay, so I have to enter the OtherWorld to locate and retrieve Andres' soul," I said. "It's going to be life-threatening for me, so I expect all of you to work with me and stay alert and report what's happening here as I go. No funny stuff."

It would be more dangerous than I thought.

Lord Elf accompanied me (those present here reported seeing it at my side once I began my search) as it always does on these excursions. It is with me nearly all the time, but becomes tangible and visible at these times. Quickly it was reported that I had disappeared. I was on my way. But where? I ended up in a space I had never experienced previously. And I just did not like it a bit.

There is no language for this. The place/space was all gray tones and strange angles. It felt like machinery or parts of machinery. It was uncomfortably absurd. Although I could not discern other entities with my senses, I knew they were present. In fact, I came to comprehend that the entire space was an entity. I was inside a monster of some sort. Yuck. I also knew without a doubt that one misstep on my part would be my last. And that if I screwed up in here, I would be a permanent resident of this space.

But there was the soul. Two eyes peered at me from beneath something that resembled a stack of boards or iron plates. I checked and knew it was Andres. But I also knew that if I moved toward those eyes or bent toward them, I would be done in. They had to come to me. They did not. This was the most passive and un-sentient soul I had ever gone after. What to do?

The eyes disappeared. Everything shifted as if in an earthquake. When it was still once again, I looked in the same area, and the eyes re-appeared shortly after. Fearful, distrustful, not of this world or our species. Yet they belonged to Andres. No doubt. I waited—this is the hardest—for things to clear and for my ability (if you can call it that) to solve the dilemma. Then ...

"Andres, allow images of your life—the best parts—to run through your mind right now. Your wife, kids, home, art, that kind of thing. Feel how much they all mean to you," I said.

The eyes paused, then the soul flew into my arms, and I wrapped it within my owl wings. It was a baby, yet ancient—the eyes old and creased but also childlike and innocent. There was little or no intelligence or memory. This is very strange. Focus. Get out. Now.

Returning to my centering place, I pondered what to do. Reuniting this poor thing with Andres would be useless. Possibly worse than useless, for it could actually absorb his energy and life force. That's it! Life force.

"I'm going away with the soul to heal it," I murmured aloud.

We entered the Source of All, that ineffable Light. Duh. Why did it take me so long to figure this no-brainer out? Of course, take it into the Light. It had no life, and now it would enter Life itself. While we were healing, I realized that this soul-part had been taken from Andres while in the womb! That long! No wonder it was lifeless. Well, it was lifeless no longer!

Re-entering the now and the room where the others waited patiently, I began "pouring" the soul part from my body down my right arm and into my hand. A soft, vague glow at first, the soul part soon took form and some solidity. I blew it toward Andres, where it entered him via his chest. As Andres breathed in his soul and quietly reunited, the rest of us spoke quietly.

"He looks more three-dimensional," Ed said.

"His legs are back," said Olivia.

"He's alive and more, well, here," said Ernestina.

I explained a little—not all—of what I knew about the soul part. The rest of it would have to wait until I could process the work privately with a student. As I process, we put our two views of the proceedings together and make a whole. It's really important. Andres and Sophia did not want to know the details, nor should they be distracted with that information.

"Andres, I have to seal up the hole in your back," I said. He stood, and I rewove his aura in that area, ensuring that it was strong but not too tightly woven as to prevent good circulation. For our energy must circulate as well as our blood, right? His legs didn't need any additional work. They had returned and seemed to be strong and in good shape.

"I have something you must do in exchange for this work," I told him. "And you must do this in a conscious spirit of gratitude and awe. Can you do it?"

"Sure. What is it?"

"Well, you'll think it's a bit nuts, but I give you my word: it is important," I said.

"I trust you," he said. "What should I do? I'll do it."

"Each night until after the night following the full moon, you are to go to a special place outside your home and set out a plate of good cookies or cake and a cup—not glass—of grape or apple juice. You must do this as if you were presenting a dessert to a respected guest at your home. In the morning, take up the dishes, leave the pastry for the insects and birds, wash the dishes carefully and do the same the following evening." I pictured him doing this near a magnificent sculpture he created in his yard.

"I'll do it, and I'll put it by that sculpture of Moctazuma," he promised.

"That's what I was thinking of, too," said Sophia.

Minds of a feather.

"Now, remember, you must do this on the night following the full moon, too," I said. "Starting tonight, when you get back home, and continuing every night through then."

"Got it."

Why do I include this in the chapter on curses, when it appears to belong in the one involving soul retrievals? This goes directly to the curse placed upon Mother Grijalva and her unborn child—and the rest of the family as well, for all are affected in various degrees. This is a demonstration of how a curse takes on a life of its own and simply continues to live on in diverse forms, often picking up strength as it goes.

A Prehistoric Spider?

Something similar occurred when a Pakistani man called me and asked a series of questions, trying to determine if I was qualified enough to rid him of "something evil." In fact, he called it a curse, but I found it to be something a little different. I met with this man, and in the course of our discussions, I told him I would have to have his wife present, since it somehow involved her. We arranged for them to come to my place.

His wife was not exactly hostile, but she was certainly not friendly. I found her reaction to me a bit odd and so observed it during our meeting. I could see a "sort-of" figure behind her. What was this? I didn't mention the figure; for some reason, I just didn't trust the situation. I felt almost as if I were being tested and—what? Challenged?

As I began honing in on the problem, a spider crawled out from beneath the sofa the wife was seated upon. Since we do not kill them, I called Larry from outside and asked him to remove it to the yard. When he reached to lift it onto a piece of heavy paper, he stopped and remarked that it sure was a peculiar spider, one he'd never seen before. I looked and agreed with him. It certainly was a strange one. I also caught a glimpse of the wife's eyes; they glittered, and I realized in passing that she was almost laughing at me.

The figure had disappeared. In its place, I saw a portal open. It took me into the deepest past. Back to when humans looked more ape-like than modern. Smallish, hairy, very primitive in thought. And a woman. Woman? Hard to tell. But "she" looked at me with primal hatred.

I stopped everything, sat back, and looked at these people before me. Then, I did something I have only rarely done: I apologized to them for taking their time but stated that I could not help them. The wife was vastly pleased. And then I knew! She had done this deliberately to him. They would have no children. She would give him nothing. It was her only way of having control in an arranged marriage to a man she felt contempt for. Her elder sister was with them, and I saw confirmation of this in her eyes also. The three of us women stood in silent communication for several seconds, timeless and ageless. They knew I knew. They were pleased that I would not intervene. The man was very angry.

"My advice to you is to go on pilgrimage. Make peace. Atone. Turn your face to your god," I said. "Only in that way will you ever find peace and joy."

He raged out of the room and into his car and sped away, leaving a cloud of dust and gravel in his wake. Oh well.

They also left me with something else.

The spider.

"Larry, where did you put that spider?" I called.

"Right there, by the door," he said. "It was really strange."

"Strange is right," I said. "Help me find the bugger. It's not exactly a spider."

We never found it.

A couple nights later, my study group came out and I told them of the encounter. All instinctively knew that the spider was a connection with that ancient pre-human. A light came on in my head. We formed a circle just outside the door. Inside this circle of caring people, I began walking counter-clockwise, going back thousands and thousands of years. And I found that ancient "woman."

She was entirely primitive. It was impossible to speak with her until I found the primal space within myself and tuned in to her. In imagery, I saw her connection with the woman who had sat before me a couple days previously. Powerful magic because it was so primal. I learned some from her, then sealed that portal. Retracing my steps clockwise, I returned to this time. Someday, perhaps, I will re-open the portal and taste some more of that ancient's abilities.

Okay, I confess that I place curses on certain people, too. It would be almost impossible for me not to. There is a real judgmental attitude about this, however, and I have downplayed this part of my work considerably.

But as you will read in "Chapter 8: Danger, Judgment, and Protection," it is simply a matter of moving from our childish and outdated "everything spiritual is nice-nice" thinking to realizing that the All Life is open to many ways.

For me, the largest portion of placing a curse is to research the entire situation carefully: the meriting of one who would receive the curse; all the possible ramifications of it, including the curse's afterlife; and the exact properties of it and benefits. Yes, benefits. Here's an example.

A man is abusive to his wife, children, and dogs. Nothing seems to alleviate his inherent evil. Okay, he merits a curse. What ramifications? He has two biological children. Thus, the curse must be formed to affect him directly, with no splashing. All right, that's planned. Now, what are the benefits: Ah, yes. Nightmares of being chained and beaten? Thirst?

Hunger? Cold nights? How about mortal fear of one bigger and more powerful than he? Hey, discovery by the company he works for that he's stealing from them? Yes. And just for fun, sore feet.

Just try to find anything "negative" in that. Even Jesus cursed, you know. Had a bad temper, that one.

Perhaps this chapter will remove some of our preconceived ideas that we are the arbiters of good and evil, even without researching the subject—and remove a bit of the bad press on curses.

Owl is Roberta's totem.

Chapter 8
Danger, Judgment, and Protection

There is certainly danger. All about us, all the time, shaman or not. In our present environment, filled beyond the maximum with human beings, living and dead, pollution is made up of far more than bad air, noise, and bad water. Our environment is filled with attacks, with evil and with nonsense zapping around the place from fools who play with things they do not understand in the name of "healing Mother Earth" or whatever. Then there are the non-humans all about us in our daily comings and goings. How many of us have had an encounter with a very strange-looking person, perhaps passing on the street—a short encounter, but one which left us feeling uncomfortable and wanting to talk to someone about it, but not knowing how? Nearly everyone I have talked with concerning this has been able to relate such an experience.

If one were never to be "attacked," I would find that unusual in the extreme. It does not mean that something is "out to get" you but probably just that you were in the way. Zap, zap—go to your friendly neighborhood shaman. I will confess to you in this chapter that all the healers and people who know better have been zapped, too. Ha. You would enjoy their faces when it comes out. "Me? Couldn't be. I know better." To be fair, here's a story on me.

I had just returned to Tucson from a trip to visit my daughter in San Francisco. While there, we had driven to San Jose to sightsee the Winchester House. This is a rather infamous place with a fascinating story involving the widow of the man credited with inventing the Winchester rifle. She was into spiritualism and was told via a medium that she must constantly build on this house in order to stay alive, that when the building stopped, so would she. One cannot help but wonder if that medium was related to any local builders or carpenters.

The place is amazing. Construction continued day and night for several years, even on holidays. I had wanted to visit there since I was a kid. We enjoyed it thoroughly. So busy having fun and looking at antiques that I put all the possibilities of a place like that out of my mind. We got a kick out of the tour guide trying to frighten us with innuendo.

Now, it's not that the place was haunted by ghosts so much as the house just attracted all sorts of energies. It served as a swell repository for things brought to it by the thousands of tourists who walked through it each year. And I got gotcha-ed.

Upon my return to Tucson, I found myself in a deep depression, quite unusual for me. It was difficult even to breathe. And nothing seemed to alleviate it.

John—a Pipe Carrier—called one day, and it was just a chat until he asked how I was feeling. I replied the usual okay, and we concluded our call.

He called back almost immediately.

"What's really going on?"

"Well, John, I'm terribly depressed, and I just don't seem to be able to get a handle on this thing."

"I'll be right there, okay?"

John brought his Pipe. We smudged, smoked, and I nearly passed out with the Pipe in my hands. I was very sick. At one point, I was smoking that Pipe, barely supporting it from touching the floor. My eyes begged John to stop it, but he would not. We smoked that entire Pipe in silence. Then I ran to the bathroom and retched.

I felt better! John soothed me with his Eagle feather, and we sat outside and had some iced tea.

"John, what the hell was it?"

He smiled—no, he laughed at me. "Well, you got got. Where you been?"

"Just to San Francisco to see my daughter. No big deal."

"Yep, big deal. You picked up something evil that was taking all your life force, lady."

"I just can't imag- ... oh, I did visit Winchester House. But ghosts can't hurt me."

"Not a ghost; something else. Yep, you got it in a big old house. I know that place. I wouldn't go in there."

"Well, I sure did."

"Yep, you did, all right. Feeling a little more humble?"

Since then, I have cleared a lot of people—very smart people who know how to take care of themselves. I have compassion for them now. I also laugh at them when they explain that this sort of thing cannot happen to them because they know what they are doing.

The best protection is to practice paying attention to everything. Simply being aware and prepared. Experience will help, and you cannot experience anything to prepare yourself for some big baddie if you keep yourself all blocked up. Take risks, get cleared, learn.

Judgment

Late one night, I received a phone call from John. Remember John, the smarty Pipe Carrier? I had only seen John once before, at the Sun Dance, where he was a dancer, piercing in his chest and back. He had also taken my flesh for the Sacred Tree and had glowered at me. This time, however, he was asking for help.

"I have sores on my legs, and they won't heal up."

I asked the obvious, "Do you have diabetes? Have you been to a doctor?"

Snort. "I have had Dorris give me medicines, and they still will not go. My piercing wounds are healed well, but these will not heal. I got them at the Sun Dance from a man there."

"But there were all spiritual people there," I said. "Surely no one there would hurt a dancer."

"I am sure it is he. But I want to know. They tell me that you can see far. Do it for me. Find this man."

"I've never done this before, but I can try. I'll call you back in the morning." How does one say no to a Sun Dancer? I could not.

I worked for an hour or so, sitting before the television and holding my crystal in my left hand. From time to time, I would glance easily into it. In far less than that hour, I saw him. The next morning, I called John.

"I found him, John."

"Good. Tell me," he grunted.

"He is Native American, has a pockmarked face and something bristly in his hair, on the top of his head. He danced there, too," I described.

A breath. "That is the man. I thought so. He attacked me last year, too. Come to heal my legs today."

"How about this evening?"

"Good." Click.

I didn't know where he was. I called Dorris later that day.

"I found John's attacker, and ..."

"I know," she broke in. "I told him you could. None of the medicine people we know were able to. Now, he can be healed."

"I'm to be there this evening. But I don't know where he is."

Dorris laughed. "You can find a man no one else can because he's so powerful ... but you can't find John here in town? Some shaman."

Native Americans like to make fun of pink people such as I. But she gave me the address and directions and said that she and her young son would be there also.

The healing went easily. Using my hands in his etheric body, I "pulled" the angry red poison down his legs, down into his feet, and told him to release that into the bowl of salt water I had at his feet in front of me. He did not respond. I asked him again, but he sat with his head resting on the back of the sofa, apparently relaxing.

"John, release the poison into this bowl of water so that I can return it to Mother Earth. Please."

He sat up, staring through me.

"I send it back to he who put it in me!"

That poison went through me like lightning. Every person in the room was affected. Dorris' little boy was sick for days, vomiting and cramps. I was stunned, physically as well as mentally. Why did he do that?

The healing was very successful. But my life was a mess. People noticed a black tarry substance oozing under the door of my workroom when we had meetings and readings. I could not sleep. Larry was sick. And it was getting worse. A woman visiting me saw the phenomena in the workroom and told me clearly that I had better get help because something wanted to kill me. I called Dorris.

"Yes, it is the man you identified to John."

"Why?"

"Roberta, no one else could see his face, although many tried. But you could. He wants you. He hates you because he's threatened by you. And to top it off, you are white."

"What can I do? Larry's even too sick to work."

"Call Ed and his wife. They are medicine people, and I believe they can help you. Do it right away."

I did.

"So *you're* the one who saw him. Hey, we're impressed. We've been hoping to meet you. I tried last year, too, but just could not see his face. How did you do that, anyway?"

"He came into my crystal. As I caught a glimpse of him, he turned his back, but I 'walked' around in my mind inside the crystal to face him. He turned again, but I just kept up with him until I saw his face," I related. It had seemed pretty easy to me.

"Wow. (Ed is a white medicine man, so he can say wow.) Well, you're in trouble now, hmm? Want to come out here and see what we can do for you?"

"Please. It's bad. I'm sick, my workroom is filling with nasty black tarry stuff, and my husband is too sick to work."

"Yeah. Don't sleep tonight, or he'll get to you. If you can, keep your husband awake also. We'll see you sometime mid-morning tomorrow. Okay?"

I got the address and directions and spent the longest night of my life. Larry was too far gone to care about anything, so he slept. I created a circle and maintained that all night. After two flat tires on the way there, I did arrive at Ed's unharmed.

"I'm really looking forward to hearing how you forced him to show his face," Ed greeted me. "I hope you brought that crystal."

I had, and I brought it out and showed him the technique. Shamans always have *one* crystal which they use for protection and scrying. We seldom have more because to have many crystals is disrespectful to

Mother Earth. Mine cost me less than five dollars and has been a best friend to me for a long time.

Ed worked on me for about two hours, and I had a lot of work to do myself, but the pockmarked medicine man gradually left my life. It also left me with a *lot* of questions. I called Dorris and met with her.

"Dorris, why did John do what he did to us all?"

"Well, he had to do it that way, to show his power over the other man. If he hadn't, that man would continue to attack him forever."

"But why didn't he tell me he was going to do it so that I could have been safe? Why did he harm me and make your little boy so sick? That's not a very spiritual thing to do."

"Who says?" Her eyebrows lifted.

"And for that matter, why would any Sun Dancer attack another *during the dance?* It's just not spiritual, and I thought these men were highly spiritual."

"Who are you to judge them?" asked Dorris. "It's their way. And if you think about it, it keeps them on their toes. Competition is good practice, isn't it?"

She had a real point there. "Yes. Today's society approves of competition in the workplace, in business, but frowns on it in religion and in interpersonal situations. But I've been getting snatches of teachings about competition and shamans. You're right. Still, why did he harm me, almost kill Larry and make your son very sick?"

"What have you learned in all this? Can you list it? As for my son, I thought I had him far enough away that he would not be affected. Silly, foolish me. And, Roberta, sorry, but Larry needs to learn to either protect himself or steer clear of you when you work. He's his own person, and he has to become aware of his responsibility in all this."

She was right on all accounts. I did not have the right to judge anyone else's spirituality like that. I disagree with what the pockmarked man was doing. And I would go after him today for a client. But I would never again draw poison toward me, and I would be more careful who was present. I am now able to protect all the people in a room.

I lost a great deal of childish innocence.

Protection

Many years ago, I was watching one of those daytime talk shows. This was before cross-dressing priests and on-screen violence. Someone famous was being interviewed about her spiritual journey, which she had put into a best-selling book. The audience had questions.

"What about protection?"

The Star replied, "Oh I don't believe you need protection. You only get whatever you put out into the universe. Be good and you get good."

I was stunned! I stormed about the place, frightening the dogs and cats lounging about, then walked outside a minute to calm myself down. What was this woman doing? People get hurt and worse doing the things she was suggesting—was selling. Madness is lurking about spiritual growth, looking for a toe hold, no matter how "good" you are.

As I returned, it appeared that they had broken for a commercial, or two or three, while I was gone. The Star apparently had been spoken with because her reply was somewhat different.

"What I meant to say was not to protect yourself, but to be careful that what you put out into the universe is what you receive from it."

I waited. Surely that's not all. Would she address protection? I was concerned, since this woman had surrounded herself with known charlatans who purported to channel entities but did so with fake accents. One even used the wrong accents for various spirits and got them mixed up! They were popular, and the Star was making the metaphysical movement more acceptable—to a degree. I referred to it as coffee table spirituality. Johnny Carson referred to it with even more humor.

As I recall, the Star never did address protection that day.

It is a question which comes up with each lecture or class that I do. For good reason. I'm constantly clearing people of stuff, even when they aren't practicing being open. Shamans do not exactly protect themselves. When working, I draw in and pull the energy that no one else wants into myself and release it later, or turn it into defecation. Tradition. Frankly, it's easier and faster to work hard to do this than to continually stop and clear, stop and clear. Besides, I often gain valuable information from nasties that I draw in. Everything has information for me.

I do teach protection. Common sense protection.

Rose came to a meditation weekend I held, and the question of protecting ourselves as we meditated came up, as usual. Before I could reply, Rose explained her technique, which she had been taught years before and was "surefire."

As she launched into this formal protection ritual/visualization cum prayer cum woo-woo, I observed some of the class actually writing this junk down. In a very small nutshell, she was describing what she did each and every night before sleep.

Rose put up protection miles out in one color, then layered the next area in another color with other prayers and visualizations, and so on, until she was in the center of this tightly wrapped cocoon of color and prayer and visuals. I wondered that she was able to move about in her sleep. And what happened if the alarm went off? Could she move? How did she awaken? What were her mornings like? Okay, I admit I began playing a fun game in my mind as she went on. And on. As she finally took a breath, I cut in and asked her about her dreams.

"Oh, I never have any. That's one reason I'm here. I don't dream, and I thought that through meditation, I might be able to return to dreaming. It's so important ..." and on she went into that subject.

Finally, I just stopped her. "If you are so very protected, how do you expect to be taught, inspired, to dream?"

Silence. A long silence.

"You see, when people talk protection, many of them are really talking about blocks. If you block anything, you are in danger of blocking everything. Real protection breathes and is exquisitely simple."

I continued, "What about simply praying along the lines of, 'Great Mystery/God/Whatever, I pray that I receive only that which is for my highest good." It turned out that Rose had not been dreaming for quite some time. Well, how could dreams get through that concrete wall she erected each night?

Experience demonstrates that no matter how well you protect yourself, something will slip through. And it's probably for your highest good, since you will surely learn a great deal if you survive, and you will be better prepared for something worse, which is waiting around the next corner.

Rose took my advice and her dreaming began again immediately.

Sheldon came to our journey nights occasionally, and he considered himself an expert in this sort of thing. One evening, as we were discussing protection and what sorts of things to protect ourselves from, he cut in with the statement that he would not enter a journey without his trusty crystal (or two) for protection and that one must have that sort of tangible protection for one's safety.

We continued the discussion as it had been going, and Sheldon broke in again, repeating his information. Finally, I explained that I believed that in the end, all we have is ourselves. Reliance upon an object, or even a spirit or animal, can let us down at the most inopportune moment. I cited my meeting with the *Chindi* (see "Chapter 9: Evil and Shadow") as an example. Yes, I had a crystal there, but I had actually killed it. What I really had was myself, my experiences, my close calls, my wits. And that is all we really have, folks.

Protection is an attitude also. The analogy here is keeping your doors closed and locked. How do you walk a big city street? Do you keep yourself open-faced, receptive to all you meet? I don't think so. Not these days. Do you leave your doors unlocked in the city? Not likely. If your door is open, how do you determine who walks through it? There are mass murderers out there, right? Thieves. Rapists.

Well, we have the same sort of energy all around us. Those murderers may be dead ones. We don't want just any old murderer entering our space, right? So we adopt the *attitude,* keeping strangers at bay. This also allows us to drop the 'tude when we want to.

There are many examples given in this book regarding danger and protection. Foreign lands and alien spirits, the "black man," fraudulent psychics and so on. The best protection is discernment and wisdom. Only then are we able to protect ourselves. Expect to be gotcha-ed from time to time, and then prepare to deal with that. Isn't that how we learn and acquire the ability to take care of ourselves in life? After all, life should be an adventure.

Roberta poses with various shamanic tools.

Chapter 9

Evil and Shadow: Walking on One Leg

Evil is interesting. Evil is complete freedom, for it is obliged to nothing and no one. Evil is seductive for these very reasons and more. Those who practice evil believe it is power over all. This may be true since one could feel pretty powerful over all other people when they are free of conscience. Early on in my work, I believed that I was here to battle Evil.

Even before the incident in this chapter, I realized through the Work that Evil and Good are the same energy. Merely energy. People have walked out of my lectures because of that statement, likely because they are personalizing Good and Evil. It's hard not to. Let me illustrate.

If I entered a room and found someone raping another, I would act quickly. I would act not only to stop it, but I would probably go wild and have to be pulled off the rapist. I consider such an act to be supremely evil. Laboratory work on animals is inherently evil. Child abuse is evil. Insert your personal outrages here. Those are evil acts out of really nasty human nature and we are actually responsible to react accordingly.

Evil, however, is an energy. It is one which we have certain difficulties comprehending, since we are all programmed to be aware of only "good" things, energies and so forth. We have been indoctrinated for thousands of years that only "light" is our friend. We must aspire to goodness. Shadow and Evil are seldom mentioned, except that we must eschew both. Logically, one has to realize sooner or later that this is impossible. There must be equal amounts of those energies in this life. Nature reveals this to us.

Once we accept that Evil exists and not just to "get us," we may begin to open ourselves enough to comprehend its presence everywhere. As there is day and night, light and darkness, there is Good and Evil. Finally, we experience that it is but energy. All true power and creation are born out of darkness and shadow. Even plants can't grow without darkness.

Only humans, of all sentient forms, have created morality, yet we remain a most immoral species. Our morality is what keeps us separate from All Life. Thus, we continue in our immorality and lack of ethics—inhumanity. What a paradox that one is!

As I began my shamanic practice, I ran into one Evil after another, battling along, doing my best to stamp it out. Nasty ol' Evil, Nightwing will getcha. I also noticed that as I stamped, there was this "mist" which would show up off to one side, similar to a person leaning against a wall, legs crossed, arms folded, head tilted, watching with amusement. I returned to that over and over, moving toward discernment of that energy and information.

For sixty some years, I've striven and prayed for sainthood; I never wanted to be a shaman. Such disappointment. But as I've pointed out to myself and other shamans: if you only have one leg, you eventually stop trying to walk with two.

It came at Wupatki National Monument, near Flagstaff, one Autumnal Equinox. It came big and it came surly and it came for me. Evil. The *Chindi*.

My practice, until I moved here to the mountains, was that each Autumnal Equinox I would travel to Wupatki and camp out. It was a working vacation, for most of the time, I would have students join me to experience the place and something indefinable.

That indefinable was the *Chindi*. I have borrowed that word (please forgive me) from the Navajo (Diné) people in that area. While I suspect it means something slightly different, it is the closest comparison I can find. It describes an evil entity, often appearing in wolf form. It appears to me clearly as a monstrous wolf-like creature, or werewolf. A young man asked me once what I have against wolves. Not a thing against them. This is *wolf-like* in appearance. I believe it is also often true of the Navajo concept of *Chindi*.

There is a phenomenon in this part of the world, on certain moon phases and parts of the years, especially strong over the Fall Equinox, which is reported in newspapers frequently. People reporting that giant black cats have leapt into their backyards and taken their dogs. People slamming on their brakes, even in town, to avoid striking dogs or cats the size of automobiles. I personally have seen this "animal" around Tucson, and even up here on the mountain. I know that certain times of the moon and year I stay inside at night. One of these monsters ran down our alley in Tucson when my mother was in her vacation trailer along the fence line. Her dog went mad, and she arose in the night and saw it. She had not believed in this sort of "folklore" previously. People from all backgrounds see it, usually peripherally but quite clearly. I believe these sightings are of a member of another species, and that we are able to physically see it when conditions are favorable. We can place the Yeti, Bigfoot, and other oddities in this category. A shaman would be the last to suggest that these things are wholly imaginary. No, we meet stranger things than this daily.

The *Chindi*. One fall, I entered the area after we had camped alone there, and I was joined by a student, Jerry. We were exhausted as we drove in. In fact, we didn't talk much during the long drive, both being tired from working late the night before on clients, packing, and the usual chores in preparation for a three-day trip. When we did speak, it was concerning how everything seemed to conspire to stop the trip—a fairly good sign that the trip was very important—and that even our mates and families were angry and blocking us.

I had experienced the *Chindi* two years previously but didn't speak of it because it seemed so nightmarish. Larry, our three dogs, and I had camped there, at a precise spot. It is lovely, the area is entirely covered with volcanic pumice with beautiful cedar and juniper trees, dark green against the black pumice and clear blue skies. There are ridges all over in there, and the entire place is filled with thousands of ancient indigenous ruins, most of which are unexcavated.

We were camped within a few yards of one such, and later on we were able to recognize a kiva in the buried village. The night Larry and I camped there, we had laid our pads and sleeping bags outside our tent door. It was lovely and quiet. Larry had just fallen asleep.

Suddenly, the air became close and humid; some odd clouds moved in and seemed to push me down. I felt so sleepy that I was dizzy. As I drifted down into that soft darkness, one of my spirits shouted at me, "Get up! Get into the tent, NOW!" I grumbled and umphed and rolled over. The spirits became even more emphatic. I awoke Larry and told him what we had to do. He also was nearly impossible to awaken.

By this time, I was aware that something truly awful was present. And I knew something truly awful was about to happen. Inside the tent, the dogs were whining. One was vomiting. Larry is tall and heavy, especially that night. But I grabbed his bag with him in it and began dragging it into the tent, sobbing and choking. At last, he awoke and helped me, and we were inside the flimsy nylon enclosure. The remainder of the night, we huddled inside. The air was almost non-existent and the sounds ... we heard something moving all about us, close, brushing the tent walls, crunching in the pumice, raspy breathing. Again, the dogs were terrified; they crawled beneath clothing, bags, whatever they could find to hide under. We were all physically sick. The sounds continued. Shortly before daybreak, the air cleared, a slight breeze seemed to clean the world again, we could hear coyotes in the distance, and we all drifted into a sweet sleep. Although we had planned to stay another day and night, we departed to another valley to camp and heal.

This year, I had brought a few students out there to experience whatever it might be. The trip did not go well. Despite my admonitions to leave our spiritual toys home and my warnings that whatever we did there would be quiet and neutral, one woman brought her extensive collection of crystals and intoned to/with them constantly, when she was not grooming herself. While I was away from camp, the others had joined effort and dug a great pit and brought in a mountain of firewood. By the time I returned, a bonfire was going. Later that night, one of the group had his boombox going with a Didijeru tape. All of these things we had agreed would be left in town. All of these things are designed to block or irritate the energies and dead of this sacred place.

So I was back with one student, who had agreed to follow my lead and to be assistant as well as witness. As we turned onto the first entrance road, we both commented on our inner discomfort. As we drove closer and closer to the site, we both began experiencing inner pictures of various things, most of them uncomfortable and most of which were more than similar. At one point, Jerry commented, "Werewolf," and I smiled ironically. Later, "It's waiting for us." That was exactly how I had first experienced it. I made no response beyond the nod.

We set up camp, buried a dead vulture we had retrieved from the highway, put out food offerings for the ravens who had been teaching me so much there, propitiated the spirits and directions, and promised to move gently there and to disturb as little as possible on this sacred land. We then ate a cold dinner and hit the tent early, too exhausted and sleepy to sit up. We were sharing a three-man tent, our bags on opposite sides with a space of three feet between and the open doorway at our feet. Each of us had placed our medicine bundles nearby. We dropped quickly and deeply into slumber, mumbling that we would waste no time tomorrow, and we would work hard to make up for today.

I knew immediately that it was no dream. I'd had these experiences before, being a medium. There was someone, or something, entering my body. I could hear Jerry breathing deeply nearby, asleep. This intruder, however, was not giving me much time to pay attention to anything beyond myself. It had "crawled" in and was beginning to enter my chest cavity. Already, my lungs were being expanded but squeezed down, my rib cage stretching and bulging as from an entity much larger than myself. I had great trouble breathing enough for both of us. Now it was entering my head and face, my facial bones stretching and my eyes enlarging. My ears were ringing from the pressure.

I challenged the presence. "Are you of the Great Mystery?"

No response.

"Are you of the All Life?"

"What?" it growled within me.

Oh crap. I knew what was happening here: this presence did not even recognize a god/spirituality that I comprehended, nothing even remotely "good."

I called upon my human spirits whom I had been channeling for so many years. No answer. I called upon my totem and some power animals. Nothing. The pressure and presence increased. I was nearly taken over. I moved my right arm down, down, slowly to my knees where I had placed my medicine bundle. Yes! Reaching in, I retrieved my crystal. All right, Evil! Super Shaman is here!

It was a grinding process, getting that being out of my body. As soon as I could speak, I groaned to Jerry, "It's after us. Protect your left arm."

I even nagged a bit because he was not responding coherently. Of course, one could rightly note that I was not exactly coherent, either.

"Call on your animals and spirit folk," I said to Jerry. "I can't help you; it's in me, too."

I reached down to my left side to help myself turn over, and beneath my hand was a squirmy, hairy low-to-the-ground creature.

"Uh, excuse me," I mumbled before turning and hurling myself into sleep.

In the morning, we went out into the warm, restoring sunshine and spoke of the night.

"How did you know it was my left arm?" Jerry asked.

"I don't know; I was just talking to keep you from being taken," I said.

"Well, it was entering that arm, just above the elbow. It was awful," Jerry added.

"How did you get it out of you?" I was curious as to his technique.

"By calling on your totem, Owl. The thing didn't seem to respond to anything of mine, even my beliefs, but I felt sure it would go from Owl. And I expected that you would have the power to take it out."

"Oh, right," I snapped. "I had my own problems, you know."

"Well, it worked."

We continued processing the experience. Jerry, an artist, drew what he had perceived in the pumice-soil. Yeah. Me too. But we both agreed that it was an accomplished shape-shifter. Then I told him of the furry one between us.

"It was my totem, Badger," he said. "I called on him first."

"It was there, for sure. I felt it move and its warmth. We'll take something out after breakfast for Badger, to thank it."

We spent the day visiting the grave of a shaman just under a nearby cliff, where the ravens had led me to the grave in a quite deliberate way. The markings above the grave identified her as female and there were two very small graves, likely children, alongside her. I always took her some beads, food, and tobacco when I visited. The sweetest sage I have ever smelled grew upon her sunken grave. Each year that I returned, the sage had increased; the last time I had visited, the entire area was covered with black rocks and light green sage. Oh, and a rattlesnake den. May they all be in peace. It was she who bestowed upon me my lasting sacred name, Nightwing.

We set up a plan for that night. We would sit outside, have a small fire to draw the presence and erect a subtle Sacred Wheel. In the meantime, the day was lovely and warm, and we walked alone and together about the place, looking at ruins, studying small potsherds, feeding the birds. Toward sunset, we found ourselves wandering back and forth through a very specific energy line. It was so precise that it felt like grabbing an electrical wire as we passed into it. Continuing our walk, we noted that the line included the graves and our tent. About five feet wide, it flowed from the southwest toward Monument Valley northeast of us. It appeared to pass through some of the excavated ruins in the distance, including Castle Ruin. Realizing that the sun had set and that it was rapidly becoming dusk, we hurried back to camp to eat and prepare for the night's battle.

That night, I met the partner of Evil. The great white Kachina which I now associate with Christ energy made its first appearance to me. It marched in from the sacred San Francisco Peaks. The very ground shook beneath the feet of this Kachina and the others who followed it. Our campsite was suffused with light—that misty white light that lives. I sat and held my power objects before me. We were ready for the *Chindi*.

But it was too much preparation. We left no openings for poor *Chindi*. I called it. I taunted it. We were aware that it was nearby, stalking and lurking all about our site, but it did not come to us. One last taunt before we retired.

"You are nothing. A newborn puppy would not fear you. You are less than my comfortable bed." I laughed and went into the tent.

Jerry covered the tiny fire, smothering it carefully. Only the smallest wisp of smoke remained. He joined me in the tent as we prepared to process the evening that didn't happen. During our conversation, we felt its presence approaching.

I called out, "Silly thing! We are too tired to wait for you to frighten us any longer. Go away!"

The dead fire burst into flame. The soil and pumice burned. There was no wood remaining, no leaves, merely rock. The flames shot higher into the sky than our original fire produced.

I called out again, "That's a pretty good trick but childish."

We heard a car. A car? In here? We were on a dirt road that went to a dead end, nowhere. Not even a road, it was a track. But a low-slung sedan passed within feet of us, filled with chanting Native Americans, each of whom wore a white cowboy hat.

"Hau, thing! Not bad. But I have seen you on a cheap postcard. If you hope to frighten us, do better," I shouted into the night.

Several automobiles drove past. What on earth? They caused no dust to rise, and made little sound. Most telling of all: they were fully lit as if it were daylight. We could see every detail. In one sedan, one of the men had his legs stuck out the rear window on to the trunk, his head resting on the back of the front seat. Several other phenomena ensued. We decided that we must be frustrating the *Chindi* pretty badly. Finally, things began to quiet down. Still chuckling and murmuring about parts of the "show," we slept. Quietly and well. Evil does not thrive amidst laughter.

The following day, we broke camp, cleared the area, and returned to Tucson. Three days later, I entered a 21-day visionquest in Cochise Stronghold. It would be another year before I went to *Chindi*-land again.

I contemplated that experience on and off for several years, and each Autumn I camped there. Nearby, not within the line. It was silly, probably, but what did it really mean, when all was said and done? I had merely played with some non-physical entity. So what? However, I had learned that this work was not recreational. The few people I tried to discuss this with seriously assumed we had been ingesting mushrooms or smoking pot. Not so. In fact, I don't believe in the distortion brought on by such substances. Real shamans do not drink or consume hallucinogens. It's dangerous to release that unreal reality into this world, and we would surely have to deal with it in the OtherWorld one day. We have enough to do there besides adding to it. Anyone who needs such assistance in shamanic work is too weak to be doing it in the first place.

In 1995, I took a much different group of people into Wupatki. Smaller and all serious students with whom I had worked for years. As we prepared for bed that first evening, our old "thing" showed up. All felt and heard it, as it "walked" through the crunchy pumice layer. We discussed the presence between our tents in the night, comparing experiences and perceptions. The following evening, it began again, but this time I decided to do something about it. I trusted these people very much; they had been present during many often-troubling pieces of work and stood firm and respectful of the What Is. This was my time.

We met outside, walked the few yards to the specific site and placed our camp chairs in a circle. I let the taped drumbeat take me.

I was there, but not there. My centerpole was before me. I touched it in blessing. The *Chindi* was there, in the form of a cat/wolf/bear thing, tongue lolling as it appeared to be half laughing. I smiled and bowed to it. It nodded in return. We ran together—out to the northeast we ran. So fast, so free, completely free, I cared for nothing, except the run.

As we neared the rim of that part of Mother Earth where we began, I realized that I now had the choice. I could continue to run freely and forever with no conscience, no regrets, no guilt, no karma—just the joyous freedom of Evil. Or I could turn around and "something" would happen as the result. Curious, I turned. We ran back toward my centerpole within the circle of friends there. I saw us all and could see that they were looking our way, as if they could follow our movements.

"Stop, Shaman, and hold out your hand. Make Evil eat from your hand," the Voice urged.

I did so. Evil stopped, stared hungrily at my extended hand. It paused. Then, its eyes on mine, it moved. Evil ate from my hand. Evil was mine.

Evil became mine to work with. It became my almost-tame energy. It increased my healing abilities multi-fold. Because of this addition to the power which works through and with me, I could more profoundly address curses, soul kidnappings. I could work more deeply with people who had some "satanic" work done to them, for example. I have never been casual about working with Evil, nor am I careless. Oh no. If anything, I have become more careful. However, it also lends me the courage I require to go into places and spaces others will not. Do I still risk life and limb to do so? Oh yes. But as I go, I do not hesitate. Hesitation in this work drains power and is actually dangerous to self and others. Thus, Evil, the *Chindi*, lends me that apparent fearlessness I need to increase my sharpness. Of course I still fear. Fear is also an integral part of being sharp. Only stupid people do not fear.

Evil works *for* me. As does Good. Our problems begin when Evil (or Good, for that matter) becomes personalized for us or by us. These are energies which we as a species have defined and labeled. No other species view life in this manner. They are too busy living a pure and perfect form of it.

Once we have Evil in our corner, so to speak, we can really do battle. Nothing faces down evil the way Evil does. One of the things I have realized is that the day I ran with Evil and brought it to heel was the day that I lost my spiritual innocence. At that point, I began growing up in this work, my childlike arrogance deflated. The lines we set to live by grew dimmer and dimmer, and I entered some confusion and chaos. In short, I became a full-fledged, matured shaman that night.

Vistas opened, some a bit uncomfortable, for we all embrace our limitations. Was my life controllable? The Work began with new perspectives and unknowns. Even the temper of the clients coming to me altered somewhat. More people called in regard to curses or soul theft. As the energy of Evil expanded in my world, so did that of Good.

Shadow: Darkness, Night, and Winter

Shortly following my acceptance of Evil, I found myself contemplating shadow and darkness more often. I have always felt that those times and conditions have been given the short end of the spiritual stick and that someone has to stand up for them. The New Age is filled with lightness and sweetness—so much so that shadow is overlooked at best, despised at worst.

Consider shadow. Half of our seasonal year is in shadow; half of our day is night; and we each contain great, deep caverns of darkness within ourselves. I think of that as caverns because we are taught and have so been taught for millennia to eschew shadow within ourselves, to deny its very existence, and to repress that powerful darkness. It is insisted that we must love everyone, forgive our enemies, return hate with love, hold all in "unconditional love," never be judgmental, and never, never hate. Rage is not to be admitted, for if we do admit to rage, we must endure counseling or psychiatric treatment for it.

Hogwash.

Until we can admit our shadow, we cannot work with it; we are only half-beings. Until we recognize that we hate and experience intense rage, we have no choices in our actions. Most of us do not even know that we have such emotions! That offers us even less choice. So, facing ourselves and human nature squarely, we root inwardly, plucking up and inspecting carefully those shadow emotions, that overwhelming power that lies within each of our psyches.

Which is not to say that I condone behaving badly. Again, such knowledge brings with it a deeper sense of responsibility for our actions, our behaviors. We find that we *must treat All Life more fairly, more the way we would want to be treated if we were in that condition.* Without this knowledge and experience, we cannot enter the All Life, but must remain without: isolated from all, including our god, our species, breath itself—and ourselves.

Ah, but Shadow does not pertain to our inner feelings alone. It encompasses what happens all about us: pain, suffering, grief, loss, poverty. These things are not personal attacks, but part of Winter, Nighttime, and the darkness of growth, regeneration, and change.

The shaman experiences this fully in her life by being viscerally aware of all life about her. Although they have not "sinned" in any way, trees, grass, animals, and insects—all of Nature—suffers, becomes sick, and eventually dies. These occurrences are not penalties, but they are merely part of life itself. The shaman takes this wisdom, incorporates it into her healing work, imparts it to the other tribe members, and uses this to reconnect humans to the All Life they have separated from by the concept of morality and superiority.

So I was prepared for the following. Gunfire was making us all a bit crazy. I had a group of four who were to visionquest, along with my helper. We had sweated the night previously, so we were especially vulnerable, and now we were setting up base camp in preparation for these four to enter the sacred circle of visionquest the following day. I tried to ignore the nearby shooting. Probably some folks just below us were target practicing and had been at it since our arrival. I was in the midst of helping to set up the latrine when I could take no more. These fools had begun with .22s and were steadily escalating into larger and larger firearms. They had just brought out some automatic rifle and were blasting away furiously. Enough is enough.

My shadow side up, I stalked to my tent, which had just been erected, fished out my drumming tape and recorder and quickly focused, entering the OtherWorld as the gunshots continued. I gathered up all my power animals, my "Hand of God," Lord Elf. I shifted into the form of Shaman, and we "marched" down the mountain to where these people were shooting up trees and foliage.

The shots stopped immediately. We heard trunk lids being slammed down and van doors closed. They left. I thanked my spirit helpers and returned to the work at the latrine.

Shadow has also opened me to greater vistas of fear. Each time I visionquest, I am taken to the absolute limits of terror, to the edge of comprehension—and then one step beyond. It is nearly unbearable. This has increased greatly since I have accepted Shadow. It causes me to be even more sensitive to everything. Worth it? Sure. Only by embracing our shadow sides as well as our lighter selves may we be fully alive and in contact with ourselves *in toto*. Only by embracing it all may we ever be freed of it.

The Black Man

I was exiting the interstate on my way home in El Paso when I first saw him, waiting at the top of the off-ramp. It was late at night, dark. This was not a well-traveled part of town, and my car was the only one around. He was at the stop sign. And I was terrified of him. What to do?

He was all in black, including a black brimmed hat. I could see glints of some silver. His face seemed to be evil incarnate. I could feel his eyes, rather than see them. He was there, and he was waiting for me. And if he got me, I would be dead. At least.

I looked around me; there was no traffic on the street at the top of the off-ramp. I took a chance, and I took a quick left and drove away as fast as I could instead of stopping at the sign. He had disappeared by the time I turned to look behind me. I remained frightened but rationalized it enough to live with.

Years later, I was visiting my daughter in San Francisco, sleeping on a comfortable pad on the floor of her bedroom. He came again.

I was on a train, in an old-fashioned European style car. He was on the seat facing me, leering at me. All black, except parts of his face. He was going to kill me. Not words, but images. Intense images. I called upon my spirits to help me; I called upon the guys I channeled. No response. He showed me how he would do it. There was no way I could escape! As he reached across the compartment to kill me, my last fleeting thought was, "No, I have work to do!"

And I awoke. Drenched with sweat. My throat (where he was killing me) hurt terribly. My spirits were all around the pallet.

"Why didn't you help me?" I cried.

"You have to fight this thing yourself. All we can do is to wait and pray," they replied. "In surviving these attacks, you will become strong enough to do what you must. If you do not survive ... well, we will be very sorry."

Boy, was I comforted.

I have dealt with "Mr. Charisma" many, many times. I now realize that he was there when I was a child too, but I had blocked those memories. He does not come anymore. I am not letting my guard down, but I understand that I have conquered him fully.

There are many of you who have met with the black man. I meet you during healings sometimes. Often, you cannot remember when I ask about it but call me or write me later. What can I do for you? Counsel. Point out tips for survival. Encourage. One of my not-going-to-be-a-shaman-yet friends has had some nasty encounters with the black man.

She came with another of our friends to visit out here one day. We were sitting around, talking about all sorts of things.

"Sara, you've been seeing the black man," I suddenly said. We had never talked about this before. It's not something I talk about often, in fact.

"I told you she'd know," Dina piped up. "We were talking about her experience in the car, driving out here. I told her to talk to you about it."

"Well?" I urged.

Sara told of a rather lengthy harassment she had been enduring by the black man. She had been trying to pass it off as a dream.

"Sara, you know it wasn't a dream," I said.

"I know. I told Ted (her husband) it wasn't. I even moved into a motel one weekend to get away from it. But ..."

"It followed you, didn't it?" I said.

"Sure did. There it was, hovering outside the second-story window, leering in at me."

"Tell all. This guy's dangerous to you," I said.

"Well, you know, our house is two-story. Our bedroom is upstairs. Lots of windows. One night, there he was, sort of floating outside my window—what, fifteen feet up? I thought I was having a dream. I got up and went into the other upstairs room. *Zip*, there he was, at that window. All in black, brimmed hat, handsome—but hideous face. I was so scared, I was soaked with sweat. I was too afraid to go close enough to close the curtains. I sat on the floor behind some furniture all night, listening, afraid he would come in after me."

"Well, he's not a dream, or even a nightmare," I said. "He's quite real, and he wants to kill you."

"Why me?" she asked. "I haven't done anything."

"Well, you have potential power, and I guess he figures he'll get to you before you get strong enough to fight him."

"What can I do?" she asked.

"You won't like the answer," I said. "Get busy and shamanize. Accept your power and role in this life. Give up your happy little homelife and get with the program. Of course, he'll still attack you, but you will have the ability to fight him off."

"Well, you know how stubborn I am."

Yeah. Actually, I do not comprehend how she has been able to bargain with this thing. It didn't seem to be anything I could negotiate with. But she is still alive, and to date, it hasn't returned. I did tell her how to use me for help with it, and she reported that it left then. But why did I have to fight it alone, and she didn't?

Most people report seeing him alongside the roads, at night. As an aside, there are also what my kids and I have always called the "hitch hikers" out there, too. I thought everyone saw them. They are dressed in clothing from all periods of time, and are apparently the memories of people who died in those areas. We see them most often on curves, I guess—at least the more modern ones. But we have seen pioneer-type folk quite often, especially when we lived in Texas.

Beware the black man. Never stop for him.

Are ordinary people inherently evil? This is a tough question, and one that I have contemplated many times—in fact, each time I meet up with an evil person. Are they born that way, or do they become evil? Or does something evil come to inhabit them? I have come to believe that it is all three.

There is an evil man living nearby us here in the mountains. I didn't know him as a young boy, so how can I say if he is inherently evil? He has undergone a certain amount of psychiatric attention for rage. He is a Vietnam veteran. Did his evil-ness happen there? Not in this case, I don't believe. For his very young son is so evil that one spots it immediately upon looking into his little eyes. His aura is dark and oily-seeming. He appears, to an inner eye, to be a clone of daddy. I had a really difficult time remaining in his presence. It was even harder to bear than his father's energy field, for he had no experience dissembling.

This type of evil is not even as pure and clean as the *Chindi* energy, for it is entangled with humanity and all its foibles and desires.

What have I done about daddy-dearest? What any red-blooded shaman would do: I have cursed him into a condition of helplessness. He is isolated and miserable. Soon after I applied the curse, his facade began to shatter. Law enforcement noticed that he was driving drunk more often than not; his superiors at work found that he had been stealing; his world is slowly crumbling inward until little space is remaining for him. He looks over thirty years older than his chronological age. What about the son? Nothing. I guess we'll just have to wait and see how that goes.

Have you ever been driving along a busy city street, glanced over at the car next to you, seen the driver and been very afraid? Many people I have talked to about this have experienced such. Perhaps you are walking, pause at the curb, look to your left and see the ugliest human in the world, dressed in strange clothing. Is it a poor street person? No way. It is something else. That automobile you saw? Was it a familiar make and model? Probably not.

Do you expect me to be able to tell you what they are? I can't. Watch out.

Poltergeists

Boy, do I ever hate these jobs. A poltergeist is a real problem mostly because they are not human, do not think, act or react as human, and have no ethics or morality, no sense of guilt or what's nice. They seem to exist solely to cause trouble and to torment humans. They are often attracted to young people entering puberty, especially young women. Poltergeists crave energy they can steal, absorb, and use. These situations are always difficult, take much work, and are touchy, since so many involve young people whose parents don't want them exposed to the work I do.

Denise called me about her former husband's aunt who lived in a mobile home in a town near here. Mary lived with her daughter, who was twenty, and Denise's son, who was in that town for a good job. She had previously mentioned the bizarre activities that were occurring in her home, but Denise didn't think too much about it ... then. Now, since meeting me, she wondered. And then, Mary called her and mentioned in the course of the discussion that the ghostly activity wasn't just continuing, but it was accelerating and becoming impossible to live with. Denise drove me to Mary's home the next day. A Sunday. Sundays seem to intensify this type of work.

Mary is a lovely Mexican-American lady, who lives in a mobile home which she has created to be cozy and maintains spotlessly. She showed me through the house, pointing out the places where most of the activities took place.

"At first, each Sunday night, there was a banging on the roof, as if someone real heavy and with steel boots was walking back and forth," she said. "Then this front door, although locked, would fly open and slam open and shut."

"What did you do?" I asked.

"I called the police several times, but they found nothing ... no footprints, no dents on the roof. Nothing. Even the neighbors heard the noise and called the police. One time, the officers heard it and ran out, but could find nothing."

"What about your daughter?" I asked.

"Brenda has been here a lot of the times. She has also been run out of her bedroom at the other end of the home and into my room. Often, as we sit together here on my bed, the pictures on the walls rattle and things on my dresser bounce around," she said. "All the walls in this room pound. We hear footsteps into the room, but no one is there."

"How long has this been going on?" I said.

"Let's see. It started when Brenda was just thirteen," Mary said. "And she's twenty now ..."

Um-hum.

But I really didn't want to deal with a poltergeist. Especially not one which has lived off these people for seven years! I fudged. We did some work on a portal I found in the living room. I urged holy pictures and statues on the women. Bring in light to each corner. Get the priest to bless the house—not exorcize. Do not tell him the place is haunted or cursed. Just bless it. I went through some real good advice. And it all was!

Denise called the following Thursday. Less than a half hour after our departure, the roof boomed, the walls banged, and the door flew open and closed. Oh, damn. We would return that Sunday night. This time, I would be loaded for bear, as they say.

"And be sure that Brenda arrives there about thirty to forty minutes after we do," I said.

This time, I took my shaman's clothing and the tapes I use to journey with. We arrived and were graciously greeted by Mary. Brenda would be along soon, and no, she hadn't told her anything. I had stipulated that, since I knew the "thing" was focused on Brenda and would probably attack her if she knew I was onto it.

We were prepared, and Brenda came home as scheduled. Thank goodness, she hadn't stopped after work for a drink that evening! She sat across from me, obviously puzzled and a little anxious.

"I realize this will seem as if we are ganging up on you," I said.

"Yes."

I explained that whatever was "attacking" her and her mother was focused on her. "And if we had told you what we would do here tonight, it might have hurt you," I said.

She seemed to understand that. But she asked, "What do you mean focused on me?"

"Well, these things are attracted to young women, usually around twelve to fourteen years of age, especially when they are starting their first moon cycles," I said. "Women that age, going through all those physical and emotional changes, emit a strong energy, and these creatures crave energy above all else. Then, once here, it grew stronger with each time it frightened you and Mary."

"Grew stronger?"

"Fear and anger are strong emotions and are almost edible by these entities," I said. "They can't handle things like laughter. But at this point, it's hardly funny, is it?"

"Not hardly. I don't know how I could laugh at something that's chasing me out of my room and into bed with Mama, and then comes in there and makes the room like a drum!"

No kidding.

"Brenda, what I need to do to rid you of this thing is to use you to contact it and take it out. Then I can heal you and make you strong enough it can't come back into your life again. Okay?"

No answer.

"Brenda, I promise nothing will hurt you. Nor will I cause anything to happen in here that will scare you."

She looked at her mother.

"Mary can sit next to you and hold your hand," I said. "Does that help?"

"Yes."

We set things up. Mary was sitting next to Brenda. They could hold hands and yet Mary would not be between us. She was situated on Brenda's right side. I would remove the poltergeist energy via Brenda's left side. I always take pains to ensure that no one in the area will be harmed in any way by my work.

As soon as the drumming began, the poltergeist made its presence known. I did not allow it to throw things or bang on walls. That was unacceptable. That is a tantrum. The women in the room experienced dramatic temperature changes and misty spots around the room.

"Brenda, I'm going to talk and ask questions, and I will appear to be addressing you," I said, "but I'm actually talking to it. What I need from you is for you to tell me exactly what you feel when I ask a question. Don't be worried about hurting my feelings or being discourteous. Just tell me what you're feeling, okay? And you other two: tell me what you see and experience in here as this part goes on."

At first, Brenda was polite. But the other two were able to describe certain abreactions of hers so that I could keep track of her physical reactions. Finally, she was comfortable enough to really work with me.

"I'm angry about that question," she said.

"Good. You know that's its response," I said.

"Yes. It's not how I feel at all," she said.

I got all its baggage together with it and began dragging it out of her, through her left side.

"Oh my god," Denise said. "It's black and oily and oozing out of Brenda's side, just below her left armpit."

"Let me know how it moves," I said.

"It's curving out and turning toward you, toward that space between your hands," she reported.

"I can see it now," Mary said.

Brenda was squirming. "I feel agitated and a little frightened. Uneasy. I want to stop and get out of here."

"Brenda, hang onto your mom's hand," I encouraged. "Not long now."

"Okay. I can do it. I just want you to know how I feel," she said.

"Good. You're great."

I brought that ooze between my hands into another dimension. When it was all in there, I clapped my hands together. This serves as a window slamming shut.

"Gone."

As I opened my eyes and looked around the room, all were agreeing that the room was very different. Light. The dark spots floating about were gone.

"The place seems empty and peaceful," said Mary.

Denise agreed.

Brenda was a bit shaken. Time to fix her up. I did a healing on her and re-wove the fabric of her aura and energy field.

"Oh, that feels so good," Brenda said. "I'm getting drowsy."

"I think it's time to quit," I said. "We'll go now. Your haunting is over. Please call Denise and report to her. It still would be a good thing to have the priest in for a house blessing,"

There were no more disturbances there.

Many people who are being bothered by poltergeist activity call in priests or religious exorcists. And often, that simply aggravates the situation. A poltergeist could care less about holy water and prayers. In fact, that approach probably just pisses them off. And each failure at solving the problem feeds it.

A pair of chicks, two of the many animals that lived with Roberta at RavenHouse.

Chapter 10
Hand of God and Shamanic Spirits

I awoke flat on my back in the semi-dark tent. Larry would be up there soon to join me and the dogs for a long weekend camping. Was it his truck that woke me? No, there was no sound outside. But there was inside. There was a peculiar sound ... on me! And now I could feel the weight on my chest. Rustlings. Chewing sounds? My body felt very strange indeed. This wasn't nice at all. Then I saw it.

Perched on my chest, staring placidly into my face, was the nastiest creature I had ever seen. No, this was not see-able. I had not even seen pictures of anything like this. None of my worst nightmares included this ... thing. It was about eighteen inches tall, humanoid in stature in that it had four limbs and a sort of head and seemed to "stand" upright. Its head was all mouth, and that mouth was filled to the brim with pointy teeth ... which were dripping blood and flesh. Mine.

Being careful not to move too much, I looked down my body and saw four more of these critters. Each one had a slightly different appearance, but they all resembled each other. And each one had mouthfuls of me. I felt it clearly. I smelled it. I saw it. I heard it. The thing on my chest "spoke" to me.

"We are here to eat you."

"Ye-es," I said. "Why?"

"To make you new. What we eat we will recreate."

"Is this real? Am I awake?"

"Oh yes, very real. The realest. Realer than what you think is real. So real ..."

"I get it. Who is behind this? Is this right to do?" I have a thing about appropriate.

"We do not bother ourselves with right or wrong. We are told to do a thing and we do it. It may not be to our taste, heh-heh, but we still do it. We are obedient to the god."

Aha, something to go on. "Is your god the same as mine?"

"At least we have an understanding of the reality of the god; yours is minimal. Less than minimal. But with this feeding and rebuilding, your comprehension may be born."

"Okay. I guess. What do you need from me?"

"Nothing. But as we get to your brain, it helps if you are conscious and cooperative. It will mean more to you as well," it said.

"All right. Say, is this going to hurt? And will I have any memory? Will I know the people I love? Will I know how to read, write, eat, and go to the bathroom?"

"Be still. Why do you care? Listen, we are the Hand of God."

"What does that mean? I'm not religious. I don't believe in a personal grandfather-god," I said.

"That's an advantage," it said. "We are sent here to take care of you, the shaman, as a tool is taken care of. We don't care about you personally. We are just here to protect you, teach you, lead you, eat you, basically be your caretakers for the rest of your miserable little life. We are to make room for and care for the shaman and care nothing for Roberta. If she gets in our way, we will hurt her. Anyone who gets in the way of our work will be hurt. That's what the teeth are for. Now, let me get busy and eat your brain."

I felt my skull being opened, the top lifted off, and I saw and felt them dipping in and eating my brain. Lights went off, and I twitched uncontrollably. It was quite unpleasant, although without what we know of as pain. As they fitted the top of my skull back on, I drifted off to sleep. The next thing I knew, I heard Larry driving up.

I was awake. Quite awake. It was not a dream. Nor was it a vision. It happened. Since then, many people have seen my "critters" during tough times in healings. When they come out—and there are seven now—they move about the room to keep anyone from moving or interfering with the work that is being done in any way. Most of the time, when this happens, several people fall asleep. Those who stay awake struggle to. As near as I can figure, this is because things are so intense that most people simply shut down; their minds will not accept what is before them.

My life with the critters has not been pleasant. They will steer me into the work I must be doing whether I like it or not. If someone close to me insults Nightwing—or if they perceive that—that person is punished, even if it also punishes me. I have never been able to negotiate with them on this point. I don't like them. I doubt they like me. They want me, today, to give up my personality entirely and become total shaman, which is insanity and would require a keeper. I am not willing today. Thus we are in a situation wherein my caretakers and I are fighting desperately over ... myself. I realize I need to give up and give in; I even know that is the proper thing to do, but to date, I have not been able to do it. And they cause me great pain, mental and physical, in their determination to win. We'll just see.

When Nightwing is not given the appropriate respect, she must respond on behalf of herself. If not, the Hand of God, or even Lord Elf, will attack. Because I did not chastise a student who treated Nightwing foolishly, she is currently being followed and harassed by cold, dire energy. Naturally, it would have been better for her if I'd decked her, but I often fail to do so, since it's socially unacceptable. I do place low grade curses on such people now, which is far kinder than doing nothing.

The Hand of God is one form of shamanic spirit. Lord Elf has become one, my UFO experiences are one, and all are determined that Roberta give over to Nightwing. This is one of the differences between medicine people and shamans. The former can have lasting personal relationships. They can marry and have sexual intimacy, even as they practice their craft. Shamans are not allowed. Power is jealous. Power wants the shaman entirely. Sexual intimacy is a deeply shared part of a person. I know because before the shaman part became insistent, I was sexual and found it a wonderful part of life. The Great Mystery called and insisted that I become its servant—in the deepest traditional sense—and I have agreed. I am able to maintain my marriage and friendship with Larry because we are celibate and careful in our dealings with one another. When we slip and become careless in even our talk, we are attacked. I protect him the best I can when we argue. It doesn't matter that when the critters harm him, it results in harm to me. Once, when he was in a nasty mood with me for some time, they got at him by hurting his back so that he couldn't work and we ran out of food. Another time, they destroyed both of our cars because I continued to try to bring in money through non-spiritual work.

Power does not allow close relationships with family members, even children and parents. They are removed from the shaman one way or another. The shaman belongs to the Great Mystery and the people. The shaman exists to maintain the connection between the humans they serve and the rest of the Natural World until such time as they are reunited. When I am doing anything that is not to that end, I am wasting time, and the thumb screws get turned yet again.

Yes, they protect the shaman within. But I have faced incredible danger alone, apparently without their help. One time, coming back from a situation where I was facing certain death and somehow overcame it, my spirits, including the human ones, were all hovering about me.

"Well," I grumped, toweling the sweat of terror from my body, "where were you guys when I needed you?"

Then I saw the concern and tears on the human faces. "We could not interfere," said Walking Hawk. "You must face these attacks and win without us—or lose. It is to strengthen you. If we helped, it would weaken you."

They are right, of course. And I can say with complete honesty that they have always been there when the chips were down. They have also promised to be there to lift me from this body when I'm through. That's a genuine comfort.

Shamans were not the wise men and women who lived in the midst of the village. No one wanted to be around them for very long. Some people considered them to be necessary evils. Others revered them and understood that it was a sacrifice to live as shaman. Still, we lived at the edge or a little distance from the people we lived to serve, to be called upon when there was need, to conduct the deepest mysteries and to take the dead to their home over the waters.

This distance and, yes, distaste was engendered by their shamanic spirits. If someone does not dislike me enough, then something takes place to cause it. Shamans seem to be so completely neurotic and even psychotic that "normal" people cannot abide them. They say strange, irritating things. At the same time, they do not appear to be romantically exotic enough to tolerate. They also serve some as the reminder that some of us live in disharmony with the world, and that can engender hate. Even our humor is strange and often incomprehensible, for we are laughing with something else. As I have pointed out earlier, shamans are similar to individuals with autism in that they see the world and all within, upon, and over it from the inside out. What is normal to human beings is frightening to shamans, and vice versa, I think. Season this with Hands of God and shamanic spirits and Lord Elfs, and we are alien indeed.

In Korea, even today, shamans are nearly always women who are chosen by spirits and are tormented until they accept their lot in life. Families react in various ways, but all are dismayed and wish to "disown" these women. Some families attempt to take the children away, husbands leave, and great pressure is brought to bear on the tyro shaman by her in-laws. But soon all agree that no one can prevail against these determined spirits. All who try are attacked and soon back off. The shaman then selects an older, experienced shaman to study with and to use as a sponsor. During this apprenticeship, the tyro will do all the labor and attend all the work performed by her mentor. Gradually, over the years, she will take over much of the shamanic work from her teacher until her teacher can finally retire.

From the moment she is selected by the spirits, the shaman becomes celibate and separate from friends and family. She may retain contact with her children, but it is no longer a warm motherly relationship. It is much more formal. People about her keep their distance, even within her home. She becomes the head of the family, subjugating her husband, since most of them remain. The spirits "jealously" remove from their shaman any semblance of emotional normalcy.

Korea has officially become a Christian nation, and shamanism is frowned upon; however, nothing can stand in the way of those shamanic spirits once they have chosen their host. I have seen photographs of one woman whose family opposed her shamanizing so much that she caved in and turned to their fundamentalist Christian church instead. Her face is empty, her body language stiff as if she holds herself tight against bending the "wrong" way. This must be a living death.

Nancy, the best apprentice I've ever had, has been studying with me for over twelve years and is one of the best healers I know of. And she loves me. Thus, since my physical health has been so very poor and the pain indescribable, she wants very much to heal me. She met us for a trip in Elaine's motorhome some time ago and asked to work on me one evening. I felt uneasy but went with it since she's always learning. As it grew dark, we all gathered in the motorhome for the session and got the drumbeat going. I remained uneasy, but I was willing to go with it.

As she worked, my discomfort grew, but I checked and was assured that this was supposed to take place for ultimate good. I gritted my teeth, and she continued, although I felt no relief whatsoever.

"Roberta, your critters are here and they're interfering. Please tell them to move off."

"Nancy, you know it doesn't work that way. They are my bosses and teachers."

"But I know I'm really right in there. Try."

"Okay." And I asked them, respectfully, to back off. They did not.

Suddenly, they attacked ... me! And badly. I was wounded. All present were quite aware of it. It was an overwhelming bomb blast in that small space. God, I was sick.

"Please, I've got to get out of here. I'm going to die," I begged. And Nancy stopped immediately.

"What happened?" she asked, stunned.

They helped me out to my tent to sleep, which I did soundly until dawn. Nancy was waiting for me to emerge.

"Roberta, please tell me what happened. What did I do wrong?" She was frightened.

"Well, Nancy, what do you think caused it? What was going on when they attacked?"

"Nothing. I was healing you. There's nothing bad about that, is there?"

"Remember, Nancy, what we were going to work on during this trip specifically," I prompted her.

"Well, you talked about my arrogance. But, honestly, I'm not arrogant," she replied.

"Of course you are," I laughed. "You are constantly trying to teach me how to do things, everything, even everyday life stuff, as if I were unschooled and of a lesser intelligence. But Nancy, most of what you try to teach me is pre-kindergarten. It's pretty insulting at the least."

"Okay, I did that when you first moved onto that mountain, but I soon learned to look at things from your point of view and check the big picture. I thought I'd passed that by."

"Yes," I said, "it's been better. But what did you do last night?"

"Just work on healing you!"

"Stop a minute and look at it. Sure, you had good intentions. Healing is a good thing, right? But it may not always be appropriate. And from the first, I've constantly reminded you that, in my case, I am supposed to be of poor health, and that the cause of that is not what it would be with most people."

"Oh. Yeah," she said, "but you allowed this."

"I wasn't sure why I had to do that. I did make it clear from the beginning that I was not comfortable with it, but you persisted despite that and did not even follow that up. Something no real healer would do. You were being supremely arrogant."

"But why didn't your critters attack me? Why you?"

"Well, Nancy, perhaps by attacking me, they got your attention. Think of that?"

"And so you sacrificed yourself for my lesson in arrogance?"

"Guess so. You're the best healer I know of, but you'd be a hundred times better if you weren't so arrogant and if you learned that what you want isn't important. It's not what the client wants. It is what the client's soul asks for. Did you check with my soul?"

"No. Got it. What about all the animals I work with?"

"Same thing. You could really screw up one of those horses you work on if you don't first ask it if this is for its highest good. You're treating them as if they weren't sentient or worthy of considering."

Well, Nancy was subdued after that, and I did frequently inquire as to her processing the whole thing. She owned that she was looking at everything through the perceptions of a more humble person. And, after all, I did survive it.

People who choose to approach a shaman or to work with him/her must take on the responsibility of doing so with respect and in harmony with the stuff the shaman brings along. Another facet of this question is that I often find that my students, especially the inordinately talented ones, are being taught and refined by my Hand. A good teacher is tough and even disagreeable. Remember, I teach via provocation (as does any real teacher). So do my Hand guys. Thus, such attacks may be received as a teaching and a blessing. They teach me, and they are my teachers. Hard, but thorough. I may not love them, but I certainly respect them. And I even know they are wise beyond my abilities and see a much fuller picture than I do. Should you meet me and them, be grateful. And careful.

Once the Hand of God grasps a person nothing is the same.

A Universal Serpent drawn as a gift for Roberta.

Chapter 11
UFOs and the Faire Folke

I have never been comfortable with UFO talk. I experienced a close encounter as a young girl, and I knew there had been more but did not wish to remember it. I never felt *they* came from someplace "out there," which caused me to feel even more uncomfortable; if they were from other planets, then they could—and would—go back. Since they were from here, there was no hope that I would not re-experience them. I endured the tremendous UFO craze of the late 1940s by peeking at it through my fingers. I shut out any talk of it the way I shut out pesty dead people and "knowing" too much. Let me start at the beginning.

At age eight and nine, I was friends with a girl whose family had a great deal of wealth. Sandy was an only child, and her parents wanted a companion for her, so we were encouraged to be together. In the course of these events, I was often invited to join them at their beach house in Newport Beach, California. This was in the late 1940s, when the place was a village and the beaches clean and free. It was wonderful. We often caught sand crabs for the fishermen who came to cast their lines in the surf.

One morning, as the sun burned off the fog, likely around 9:00 or so, we wandered through the streets in a roundabout way to the beach. We saw it come toward us so quickly it was almost as if it suddenly appeared—a silvery saucer-shaped thing, which hovered before us. After that, I had no memory—nor did Sandy—until the thing was no longer there, and we proceeded to the beach. We were uncommonly quiet that day. Her parents even remarked on it. That night, as we prepared to drift off to sleep, we whispered.

"Did you see that flying saucer this morning?" Sandy said.

So she had seen it too! "Yes. But suddenly it wasn't there anymore. Where did it go?"

"I don't know," Sandy murmured.

We were quiet again for a few moments. I searched my memory hard, trying to find something which connected one moment with another.

"Roberta?" Sandy again.

"Yeah? I just can't remember."

"I can't either, but we must have stood there a long time, because when we walked to the beach, it was lots later," she said.

"How do you know?" I asked.

"Remember how bright the sun was when we started walking again? It had to be later," Sandy said.

She was right. We never discussed it again; it was too frightening. It wasn't long afterward that Sandy was sent to boarding school, and I never saw her again. She became a mother superior of a Catholic teaching order ... and I became a shaman. Is there a connection?

It is common knowledge that most contactees experience profound changes in their lives. And there is such a strong body of folklore regarding this subject that one has to believe that there is strong history here. It has always been believed—in all cultures—that when one has a deep experience with these beings that one returns "mad." Parents have always protected their children from such contact. In each anecdote, we are warned not to eat with them, for example. Not to go with them. To be careful of the deep forest. There are children who are stolen in the night only to be returned terribly altered—changelings. It is believed that these children's souls are removed so that one of "theirs" could now inhabit that empty body.

Most of the people I have talked with regarding UFOs, in whatever form, exhibit extreme fear and terror. It appears often to be way out of line with the recalled experience. Why is that? Why such horror? I believe it is a result of the dread built into our DNA, the very cells of our bodies, from ancestral exposure to a species so alien and so much more powerful than us that we can neither relate to it nor comprehend it without a response of extreme fear. As an example, consider our modern responses to snakes. They are a recognizable species, but still alien to us mammals. Until the spread and teachings of Christianity, people were comfortable with serpents. In fact, they were often associated with the gods and goddesses of the Earth. For that reason, Christianity eradicated our friendliness with snakes, substituting not only a horror of them, but even an urge to rid the world of them. This was a metaphor for paganism; however, it grew within our minds and then bodies until we reached the present, where we are fearful of, dread, and even hate reptiles. This example is a mere two thousand years old. Consider, then, the dread locked within our bodies from a prehistoric fear of the Faire Folke, the Ancient Ones, the Old Race.

Everywhere I went as I traveled, while lecturing on shamanism, holding workshops, and healing people, I was asked to address the subject of UFOs. And everywhere I went, I refused, explaining that UFOs had nothing to do with Earth spirituality and shamanism. What those people couldn't know was that each time I was asked about this subject, it was like pulling psychic fingernails out. The very phrase made me tremble. I also refused to read anything about it. Most of what I had seen was silly and unbelievable, apparently written by people who simply would not view the subject objectively and were so naive as to believe anything told to them, no matter how (no pun intended) outlandish. In fact, it seemed that the more ridiculous the theory, the more fans it had. I simply could not credit anything that was going around.

The dozens of conspiracy theories! I have worked with the government enough to realize that the United States government cannot support a conspiracy. Those people who have the "inside dope" and "expose" government UFO cover-ups are, for the most part, foolish, uneducated, and poor actors, hams. Many are outright deceivers who are in it for the notoriety and money.

It seemed contradictory, then, that the more profoundly I entered the world of the shaman, the more I feared UFO contact and the more I felt beleaguered by *them*. What was going on? I realize now that as I traveled and worked among hundreds of strangers, many of whom with which I was establishing lasting attachments, I was also opening to their experiences, even when those were not on an overt level. The tension was building. I realized that I was waiting for something to happen. Hell, I was actually physically looking over my shoulder!

One evening, Larry and I returned late from an errand. As we walked into the house, the television was on, and there was Johnny Carson talking with a strange-looking man. Even without being able to hear the conversation, I stood transfixed. Larry turned up the volume, and I could hear the interview. By then, tears were rolling down my face, and I was shaking like a leaf. It was Whitley Strieber. I did not connect with his words, but only with his message. I bought his book at the supermarket the following day and read it. *Communion* (Avon Books, 1987) resonated with me and my experiences as greatly truth and partly error, and it was disturbing at all levels. And it was the first of its genre to make any sense at all to me.

It was nearly three years following this that I came face-to-face with my personal *Communion*.

Suzanne, a sister shaman, came to work in Tucson, staying with us just outside the city. We had to drive through the Tucson Mountains on the western edge of the city to get home each night—a beautiful drive, but often a bit spooky. The moon was gorgeous as it reflected off the giant saguaro cacti we passed. The area of the mountains our road cut through was known to be a space of spirits, where the Old Ones often took the dead to rest. Even now, murderers find this area to drop off their victims. Night after night, we drove through there on our way home, quiet and contemplative ... and alert. My senses, always keen, were becoming very edgy, my psychic hairs on end.

On her last night with us, Suzanne asked for something from the *casita*, our guest house, and I offered to get it for her. As I went to the door to return to the main house, I could not open it. *I knew they were there.* Pulling myself together and calling on every bit of strength and power I had, I wrenched open the door and ran for the house, only to be met by Suzanne and Larry, who had felt something amiss and were coming out to get me. We nervously laughed it off.

The following day, as Suzanne and I prepared to take her to the airport, I noticed the dark circles beneath her eyes, just like mine. I had also noticed the marks upon my body when I showered. I asked her if she had any.

"Oh yes. I always have marks like these after meeting with them," she said.

"With whom?"

"You know. Them. The ones who aren't us. The Old Ones. From the UFOs," she said.

"I don't believe in UFOs," I insisted.

"Well, I do. I have to. They're real to me," she said.

"Suzanne," I said, "I was taken somewhere by them as I slept last night. And it's happened before, but I've always been able to deny it and stuff it away."

"Yeah, I know," she replied. "I've tried to stuff it but have never been able to. As early as three years old, they've been coming for me. I don't think they have ever hurt me, but I've always been a little afraid of them. Well, my body is very afraid, but my mind is kind of fascinated."

That was a fine description of the phenomena.

At the airport, we had extra time, so we entered a book store to browse. There was *Dimensions* (Ballantine Book, 1989) by Dr. Jacques Vallee. In an airport! I took it down and read the back cover. It was exactly what I *knew*. Buying the book with trembling hands, I looked over to Suzanne's smiling face.

"Well, you're going on quite a journey now," she said.

So true. And it was just the beginning of the most amazing journey, most of which was packed into the next several weeks. As I read the book, I entered a state of spiritual chaos, sliding out of all control, into a great epiphany. By the time I was through these two months, I would be affected so utterly that my very molecular structure would be altered. It was a terrible time. Today, I believe I rejoice in it. I responded to the book totally; everything was true to me. Yet I was in a state of deepest fear. I slept on the floor because I kept falling out of bed. There were voices speaking and singing, apparently from beneath the floor. One of our cats, a Siamese, spent each night at the side of my face, staring down into me so that he and his deep blue eyes were present whenever I awoke. It kept me sane.

After seeing Suzanne off at the airport, I drove the fifty miles home and found that I was being followed. Not by long black limos or sedans but by white pickup trucks. When one left off, another took its place, even through the country dirt roads and right up the dead end lane to our gate. Years later, talking with a member of a UFO group about this oddity, she laughed.

"Of course, it would be small white pickup trucks for you," she said. "Black sedans are expected. They must know your sense of humor and are playing along with you."

Could be. It has always been this way in these experiences. Dr. Vallee uses the word *absurd* often in his descriptions of UFO activity, and I have found that to be the rule in not only my experiences, but in those of all the clients I have worked with. It follows an ancient rule of shamanism and Earth spirituality: riddles, absurdity. This technique is applied in order to break down our rationality so that we become receptive. It is also absurdity, the unfathomable, which most touches our psyches. You read more about this in "Chapter 3: Illusion, Realities, and Rationality."

That evening, when Larry came in from work, I casually asked him if he had had any peculiar dreams the previous night. He moved away, averted his eyes and mumbled something in the negative. How unlike him! I pursued this. Still not looking at me, he related the following experience from the night before.

"I was asleep and woke suddenly, needing to use the bathroom. But just as I was about to get out of bed, you rolled over to me and began to move against me suggestively. I was shocked and frightened since that is something you would never do (we had been living a celibate life for several years by then). I was too afraid to move but finally got up nerve enough and rose and went out of the room. I was afraid to look back at the bed but glanced from the corner of my eye—and *it was not you in that bed.*

"As I tell this now, I realize that my actions were not normal, because after using the bathroom—and I stayed in there as long as I could, believe me—I came back to the bed and got in. 'You' had moved back over to your side. I clung to the edge of my side of the bed, fell into a sort of paralysis and finally to sleep. I knew that something was going on behind my back. There was an odd odor, a lot of movement, shuffling on the floor and strange breathing sounds. I kept my eyes closed tightly. After a time, I felt something touch my forehead lightly and I slept deeply until time to get up. I remember now that this has happened often over the past several years. I can't stand it and I believe that's why we don't get along very well lately. It's unbearable."

We moved Larry into the spare bedroom where he slept reasonably well from then on. No one who has stayed at our home has been able to pass my bedroom door or windows comfortably. Neal reported flashing lights and mirrors. One young woman simply would not enter the main house at night.

These phenomena are entwined with my shamanic spirits, who require celibacy and are "jealous" should I be close to anyone. All shamans have them, and it is one reason we have traditionally lived alone outside the villages. It may sound mean-spirited to another, but it is completely sensible to me. Nightwing requires that Roberta vacate her life so that the shaman can live fully within her body. The other thing that is going on each night is that, as Roberta sleeps, Nightwing works and learns, often with a great deal of activity—both physical and nonphysical. Combining this with my connection with the UFO phenomena, I am sure that things were pretty busy those nights. Again, I am glad I was *in* it, rather than being a witness to it.

As it happened, I was introduced to a man whose father led the oldest continuing coven of practicing witches in the world. He would have been interesting to me regardless of the circumstances, but he was even more so now. Vallee refers to worldwide and ageless belief in beings that I, with my roots enmeshed in Britain and Western Europe, think of as the Faire Folke. They are also known as the Ancient Race, Old Ones, and so on. Each race of humanity has its descriptive names for these entities, and they all are described in very similar ways. Here in the Southwest, the Navajo, Hopi, Zuni, and Pueblo peoples all have their gods which are quite similar to those in, say Great Britain.

Generally, most races believe that the Old Race was the race previous to humanity and that, as we advanced into this world, they moved into the forests and hills and waters and finally, I believe, into the very etheric body of the Earth. They can—and often do—present themselves in quite physical ways, likely at will. My impression of them is that of a strong neurological makeup with a tremendous ability to image and cause those images to become a certain reality, especially in their interactions with humans.

Most of these interactions are absurd and/or of a spiritual nature. Vallee cites dozens of nearly simultaneous sightings of beings in flying boats hundreds of years ago—beings which would throw down ladders, come to earth, "speak" soundlessly to the people gathered there, ask for gifts, and fly off into the sky in their ships. How is this different from the flying saucers of today? It is absurd and touches the psyche deeply with a riddle which we cannot quite grasp. He further cites the many religious visions and experiences, such as the "miracles" of 1917 in Fatima, Portugal, one of which was beheld by thousands of people as the sun appeared to leave its place in the sky, spin about, move rapidly to Earth, then return to its normal position. Absurd. Powerful and life-altering. *As all UFO-related phenomena are.*

A few days following my meeting with the son of the coven leader, I took some people out on visionquest. Alone while they were out in their circles, in a magic place that was powerfully eerie anyway, I went through some real terror. Finally, a friend who also knew the "son" came out. I confided in her what was going on. She told me that he had also confided in her that something frightening was happening with him, although he was unsure what it was all about. She stayed with me through the last night out there.

Two days later, I was "told" by my spirits to go to California with Suzanne—and a few other people to act as witnesses—and "join" with a being from the Faire Folke. Apparently, I was born to do this. My past lives were preparation, as was my genetic makeup. On their part, the being I came to know as Lord Elf had been "created" (born, hatched, whatever) for this and had been prepared and educated for ... they do not use numbers with me, but I gather it was thousands of our years. They explained that many were now being joined with their Old Race equivalents in an effort to save our mutual Home (Earth) from *us*. We had some choice in the matter. Did I want to go through with this? There was also some danger, since they had just recently begun this activity. Of course. Anything for Mother Earth. I left for California.

There were about a dozen people present as I lay upon a sofa at a friend's home in Southern California. We lowered the lights, and someone set up a tape recorder. It was a diverse group: a registered nurse, a civil engineer, the owner of a large business, a psychologist, and others whom I chose for their interest and intelligence—and because they were not the type of people to fall for just any old thing. I began relaxing and entering a receptive state.

I found myself seeing a brown forest. A creature was approaching. I felt much as I did when I saw that first flying saucer: a mixture of physical fear and intellectual interest. I was able to describe what was happening verbally as it occurred. Lord Elf stool tall before me. It appears variously tall: sometimes over ten feet, sometimes only seven or eight. It seemed brown/black and hairy then, with what looked like bat wings folded down to its feet, which were (as its hands) long-fingered and taloned. Its face was bat-like with large pointed ears. Its eyes were red furry orbs. We bowed to one another. It seemed so familiar to me. Then the "joining" began.

As Lord Elf moved into me, my body began to alter radically. I could hear the others in the room describe it. They particularly saw my hands, feet, and ears change. Since this took place, whenever I perform any dangerous work, my ears become long and pointed, poking through my hair. Those who know me well enough back away at this. The joining took a real toll on my body. I had difficulty breathing. The nurse was concerned and voiced that. Lord Elf referred to its "people" who suggested certain foods and drink for that night and the following days until

I normalized. Later, I found that my electrolytes were in utter upheaval. Remember that tape recorder? It was found later, the tape blank except for a dull roar. All that night, I dreamed the most marvelous dreams about places they call "Home." I dreamed of the history of this planet, of our peoples. I dreamed of what is to come for us all and how we can mitigate it, although we can no longer stop it from happening. The next morning, the telephone rang. It was my friend who knew the son of the coven leader.

"His father died late yesterday. He's on his way home for the funeral rites and the election of a new coven leader," she said.

"What did he die of?" I asked. "I thought he was only about forty."

"He was thirty-nine. His body just crashed. The doctors said that, by the time he got into the hospital, all his organs had ceased to function."

"Had he been sick?" I asked.

"That's the odd thing," she said. "No. He was healthy up to just an hour or so before he went to the hospital. They said he had gone into his study to meditate alone, came out a bit later, and said he had to get to hospital."

The medicos never discovered the cause of this man's death, but we know what happened. Fortunately, the joinings got better and easier, since we all learned much from each one. Later on, I assisted at some, and they were quite natural and left no severe physical aftereffects.

The following night, I had a workshop scheduled involving hypnosis. Just as I had my volunteer under nicely, working well, a student came in late, standing behind me. I nodded grumpily at him as I continued with the woman subject. Jack lit up a cigarette! Smoking was never allowed in my workshops, except the ones involving sacred smoke. The smoke curled around me, choking me, as I tried to keep my voice even for the hypnotic subject. I turned around once to glare at him. He walked out the door, and I have never seen him again. His wife met me later and told me that what had turned toward him was a dark monstrous head with pointed ears and red eyes. He decided that he had seen my soul and that it was evil.

That was a problem with having Lord Elf within me. It is protective but did not, for some time, comprehend life around me. Some weeks later, as I sat engrossed in typing at home, Larry came in the front door, approached me from behind, and touched my shoulder. As I jumped and turned in my chair, I was also startled to see him flying across the room, over the sofa, and into the wall by the door. He still never surprises me and has learned that if we must argue, he must address Lord Elf first and neutralize things.

Other amazing things occurred following our joining. It was as if I had never seen ordinary things before. Part of me was seeing an airplane for the first time, for example. It wanted to watch television all the time. "Why?" I asked. The answer was to learn about my people. Finally, I found myself before the television twice a day, every day, to watch two shows that I wouldn't look at for money. Suzanne called me one day, and I told her about this.

"What shows are they?"

"I'm embarrassed," I said. "One that I stay up at night and watch is 'The Dating Game.' Ugh."

She laughed. "What goes on, on that show?"

"I don't know. I don't actually see it; I'm just there while it goes on," I said.

"What's the other show?" she asked.

"I don't know that either," I said. "It's some soap opera for godsake."

"Pay attention tomorrow, and call me. I'm curious." She laughed at me.

I did. The soap opera was "Another World." Of course.

When I grumbled about this non-choice of entertainment, pointing out that there were wonderful things on the History Channel and Discovery, Lord Elf insisted that it was getting clearer information about humans from these two shows.

"But, Lord Elf, people aren't really like this," I said.

"Yes they are," it said.

And, you know, I think a lot of us are.

My adventures with Lord Elf are many and varied. It has brought an immense facet to the shaman within and opened great doors to work and thought. For example, when I now threaten entities during a soul retrieval, I do so with real teeth. That alone has made my work easier.

Much of the UFO literature and the people I have talked with who have had close encounters of any kind agree with me that the human contactee has been challenged and opened to some spiritual growth in each true case. Contactees become concerned about the environment and their fellow human beings, and they begin a deeper search for meaning through religion or non-organized spirituality. Many stop eating flesh and join groups to protect the rights of our fellow animals. A caring for Earth and all upon her is born.

Perhaps this process takes some time after the contact. I have met several clients who continue for a while to whine about "being used" or "why me" or "don't they know I'm a human being?" So what? We treat all other species as objects for our use with little caring for their comfort or rights as living creatures—more perfect creatures than we, in fact—why should we expect another species to consider our feelings or "rights?" It seems to me that any little thing we can do or participate in to help heal even the smallest portion of the horrendous damage our species has perpetrated upon this planet should be embraced fully and immediately, with joy. We can never undo the damage we have wrought here, but we can participate in some measure of healing—or at the very least begin to cause the least amount from now on! Try to think of any one thing that our species has done to improve Nature ... there is none.

Thus, we need to face the fact that we are also the termites destroying the home of the Ancient Race.

Are all these entities "good guys," working through us or around us to heal the Earth? Not according to Lord Elf, nor from my experiences with a wide variety of them. I compare them to humanity in that there are altruistic ones, some who just do not care about the results of their actions, and some who simply enjoy causing pain. So I am not surprised at the reports of painful "experimentations" or other negative contacts. I think each contact must be viewed individually and with a great deal of objectivity, observing the situation from all viewpoints possible, and as neutrally as possible. Without coloration from current UFO jargon. In short, we should approach such contact a little more scientifically—an odd idea from an irrational shaman!

Much of what the Faire Folke or UFO beings attempt to do with us is educational. There is a story here in southeastern Arizona about some men who frequently went out at night in their pickup truck with bright lights and rifles to poach deer, blinding them with the light and shooting, killing the helpless animals. For fun. One night, while chasing a deer down a dirt road, whooping and hollering, they came to a screeching halt as a gigantic light came on before them, blinding them. The light moved closer and closer; it appeared to have no source, and there was no sound. They were at first angered but soon became very afraid. Then the light blinked out. There was nothing there. Their watches showed them that some hours had passed during this encounter. The man I spoke with who claimed to have been one of these mighty hunters did not want my help as shamanic healer. He didn't want to even think about it any longer. Had he changed his lifestyle? Did he understand that he was being shown how it felt to be a deer? No. He was angry, fearful, and insulted. But he had stopped going out with the boys at night on dark dirt roads.

UFOs, Sasquatch, the Yeti, werewolves, vampires, things that go bump in the night. How does the shaman view these things? Extraterrestrials, legends, folklore—imagination? I live in an oak forest in the mountains of southeastern Arizona. I have visionquested in the deserts and mountains for as long as twenty-two days at a time. As much as I have worked with these creatures, there are times I still refuse to go outside on certain nights. There are times camping when I urge all there to get inside, when our time to be under the stars isn't really ours. We need to learn our place and space in the order of things. All these things exist to me. I have met and interacted with many of them. What are they? Shamans know them simply as other species in this wonderful planet of many, many life forms.

Implants

"... and this blue planet thing follows me everywhere I go! I go to work early in the morning, before light, and I see it pacing my car. At night, I open the curtains in the kitchen, and there it is. It's making me crazy. I'm so afraid. What about my kids?" Angela was clearly at the end of her rope. Sister to one of my students, Clarissa, she came to me for help for this peculiar form of "stalking."

I journeyed. Angela would view this from a Catholic point, I realized. However, she was also familiar with my work just enough to trust me without explanations, since I had healed her daughter. Good. Clarissa would be my assistant; she had been present for many soul retrievals and healings of all kinds.

"Angela," I said, returning from meeting her soul, "you have something inside you that doesn't belong there. It seems to have entered you through your left shoulder, at the top joint, right there ... when it was opened for some reason. You've had surgery there?"

"Yes, a few years ago. After an accident," she said.

"Good. It's never been quite right, has it?"

"No."

Clarissa seconded that. "Can you fix that, too?"

"Sure. They're the same thing. I suspect that since the item has been in there, the entry was unable to heal properly inside. In any case, it will make it that much easier for me to extract our little bugger," I said.

I began. It was an implant from a UFO or the Faire Folke—or in Angela's belief system, demons. I entered, checked it out to determine its origin (to harm or to help?), and purpose at this point (tracking, healing, goading?). It was placed originally to help with spiritual growth, to open Angela to possibilities not ordinarily in her space, but when that did not occur, it was being used as little other than a tracking sort of device. No, not even used. It had just become that, had run out of use and was just jetsam in the spiritual space that is. As a result, this blue-light "craft" was still following the "beam" from the implant. It was all quite useless, and it was time to get it removed, freeing everything involved and making Angela's shoulder "all better."

I located the implant, a small rectangular metallic/plastic sort of thing I have found often in people. It was positioned behind her left ear, and I began moving it gently down her neck and into her shoulder.

"I can see your blue light glowing around my sister's head, neck, and shoulder," Clarissa reported.

Angela stated that she felt "something" cool and warm, moving, and that there had been some tugging discomfort behind her ear, in the bone.

I was at the point, in the shoulder—should I remove it here? Yes. No. I waited. Yes. Down through the arm and out of the wrist, where the artery is distended. Perfect.

Clarissa said, "I see your light moving down the inside of her arm now."

"I feel that," Angela said. "And I can see it, too."

I checked for "roots" to see if the implant was attached to anything or if I had left any small parts inside her body. Then, opening her wrist, I brought out the implant.

"Wow!" Angela said. "I feel this ... I don't know ... a big let-go kind of thing in my wrist. It's hot but not uncomfortable. I feel like giggling."

Clarissa reported that she felt the release in the room. "Is it okay to move?" she asked. "Is anything in here going to attach itself to me?"

"No. Gone," I said. "I've got it inside me where it's safe. I'll take care of it later. Now, let me go back and check Angela out all over."

I made a few adjustments, healed up the shoulder after draining some etheric goo from it, and then went out to the upper atmosphere. No blue-light "space craft."

All done. "That's it, Angela. No more blue-light specials. You may feel lonely now."

"My shoulder doesn't hurt," she said. She was rotating her left arm all around. "It's hurt since the accident, but not now."

I stay in touch through Clarissa. All is well. No more lights following Angela, and years later, her shoulder is one hundred percent.

Implants are discussed a lot among UFO people. Most believe them to be sinister. Many think they're tied to the United States government in some sort of conspiracy (they have a very high regard for the ability of our government to be anything beyond bureaucrats), and only a few view implants to be in any way beneficial. There are those "out there" who make a good living removing implants helter skelter from anyone who feels badly. I was on a television panel with one such. She insisted, off camera, in "testing" everyone she came into contact with for implants. Even the most gullible in this group was disgusted with her machinations. My approach on the show was much as it is in this book: we have to take a look and deal with each possibility as it comes. I just don't believe in wholesale intrusion into people's bodies and psyches.

The show centered about two people who had implants removed and had the actual implant in hand. One of the implantees was a student of mine whom I had worked on a few months previously. I had removed an implant from his brain one night. He experienced it, and I thought that was the end to it. Should've known better. The phone call came the following morning.

"Roberta, this thing just came out of my nose. Do you want to see it?"

"No, Josh, I don't want to see anything that comes out of anybody's nose. Don't take this personally, but nose goop is yucky."

"No, no. I was drinking some water, and suddenly I felt this thing in my throat, and it came up my nose and into my hand. I ..."

"Josh, what the hell do you think this thing is? A booger or what?" I asked, wearily.

"It's rectangular and kind of beige and metallic."

"Are you hurt? Bleeding? Should you see a doctor?" I asked, a little alarmed.

"No. Roberta, I think it's the implant you worked on last night," Josh said.

"I took that out. It was gone. How can it be in your nose today?" I asked.

"It's not in my nose. It's in my hand now. What should I do?"

"Throw it away, I guess."

Now, months later, Josh had me on this television show discussing something I found distasteful, since most people think it has something to do with outer space. And to top it off, I was sharing this with a woo-woo from Sedona who is making a mint—and on the Internet, too—by taking out non-existent implants! I have seen the video tape, and I was noticeably cranky. I despise frauds, even deluded ones.

As Josh was being interviewed, he was asked if it was important to him to have actually seen and handled the implant.

"Yes. I have to see it to fully believe it," he said.

What? But he had told me he had felt and experienced its removal before he coughed the damn thing up! The tape shows me having whiplash as I turned toward Josh in astonishment.

The interesting thing about the evening and about the video is that also on the show was a woman who had an implant spontaneously pop out of the crown of her head. And ... it was nearly identical to Josh's implant! Later on, the moderator of the panel took both implants to a metals engineering firm in Tucson to have the makeup of them identified. They were of unknown origin.

Now, I am as curious as the next person. In fact, I have to work hard to control that curiosity, since it is not pertinent to anything. If I allow myself to think about it (and of course, I am as I write this book, may all the gods help me), I really want to delve into this more. But I will not. I just take them out when their usefulness is at an end, or when they are doing harm. There was some debate as to just what resided in the depths of the carpet in my office.

Angels and Demons

Lord Elf could be identified as an angel. I think of it as something of an angel. If you want to view your angels as white-winged, harp-playing, halo-wearing sweet guys, go ahead. Mine is now black leathery, up to nine feet tall, and red-eyed. It plays with people, and it has a temper and little in the way of sweet. It is especially partial to cats, moths, bats, rodents of most kinds, and other night creatures.

Whitley Strieber remarks in his book *Transformation: The Breakthrough* (Avon Books, 1989) that his UFO encounters are often accompanied by owls. It is in this second book of Strieber's that he appears to be moving away from the likelihood that the "visitors" are extraterrestrial in nature, but rather that they are more probably local folk. He points out many corollaries with the folklores of Western Europe and even the Gaelic language. Interesting reading. I do not always agree with his take on his experiences, but I do certainly admire his position that these beings seem profoundly compatible with our deepest genetic imprintings. There is no doubt from all sides of these debates that these entities have the deepest effect upon us all, even those who do not recall a face-to-face encounter.

A quote of Strieber's has become a mantra for me: *Learn to live at a high level of uncertainty.* I can recall a time of certainty when I was a child. People knew what to expect from life and living. There was almost an outline one could follow, and this and thus would result. Not so any longer. Everything about life and living has become uncertain. I see youngsters leaving their schools in the afternoon, their eyes watchful and wary, always moving about, checking out their environment. We have left certitude behind us in history. We must, indeed, learn to live with the new order: uncertainty. And I have no doubt whatsoever that the Faire Folke, demons, angels, however you personally view these entities, are a major part of this.

Sometimes, as I work with the Catholic peoples here in the Southwest, I find these UFO/Faire Folke creatures in them or in their homes. I do not believe that it is my place to educate people to my way of thinking or to alter their perceptions about religion and spirituality. I go with their concepts.

I also make mistakes.

"... and after you do that, go to the church and light a candle in thanksgiving," I was telling a Meso-American woman, whom I had assumed to be Catholic.

"That's evil, a sin." She was very upset.

She was a member of a rigid Pentecostal church.

Oops.

You want angels? You should see what I see behind someone when they talk to me about his or her guardian angel. Teeth, ugly (to our perception), hulking, nasty-tempered, and don't-mess-with-me. Hey, read the Bible, if you want to live with a biblical type of angel. You do not find a nice guy in there. They are mostly hit-men; god's mafioso.

One of my students went on visionquest to find her Faire Folke to join with. She came back with a) the silliest, cutest sacred name you can imagine, and b) her Faire Folke. It was ugly- and powerful-looking to the rest of us, who could plainly see it, but her description baffled us: a cute little shmoo-like creature from Lil' Abner. Well, I believe it was what she could deal with. Perhaps by now she sees it as a more powerful creature. I began by perceiving Lord Elf as brown and hairy, but I soon saw it as black and leathery. I think I would have had a hard time at first with leather. Hairy seemed less threatening.

Shamans do not present the world and Nature as what is palatable, but as it is. Simply because we are trained to view only certain things as "good" doesn't mean that it is so. We need to open our minds to other forms. Many of our science fiction writers encourage that.

Real Demons

So what is a demon then? I have to make judgments, often very quickly, when in the OtherWorld, and I had better be correct! I make mine through experience, definitely paying attention, making some mistakes and hoping I survive them, and by "feeling" the evil when it is present. I also call it "the Lie" or "Liar." But it is easy to be fooled.

An example. The class in rock reading in Yuma was going well. Everyone was having fun and "getting" stuff that was right on, and there was a lot of great feedback. One of the last to read her rock was before me now.

"I see ... Moses ... no, Jesus ... no, I think Moses ... he's coming out of the cave toward me, and it's just wonderful," she warbled.

"Stop it, Betty," I said. I could see what she was seeing, and it didn't resemble in any way the description coming from her mouth.

"He's beautiful. At last, I'm meeting a blessed apostle. Ohhh ..."

"Betty!" Very stern, now. "Put the rock down and pull out. Do it this instant!"

She went on, eyes glassy.

I entered her "vision" and faced down her "Moses."

She yelled and dropped the rock. "How awful! How could you do that to him?"

"Betty," I said, "you were being fooled."

"No, he was beautiful; he couldn't be evil like that thing you turned him into," she cried.

"That's what he really looked like," I said. "He was trying to suck you in and take over. You could have been possessed by something there." Turning to the rest of the class: "You have to always be on your guard. I don't say not to do this type of work. If I believed that, I wouldn't be teaching it, but you do have to be careful and do not ever believe in everything you see! It could be something Other."

Betty left the class and withdrew from the remainder of the weekend. She put the word out that I was doing evil stuff.

A Coven of Owls

Owls are special to me, as you'll come to learn more about in "Chapter 15: Totems and Power Animals," and they were present on my way to my first visionquest in the Pinaleno Mountains in southeastern Arizona. The place where I had chosen to fast and pray was familiar to me, a site where I had camped alone many times. I was there in the deep forest with the owls, the raspberry bushes, and a resident female bear with whom I had established a relationship of respect.

Here I was, setting up a small camp in this sacred place, high in a forest which was remote enough that I was able to hide the rustic dirt trail with brush. I would be joined on my last day of fasting by two students and Larry. Until then, all I had to do was to sit and be. I placed seed and dry dog food out for the birds and rodents and sat in my circle. On the fourth day, Larry, Alice, and Rosemary arrived, quietly setting up their parts of the camp, doing their best to avoid disturbing my space. After their dinner, they came to my circle, and we all watched the sun set and that glorious transition of day to dark.

Upon darkness, four owls began calling to one another across the meadow. We all sat in wonder and serenity. Larry went to bed as the full moon began to show itself over the pine trees, but the two women asked if they could sit up with me that night. They brought their sleeping bags close, and we watched the moonlight reflecting off the meadow grasses and pine trees and aspen all about us and listened to the forest rustlings nearby. We heard lady bear at one point as she walked by our area down toward a stream a couple hundred yards below us.

Then the owls began floating back and forth across the meadow, just in front of us. It was magic, the huge full moon, silver by now, and owls flying before it, seeming almost silver to our eyes. I began to feel odd and looked over to Alice and Rosemary, but they were both asleep. Asleep? They had just been talking in low voices not one minute ago. How odd. I turned back to the owls. I felt as if I were swinging, almost as I did just prior to channeling ... Then I saw it. A UFO. And the owls. And ... I "woke up" in the pre-dawn gray. Sick. Oh, so damn sick. I crawled into the forest, hoping the bear would not come upon me as I was weakly sick from both ends. And the pain! All over, but my head was especially aching. Like it was on fire. Not a migraine. Something else. As if it had been struck open with a sword and put back together. Please let me die.

Larry found me crawling back to camp and got me into a tent and sleeping bag. So cold and sick. I sipped ginger ale and puked some more. I would have to feel better to die. We both wondered that the two women could sleep through all this. The sun was up by now, and we could see that they lay directly in that sunshine. I asked Larry if he had slept all right, and he replied that his dreamtime had been extreme, although he could not recall the specifics. They were very disturbing dreams, however.

By mid-afternoon, I was able to get up and out by the campfire with a little help and sipped at a cup of soup. As I looked up over the rim of the cup, I noticed that all three were looking at me expectantly. There seemed to be an edge to things all right. Had I missed something?

"Can you talk about last night yet?" asked Alice.

"Sure. What about it?"

"Well, we have compared our experiences and memories of last night and are really anxious to hear yours," Rosemary said.

How odd. What experiences?

"Well, I recall the beautiful sunset. You guys moved your bags near me. I recall your voices as you talked. The bear went past us. The moon rose. And the owls began to fly back and forth probably hunting for …" I began. Then stopped.

"Wait a minute," I said. "What happened? The owls. The moon. And this other … thing in the sky. You were both asleep, and …"

"No, we were not asleep," Alice said. "We saw you look at us. We could no longer sit up. It was as if a big hand pushed us down. Right, Rose?"

"Yeah. Big hand. Are we going to stay all night tonight?"

It was quiet for a time. We all stared into the fire. The dogs had crowded up to my chair, and I absently scratched their heads and ears. Comforting. But why did I need to be comforted?

"What's going on?" I asked. "I think I remember falling asleep. But I don't think I did, either. I wouldn't sleep on a visionquest. And something happened. Is that what this is all about?"

"Roberta, I saw you look at us. The owls were flying back and forth. And in that moonlight, I swear—a UFO came into the clearing, right before us. It lowered, hovering at eye level, I think. And a door or *some-*

thing opened. And ... *you sort of walked/floated up into it!* I tried to get up, call to you, or something. I saw the owls continue flying and they began calling again. One was in the tree over where you had been. But I could not move or speak. I couldn't even move my head. I dozed on and off until almost first light, then I saw the UFO coming in again and fell deeply asleep."

Rosemary nodded. "That's what I saw, too. And I also could not move or speak, and I was awake until I saw you—I guess it was you—coming back. Can we go home?"

We all went quiet again, thinking. I was trying to remember.

"Listen, all during this visionquest, the owls have been coming in to me. One often roosts in the tree over me at night and calls. I've never felt alone nor fearful with them there—sort of guarded by them," I said. "Last night, they were behaving differently." I thought it was because there were more of us.

"But I don't know about this UFO stuff. I have always chosen not to think about them. It scares the crap out of me." We all agreed on that one, with Rosemary still asking to go home right away. But we did spend another night there as we had intended to all along. I felt I needed a little more time to recover from being so sick. I still felt bad.

"We'll be in tents tonight," I said. "We shouldn't have any of *those* kinds of experiences again. Now let's do something normal and get grounded. Okay?"

We went for a hike and picked raspberries and ate them with relish. That night was calm, and we all slept well.

A Vision

I was awakened suddenly. It was early morning of the day I was to enter a visionquest I had chosen to do in the desert inside a totally dark sweat lodge. The air was sweet as it is in the early times in the desert.

Birdsong and small rustlings. But why am I awake? I look out the tent, which I always keep open, crawled out, and turned to the northeast after seeing something in my periphery.

It was huge, a planet rising over the distant mountains. Huge? It was the size of our Mother Earth. Blue and white, almost solid. Rubbing my eyes and shaking my head, I looked yet again. And it was still there. Testing, I grounded myself and found that there were now no sounds at all, just a deep stillness. What's going on? I haven't even entered visionquest yet and already some sort of vision? But it's too real. Okay, visions are quite real and solid. But this?

I sat on a nearby boulder and watched the new planet, awaiting information. And it came. *This is Mother Earth before you, Nightwing. As you are aware, the etheric energy of all life moves ahead of the physical body. And so it is with the very world itself. What you see here before you is the future, our home with a new polar arrangement. Tilted axis, we think it is called.*

"When will this come to pass physically?" I asked, still in awe of the enormous beauty before me.

C'mon, you know it doesn't work that way, Nightwing. We don't comprehend your artificial senses of time and "years." They're nonsense. And as we have discussed often before, all sorts of things are going on which have direct cause and effect upon the timing of these phenomena. But you will live to see this movement into the future. We present to you the vision of that, a prophecy, if you will.

"Are you of the Old Race?"

Indeed. We are those who share this perfect home with you. You have such passion for the best for our Home that we give you this vision to share with us. Now, prepare to enter the darkness of that humble lodge with this vision.

I hear people carrying on about the UFOs (simply that: unidentified flying objects—unidentified, not extraterrestrial) and their anthropomorphizing of the phenomena (the same as we do all other species on this planet) and even apportioning various appearances into good/bad, angels/demons, such states being impossible for us to even comprehend, much less judge. And so many of us decry their habit of "kidnapping" us to—what? Experiment on, etc. But what I suggest to you is that when we decide to cooperate and join in their desire to save our mutual Mother … it is no longer kidnapping. Hmm? At that point, then, we can consciously unite our actions.

Nanu nanu.

Roberta with a deer she saw grow up (Cute'Ems) and a doe.

Chapter 12
Teaching and Learning

As I traveled, lectured, demonstrated shamanic work, healed, and counseled, I found that classes were becoming necessary. It was fun, and I met more people in that venue. It was also fantastic to see people awaken to so many more possibilities than they had known existed. It furthered my abilities in giant leaps as well.

Of all the classes, perhaps the most popular was the one on spirit journeying, and that evolved accordingly. I tried to leave on-going groups of journeyers a few times, but it never seemed to work out and usually deteriorated under the weight of persons who wanted to "run" things. For my part, I found it impossible to bring these groups forward over a long distance while still maintaining the integrity of the journey work and helping them grow.

When a group formed in Tucson out of a spirit journey class which didn't want to stop, things really moved. People were allowed to join the core group after taking a weekend-long class on spirit journeying, and working with the new people seemed to keep us fresh. At first, we were concerned about those who joined us who were pretty "far out there" and not necessarily down-to-earth about journey work, but those folks generally didn't stay long. One of the things that arose from teaching and working with such a tight-knit, on-going group was my set of rules for shamanic work:

1. Pay attention.
2. All life forms are sacred.
3. Pay attention.
4. Integrity in the work is essential.
5. Pay attention.
6. What you see may not necessarily be what's there.
7. Pay attention.
8. Harm none.
9. Pay attention.
10. Challenge everything.
11. Damn it, pay attention!

Today, I would emulate the Lord Buddha's admonition: *at all times be present!* And that seems to be the hardest "rule" to get across. In fact, a few students seem irritated by it to the point of total rebellion. Such a simple rule, too. As well as an obviously essential one. How can anyone ever expect to perform *any* sort of spiritual or healing work without being completely present at all times?

That includes during meditation. People have acquired the impression that meditation means checking out. Perhaps this is from the fad of the 1960s and 1970s: Transcendental Meditation (TM), which I was part of. I loved TM. I got so that I could look at a spot on my left wrist and whssh—gone into the ether! My first teachers got me started on TM. It was a great idea—it was—but taken too far and without the admonition to be present. We had the idea that meditation required absence of our consciousness.

Not so. Meditation is, simply put, being receptive. Certainly that requires some cessation of being caught up in things like worrying about temporal matters. However, it does not suggest that we be unconscious to our surroundings and things like time and discipline. Or the house on fire. Or the children requiring our attention. As a friend once said, "If we are so out of it in meditation, we might as well be all drugged up." Or confusing meditation with medication.

The same is true with spirit journeying or any healing situation: one must be present enough in *both places* to be able to discern and use one's judgment. Always. Lollygagging about in a semi-dream state is *not* spiritual work. It is merely day-dreaming. How can one expect to heal anybody if one cannot keep one's mind on what one is doing in the first place? And that carries down to all aspects of our lives. I am losing a lot of memory ability as I age. My inner computer is pretty full. I make lists now. And I work hard at recalling where the lists are! Some folks, when they first meet me, seem to expect to find a woman who is dreamy or floating about, speaking in a soft voice about ethereal subjects. Surprise! I am altogether here. In this sturdy body, attached strongly to Mother Earth—and to what is happening right now. That is the shamanic way.

Once we begin practicing presence, we may become discouraged because it isn't as easy as it sounds—and it is all the time, rather than just sometimes. This correlates with becoming aware of everything around us: once we learn to see (hear, smell, taste, feel, know) all the beauty about us, we are also that aware of the pain, suffering, and ugliness which exists—as well as our part in it.

A major lesson for me: I was so busy teaching, healing, and channeling but still had errands to run. As I drove about Tucson, my mind kept drifting ... actually *in* Walking Hawk and Rahotep. The light turned green, and I took a left, nearly exchanging paint with the oncoming man, who clearly had the right-of-way, since I "skipped" my turn arrow. He was furious, and I nearly had wet jeans.

From then on, my guys and I had a solid agreement about channeling. Still, dead people and stuff would intrude. But I had a bad tooth which I chomped on to keep me present when I drove.

Pay attention. Be present at all times. It just takes awareness and practice.

I enjoy teaching very much. Besides spirit journeying, we had workshops on reading rocks, healing techniques, mediumship, how to work with one's spirit guide, awakening ancestral memories, dreamtime, the Medicine Wheel, meeting one's potentials, and various women's issues (since I am, after all, a woman). When I started our first women's group, several men left our regular Tuesday night meetings, citing my "prejudices and male-bashing." Pretty silly, since we rarely discussed men at these meetings, unless it was pertinent to the topic. Of course, on the other hand, I enraged a number of women at a women's conference once when I demonstrated what they felt was male-preference. In fact, they behaved almost exactly like the men they were upset about! It seems a shame that, as we are all (on some level at least) trying desperately to return to At-One-Ness, we continue to maintain and even create new barriers.

Much of my work has been—and continues to be—with damaged people ... at least, people who are willing to admit they are damaged in one way or another. It has all been gratifying, as well as uncommonly instructive. This book should be dedicated to all who have sat across from me during these years, for I have learned much from each. As I have charged my advanced students, there is nothing that will teach you so much as teaching.

Eduardo

My first meeting with a great shaman may not have taken place if I had not really, really wanted it to. And therein lies the crux of this anecdote: how to approach a shaman, or any respected spiritual teacher, for this is reinforced by a conversation I recently had with an advanced teacher of Buddhism.

Someone I respect suggested that it was "time" for me to get some help and meet with Eduardo, a well-known shaman in our area, who is from a long line of familial shamans. I put the phone call off for some time, feeling that I might not be in "bad enough shape" to "bother" this man. Finally, some of my earliest teachings reached my poor mind, and I humbly called him. I would trust his judgment regarding this.

"Hello," he answered my call. Going pretty well, so far.

"Hello. My name is Roberta Lee. Alice Gerston suggested I call you. She feels you can help me move ahead greatly in my Path."

"Uh." Long silence. Finally, "What do you want me to do for you?"

Breathing again. "I'm not sure."

"Well, what do you do?" Is that impatience in his voice?

"I channel some spirits to teach and heal each Tuesday night. Alice comes there. She says it is partly because you have instructed her to do so." Hoping to identify myself a bit more.

"I know about you and what you do. I wonder if you know. Call me again when you are clearer about what you want." Click.

Okay. Shaking just a little, I sat down and began processing the phone call, the words, the nuances. I didn't do very well. He was terse, but not rude—his voice did not come across impatient or angry. I'd work on it and call back. I spent a couple days and nights meditating and being receptive to whatever I was to do with this man. I called him again.

"It is you again," he said.

"Yes, it's me," I said. "I have meditated and been as receptive to information as I know how, and I believe I have a better grasp on what I need from you."

"Let's hear it." Is he laughing at me?

"Channeling is a beginning. The spirits I work with are wonderful, filled with information, caring, and willing to give as much as we will receive. But I think that I am supposed to be doing more. Perhaps more from myself, somehow. They will not spell it out for me, of course, and I am in some quandary about it."

"You're getting warmer. Try again." Click.

That's hopeful. Maybe I'll get it right by old age. I went back to my meditating. I channeled the spirits, who simply laughed at me. I relaxed as much as I could to allow it to come to me. Bingo.

"Hello," he said.

"It's Roberta Lee again," I said. Was that mewling?

"I know." Chuckle. "What do you have for me today?"

"I need what we think of as a lift-off shot to get me going into my real work, my life work, and my spirits indicate that you are the man to see. I spoke with them this week, and they are clear about you, although purposely unclear as to why."

"Can you drift into contact with them right now?" he asked. "Let me ask some questions?"

"I believe so. Give me a minute."

Rahotep came in. "Greetings, Brother," he said in his deep voice. "It is good of you to give time to our little one here."

Eduardo responded. "Greetings to you, Brother. I am unclear what she requires of me. As you know, part of what I have for her is for her to determine ahead of time. I am here for her in a sacred way, and thus far, she has come to me also in a sacred way. Is this your teaching of her?"

"Not at this time; it is her awareness of how to address a Teacher. I am proud," Rahotep said.

"Brother," Eduardo was getting to the point now, "I am a shaman—not of her tribe or culture—and I sense that she is also. What would you have me do? She has great ability, and I sense she will do fine things, but it will be out of her own tribe and culture."

"That is true," Rahotep said. "There are few real shamans who are available at this time, and you are traditional, which is what she requires. Her heart is traditional, and all tribal traditions are close."

"That is true, Brother," said Eduardo.

"She sees the crack in the Universe but needs the means to slip her fingers into that crack and pull it apart for herself. That is what you have for her."

"I see. Thank you, Brother. Walk well," Eduardo said.

"And you, Eduardo," said Rahotep. And he left me.

"I saw the picture he made for me!" I said. "It is the Grand Canyon, and I am on the cliff and can see only a sliver of it. I must see it all!"

"Come to my office tomorrow night," said Eduardo. Click.

We worked the next night for a little over an hour. He cleared me so that I could "see" better, and he basically did what all my soul requested. I was humble and did all I could to not waste his time, and afterward I was diligent in performing the tasks he set for me. As he told me, I never discussed the details of the session, although the people I saw the following evening at the channeling were vociferous in their awareness that I had been altered physically, as well as in other ways. I just told them that I had been to see a shaman and that he had done some wonderful work that I felt would move me along more quickly.

I never saw Eduardo again.

Some teachers will not meet with a supplicant for days following the appointment. That is to say, the client arrives at the appointed time and waits for three days to be seen. It is important. Personally, I insist on punctuality, respect, and thoughtfulness. That's not much. I want my clients to be receptive and in a state of humility. Otherwise, nothing good can come of a meeting. I can give to a person only what that person values enough to receive, thus I expect remuneration—enough to be uncomfortable, to get the attention of that person. I expect a "medicine" gift which has had some thought put into it. Living in one room as I do now, I can't use bric-a-brac that people like to bring. When we go to the reservations, we always take boxes of food: non-perishables, coffee, candy, fruit. We put ourselves in the place of the medicine man we are to see—his family situation, his home, the conditions he lives in—and we take things accordingly. We put thought into it. Once there, we unload the gifts and take them into the house. The medicine man may smile, but we do not expect him to go through everything and ooh and ahh. If there are kids, they do that. If he accepts the gifts with a nod, we know that we have also been accepted. This is the sacred way of gift-giving. And this is the sacred way of meeting with a holy person

The Smoking Pipe

We gathered each Tuesday night for a Pipe Ceremony, some drumming/rattling, and then a healing circle, followed by channeling, usually from Rahotep or Walking Hawk. This night was ordinary, the altar was set up on a small round table in the center of several chairs, and we gathered about for this ceremony which we found so healing and powerful. The lights were dim, but not out; we could see detail well. A cooler was on (it was mid-summer) at one end of the room, but it was set on low to keep down the humming. As we all became quiet, I packed the Pipe with tobacco.

Once loaded, I set the Pipe upon the deer antlers I used for a stand and began the ceremony. As I looked up from my moment of meditation, I saw smoke flowing from the Pipe before me. I had not lit it.

Looking around the table, I asked, "Anybody see that smoke?"

All eyes were upon that Pipe. "Sure."

The smoke flowed heavily—so heavily that I had difficulty seeing the persons across the table from me at times. As usual, I looked for a "normal" cause of something which seemed not normal.

"Who lit it?"

Dumb question. "No one, Roberta."

"Really?" I asked.

"Roberta, I was watching the Pipe constantly after you loaded it, and no one came near it," Larry said.

Several others agreed with him.

By this time, the smoke was filling the room, which was not small.

"Maybe it's coming in through the cooler from outside," someone ventured.

Immediately, the smoke from the Pipe moved *against* the air flow. We all laughed.

After nearly fifteen minutes of watching the smoke "play" with us and some sporadic respectful discussion, I reached out for the Pipe to begin the ceremony. Smoke was still pouring from the bowl and into my face as I peered into it. The tobacco was fresh and unburned.

I struck a match and put it to the tobacco, and we proceeded with our ceremony as we ordinarily did, except that the prayers were more focused on our miracle. Afterward, we engaged in some discussion about miracles and what goes with them.

"It seems to me that a tremendous responsibility comes with this ... that we are required to live an even more spiritual life and to keep this in mind always," said Norma.

Several agreed. This made sense.

"I know that after tonight, I will be far more diligent in my meditation and getting here each week and praying for those in need," said Glenn.

"Roberta, what do you think happened here tonight?" Doris asked.

Here it was. Would I choke? Yes!

"It had nothing to do with me; it was the Great Mystery causing that smoke. I am just a channel of His power," I said piously.

In less than one month everyone present at that altar that night had left our Tuesday nights except two. And that is how it has been in all my work: as soon as things get real and tangible—which all who come to me ask for—everyone leaves. Why? It requires something back if it's real!

And what about me? What about the Pipe?

The Pipe never smoked on its own as profusely, but it does continue to emit smoke prior to each ceremony and often during the ensuing prayers. Each time someone noticed it and made mention, I said that the Great Mystery did it, not I. My spirits remonstrated with me in their own sweet way: "Hey, Dummy, the Pipe smokes for you!" Sacred words like that. My teachers know how to keep my attention. But like so many, I did not follow their teachings. I continued to insist that the Pipe smoked from the Great Mystery.

Things came to a crashing halt during a visionquest the following Winter Solstice. I was instructed that true humility is—just what Sudy and Barbara, my first teachers, taught me—*the truth*. In this case, the truth is that the Pipe smokes when I ask it to. And, of course, I would not request that without cause. It even tells me who at the ceremony will see it and who will not. The phenomenon is for me. And I refused it. *I refused to take responsibility for it.* That is egotism. That is a lie.

As I came around, the Pipe has continued to smoke, but never with the density as that first time. Often densely enough that people new to us believe that I have lit it, but never so that we cannot see through it.

I must admit that sometimes the Pipe smokes just because it wants to—or at least that is how it appears. I had a student join me as I visionquested some people in the Santa Rita Mountains. As is my custom, I smoked the Pipe in my tent door in the dusk each evening, to join with the questers in their prayers. Joyce joined me, and then, after praying, she went to her sleeping bag at the back of the large tent and snuggled down. I lay in my bag near the door. The Pipe was propped against a small bush at the tent door, by my feet. We were talking quietly when Janice nearly shouted.

"It's smoking!"

"What?" I said, afraid of forest fire.

"Your Pipe!" She was very excited.

I looked. "Yes, Joyce, you know it smokes."

"But I've never seen it before. And I thought it only smoked before you lit it," she said.

"Not always. Sometimes it smokes in its bag in the house," I said. "That's when it wants my attention. Out here, I suspect it is on guard for us and holding the space for the visionquesters."

I fell asleep while Joyce continued to sit and watch the Pipe smoke over an hour later.

Before I return to the subjects of humility and responsibility, let me stay with the Pipe. It is a stern but loving teacher. It seems gentler to me than my others, but I become a little ill whenever I smoke it. Again, the modern thinking is that it can't be good for you if it isn't comfortable, but in this case, as in many others, the fact that it is always uncomfortable for me to smoke means that I never do so without good cause and without great consideration. When I offer a Pipe Ceremony to someone for healing, for example, or because they are in some emotional need, I do not suggest it frivolously. It is going to hurt, and I will feel sick after the people leave (feeling great). My Pipe is a big one, and the bowl must be filled and smoked completely each time—that is another consideration.

Thus, I approach this great teacher with awe and some dread, as we all should approach our teachers.

The Pipe, as does the Sweat Lodge, tells me what should be done. The fire at the Sweat Lodge, for example, creates itself, for I use no rigid ritual as many do. If we believe in the sanctity of that fire, why would we tell it how to burn? The trick here is to know how to listen and interpret what our teachers are telling us. This is done first by being humbly receptive to what we claim is sentient power, then by making mistakes and paying for them.

Mace, Penny, and Joseph lived in the same house. They were all Native American medicine people and pipe carriers. Mace called me one morning.

"Roberta, we're having real trouble over here. We are fighting, there is tension, the children are reacting. We do not know what's going on. What do you think?"

"Mace, give me a few minutes. I'll call you back," I said. I was just getting into the shower.

I showered and meditated as I did so. Showers can change the entire world for me. And, of course, there was the answer.

"Mace, have you guys smoked the Pipe about this?" I called them back.

"Shit! And a white woman knows that!" he growled, disgusted with himself that they hadn't thought of that before even calling me.

They smoked, and it worked for them.

When I perform marriages, I often have the bride and groom buy a simple sacred pipe which comes apart, and I integrate that into the ceremony. The bowl is held by the woman, and it will always represent her; the stem is the man. When they join it and fill it and smoke it, they are united. I tell them that this is a fine way to start any new project for the two of them, to begin settling a disagreement, or just to improve their intimacy.

Larry and one of my students had been working on the student's car for most of a day and were frustrated and apparently no closer to solving the problem than hours ago. As I walked by them during my chores around the place, I urged them to smoke the pipe with the car. It worked. The engine was purring in short measure.

I started out with a corncob pipe I bought for less than ten dollars. You can use anything. It is *not* sacred to use marijuana in your pipe. I use an herbal tobacco created by a woman in Bisbee, Arizona for people who are allergic to nightshade, which is what regular tobacco is. The Native American pipe carriers I know use cheap tobacco, since anything extra nice has too much oil for the health of the pipe. There are natural tobaccos growing almost everywhere in this country. And there is a company in Santa Fe, New Mexico—American Spirit Tobacco Company—which sells natural tobacco with no additives, very good for Pipes.

As with any sacred stuff: beware. If you begin to smoke in a sacred way, it becomes your teacher, and teachers have requirements! I also urge you not to start with a big, fancy pipe. That's just for ego.

You hoped I would forget. Responsibility and humility. I have struggled with my ego since I met Sudy and Barbara, back in 1966. I know my ego intimately now—it has caused me the most trouble. It has been a focus in my life: to rid myself of my slavery to it. The more I work with ego, the more subtle it becomes, as it hides here and there, doing all it can to maintain some sort of connection to use me again. The most obvious form of ego is the exhibited overtly "look at me" stuff, the greatest symptom here being lying. With a strong teacher who will call you on it, you can eradicate this form pretty quickly—if you truly want to.

Then there is the form which causes you to be the nice person, always doing for others, being good, selfless. That's pretty easy to spy, although amateurs get this one confused with true selflessness and even common courtesy.

But let's get down to people who have worked on their egos for years and are walking their walks. Taking responsibility for what we are doing. I know a powerful man who is a born shaman but will not shamanize, who heals but insists that it is not he who effects healing. And so on. He insists that that is true humility. Balderdash, I say. He even puts forth that he does not think about his healing work much because it is not he who heals. Urk. Argh.

So his (metaphoric) Pipe is not smoking much anymore. The smoke is getting thinner and thinner. Why? Because he will not take responsibility for himself and what he himself is doing. You see, the Great Mystery sets up our bodies, for example, to be good at healing, and we use it. *We* decide to use our bodies for that. It is our choice. And we do it—not some etheric granddaddy in the sky

Therefore, whenever we work, we should process what took place to ferret out our part in the situation, to find ways to better ourselves always and our approaches, to hone our skills and crafts, and so on. When I hear people describe themselves as "just a channel for god," I want to go to sleep. These are boring people who do not participate fully in life. Pipes that no longer smoke. Let's get rid of the nonsense and find our passions for all life and get busy. That's humility.

Well, being sensible usually results in humility. I would love more than anything to be able to heal poor Mother Earth, but I realize that I do not know what is best for Her at this time. Rather than do anything, I just pray and yearn for what is best—soon. And I do all I can think of to stay in harmony and to not hurt Her any more than I have to. That is one of the first laws of healing: do no harm.

So let's describe humility as being sensible. A step further in humility would suggest a strong teacher, one you can count on to tell you the truth and insist upon that. Here, however, you must be sensible about a teacher; there are so many woo-woos out there. Is nice what you really want? Is light and love what it's all about for you? If not, then find a down-and-dirty teacher. If nice is what you want, then get that—but likely you have stopped reading this book by now anyway. As Anonymous says, *"The trouble with most of us is that we would rather be ruined by praise than saved by criticism."*

Most people who come to me to learn something about life expect—and demand—the simple "Dick and Jane" method of teaching. Of course, that cannot be. My teaching power animal is Coyote, who teaches us by confounding us. In fact, all of shamanic teaching, learning, and healing is comprised of paradoxes, dichotomies, and absurdity. We modern humans don't like that. We want everything spelled out for us. But life itself is a paradox and riddle supreme. When someone comes to me—and they do—for the "meaning of life," I have to suppress my laughter. *There is no great meaning, folks! There are only the questions.*

When I teach—and equally, when I am being taught—there are the questions. No "see Spot run" stuff here. Teaching occurs while life is being lived. Very often, students become frustrated with what they perceive to be no teaching going on, and, just as often, they are angry about the teaching, or at least the form it takes. The solution to this is commitment and humility. I have told some of my students that I have learned that, even when the teacher is wrong, he or she is right. That was true of my first teachers, and it is true of the spirit teachers I have now. Sometimes, these spirits tell me to do things which do not work out. In all honesty, however, I must admit that I learn from these "exercises in futility." And perhaps I have just misinterpreted their orders. My students misinterpret mine often enough.

The Shamanic Practitioner

Nancy is probably the best shamanic practitioner I have ever known. She is not a shaman, and does not wish to be one. I often question the Great Mystery about her: why isn't she a shaman, so that I could give her all the power I have worked with? Why won't shaman apprentices work as diligently as she has? Wah!

I met Nancy in Oklahoma City many years ago. She was at my opening lecture and demonstration and took the weekend spirit journey class. She has never quit. We can only work physically together each summer, as she visits Arizona during school break. We exchange tapes the rest of the time. She understands why students come to despise me, but continues anyway because she wants what I have to teach her. The perfect apprentice.

Nancy is able to spirit journey very well and gains precious information for clients in that way. Her forte, however, is physical healing, which she accomplishes through shamanic imagery and using energy and void. One of her lessons appears in "Chapter 10: Hand of God and Shamanic Spirits."

She is now learning mediumship. Certainly, talking with the dead is something one must have some native talent for, but we can really go with it if one has a modicum of that ability. She does not perform soul retrievals, although she can help people with psychological and emotional retrievals. She cannot physically go into the deepest OtherWorld to retrieve, say, a kidnapped soul. She can—and does—recognize the condition wherein one should be performed and refers the client to me. Nancy has integrity. And she has shown the willingness to walk the distance.

Another example of a shamanic practitioner was Milo, who worked with me for several years. She was always there, someone I had come to depend upon. She made my work easier and more powerful, just by her presence. And then she left. This was pretty early on in my work, so I didn't know how to promote her abilities into that of a shamanic practitioner. Her talent puzzled me—what to do with it. It seemed that it was a waste to use it simply to help me, but I did not know what else to do! Today, I would urge her toward her own practice so that many others would benefit from her great talent.

Medicine Men and Women

I had the distinct honor and pleasure to work with a group of people on a weekly basis for about three years. All of these people could easily be described as shamanic practitioners and/or medicine people. Working with them so regularly strengthened my abilities beyond measure. We worked together each Tuesday night (spirit journeying and studying), we sweated in the lodge together often, we visionquested, and we all grew in powerfully spiritual ways.

Then, as a new energy of people came to join us, the whole thing blew up. Within weeks and months, it was over. Violently, in an upheaval, which left, I believe, all of us wounded and a bit puzzled. Processing the "end" with the few people I am still in contact with, we have often wondered. Each person who left did so with different excuses, none of which even made sense. One actually created a situation and lied about it in order to leave.

We have formed some conclusions: these were all powerful people, medicine people and shamanic practitioners, and that is quite a bit of power to exist in one space, physically and spiritually. Power needs to be spread around. There was a profound intensity whenever we got together, although we were also having a lot of fun.

Further, we had become very intimate. That is, we knew each other deeply—we had journeyed multiple times for one another and had seen each other in that completely vulnerable state of visionquest, of the sweat lodge, not just once, but many, many times. We had come together for deep emotional and psychological healings; we knew each other's darkest secrets. It had nowhere else to go but to explode.

Traditionally, shamans and medicine people meet only occasionally and for brief periods of time, to work together and to compete, to hone their crafts. Now I can see why. This was the most joyous time of my life, and its end was the most grievous. I can see, however, that being hurled out on my own pushed me into a higher level of growth.

But we really had something special.

Channeling

The gold cliffs came back to me in my dreams over and over. I knew they were in the Superstition Wilderness, but I could not find what the spirits were nagging me about, although I had gone there many times. This time, we were going in with a friend—who had hypnotized me a few times and was interested in what might be there—and Larry and three other people. After a late start, we got to the site I had been shown, too late to search much, but we set up camp near a stream in the basin at the foot of the cliffs.

After dinner, Terrell hypnotized me.

I was in a black tomb, my body reclining on a stone table. I had just awakened from, what? Sleep? It didn't seem as if I had been asleep. Where was I? Why was I here? Where was here? Well, I knew it was a tomb of some sort, but I didn't recall dying. Instinctively, I anxiously awaited ... him. Who was him?

At this point, my body in the sleeping bag began shivering violently, teeth chattering. Terrell inquired as to what was causing me such distress.

"I'm afraid of who is going to come into the tomb," I said.

"Why are you afraid?" he asked. "Do you have an idea of whom it may be?"

"No. I just cannot bear it."

Terrell calmed me and tried to draw me back from the experience a bit, to be an observer. That didn't work. I was in this experience for better or worse.

Light seeped into the tomb. Then a bright, harsh light. I placed my hands over my eyes, rigid with terror. I heard voices—concern, caring. Then, there were strong arms lifting me and holding me to a hard chest.

"She lives." His voice.

My fear vanished. It was Lord Rahotep.

My face covered against the light, I was taken from the tomb and into a shadowy room. There were several people there, all exhibiting joy to see me.

I had survived my ritual death and was now ready to prepare for my work as "Oracle" of the temple. Rahotep was the head priest of this temple of cats and oracles, and he would be speaking through me for some time. I still wonder at the fear I first felt, for Rahotep and I are very close and have been since that time so long ago.

The following day, I was sitting in camp, sad that once again we had not found what I was told was here for me. I entered a light state of trance and heard a new "voice."

"Stand up and look toward the golden cliffs. Find the pointer cactus and look to the top of it. That is the place."

I stood, saw a saguaro, looked immediately above it ... there it was! I walked directly to it—well, as directly as dense desert vegetation allows one. It was a rock shaped like a loaf of bread, about fifteen feet high, with access from either end. At the northern end of this rock, there was a "seat." I went directly to that seat, just as I knew I had done often before, and sat down. This was it. I looked to my right, toward the south end of the rock; there is a relatively flat spot there. That was where the little lodge was where we ... rested? Just below me, on the east side, amidst what is now a grove of mesquite, was where ... Old Widow woman had our camp?

Returning to the present-day campsite, I waited until Larry came back from a hike and told them all what I had found. We all went there. This rock was in the center of a basin surrounded by ridges and tall cliffs of magnificent beauty. It was also the center of a vortex, an energy pool. It was breathtaking.

Terrell placed me into a trance, and I channeled myself as I was in the early sixteenth century. I was Mourning Dove. Walking Hawk, the shaman of a small tribe, had saved my life when my parents died of some disease, and I lived with him. I adored this little man.

"We come here so he can 'make his magics', and Old Widow and I take care of him because he does not sleep much or eat if we do not insist," I chirped. "I like to sit here against his knee while he prays and awaits instruction from the spirits. He is warm, smells good, and his chant is beautiful. I like to see the birds and animals come to us here," I went on.

"Walking Hawk makes me go into the lodge to sleep though, when it gets late and is cold. I don't want to, but I do what he tells me. Then I bring him another robe to cover himself with. But he hardly knows it is there, so I have to crawl up and put it over him. And I cover his poor feet. I bring him water, but he forgets to drink it until I cry."

A few evenings later, Walking Hawk came in and channeled after Rahotep had had his say. He is a gentle old man who was injured as a boy and paralyzed on his right side. He and Rahotep both share an amazing sense of humor and seem to enjoy teasing each other.

As I channeled before a standing room only crowd for months, and then a smaller regular group for two years, the Oracle began to come in occasionally. She was quite small and quiet. Toward the end of my public channeling, my ancestor from Western Britain, Wulf, spoke up. He is a pretty wild man who lived about seven thousand years ago. We do not do so well publicly because his personality is a bit more dramatic than mine, and he constantly urges me to be so too. But we commune often privately.

One evening, during the Q and A session following a channeling by Rahotep, we were asked if he or Walking Hawk were avatars.

"Haw, haw, haw," he chortled. "Avatars," as if that was the funniest word in the language—and perhaps it is. "If there were as many perfect souls as you seem to think—and as have been represented to you—there would be no just-deads here. No, we are just dead men who wish to share with you what he have learned over thousands of years."

These "just dead men" were able to instruct, counsel, and heal folks for many months. In fact, they still often do, since they live within me now. As we continued to channel, I found that we became increasingly connected, until Rahotep, Walking Hawk, and I are one now. Wulf is here but not so intertwined.

I recall a few special evenings with the guys. One, we were outside, and someone asked Rahotep where the comet he was discussing would come from. We stood, and he had me point to a spot southeast. The questioner was disappointed, for he had hoped for some sort of mathematical description. But over ten years later, I was visionquesting some people in the mountains, when I walked out of my tent one night and saw this enormous comet—in that spot that Rahotep had pointed out to us. As it moved across the sky that night and out through the northwest over the following week or so, I held in my memory that breathtaking moment when I first saw it. So large that first night, so bright, and right where he said it would be.

One evening, we had met for their teachings, and it was over. They announced that since we were so At-One now that there was no point in their coming in so formally. They also displayed some irritation that people would not heed my counsel "except when her eyes are closed. We go." That was it. There was another reason: channeling was causing me some real physical distress. I might be ill for days following a session. I channel the guys now, very occasionally, for certain people, but the trance is lighter—and I am aware that my head will ache for days after.

We continue an interior dialogue and are writing a book containing the life stories of Rahotep, Oracle, Walking Hawk, and Wulf.

Find Your Teacher

It seems to me that people who do not use their abilities on behalf of our shared Mother Earth are not only missing out, but sinning by omission. It's certainly not enough if one has always been blessed with visions, foretelling, and spiritual or even mundane experiences of the "psychic" type. Remember, death row is filled with psychics. Being psychic is no big deal. It is how we work with it for the good of all life.

Here's an example: even if one knows how to play the piano and has skill at it, one is still not a musician until one studies, improves, and plays for others.

What a waste! To me, that is criminal. Being psychic is just another of our senses, like sight. A person who has good eyesight is a real fool for not appreciating the beauty which surrounds us all—for not sharing that somehow with others.

Where's the passion? I find so little of it anywhere. Who is willing to go the distance, or even halfway? Who is willing to give up some spare time to expand their natural talents for the good of us all? How sad. What about working diligently, with discipline? Giving up the "I wants" for the joy of helping others? Of all species?

Given that we have the ability and desire, where do we find our teachers? Okay, I found my base education with Barbara and Sudy, long, long ago. Since then, it has been primarily through fasting on the ground with the All Life for long periods of time. Allowing the Hand of God to shape me into using my talents wisely. Working diligently toward being Wise, rather than talking about it, rather than just being intelligent and educated. (Please, I am not dismissing education, okay?)

The one thing I can guarantee anyone is that should you hurl yourself into giving yourself to Power (as far as you feel you are able to go) and living in respect and harmony with the All Life, your life will become so filled with joy and reward that you will naturally want to go farther. Try it. Find a teacher. A real one, not some smooth-talking self-deluded fool.

You will receive the teacher you truly want, one way or the other.

Chapter 13
The Failed Shaman

Toward the end of my spirit journey, I walked down a hard switchback trail ladened with a heavy frame pack. It was snowing and sleeting. Icy. All along the trail, as I forced myself to trudge along, were bodies. Some frozen in the position of walking, some curled up, some with rage still etched upon their faces, some holding books to their chests as if to keep warm by them, some with children. On and on, hundreds of bodies seen by me in great clarity. I viewed them and felt tremendous grief. But I continued trudging, in pain and grief and some despair, knowing that I would join them if I stopped for even a moment to express my sorrow. As I moved from this place of frozen death, I was told that those bodies were the failed shamans of today. So many! Why? Why are there not people who will passionately devote their lives to Mother Earth and all who dwell within, upon, and above Her? Is it really too much to ask?

Nearly every "baby shaman" who comes to me to learn, does so expressing great humility and promise of commitment. None have lasted more than a year. Why? Each time a new prospective apprentice approaches me for teaching, he or she tells me the same things each one who has gone before does. Each one is positive that he or she truly understands what I am saying, how I am describing the hardship that comes with the Walk. Each one assures me that he or she will not fail as others have, assuring me of dedication. They insist that they do not romanticize this way of life. But they do. They all do.

Soon, however, they find that shamanism and humility and awareness dwell in how one washes dishes, drives a car, cleans out the stables, shops, cleans, interacts with family and friends—in short, daily life, however dull and mundane it may seem on the surface of things.

Like most of us, each one wants to know, not to learn.

Goal-setting is deadly. It is the process, the journey, which is all-important. There is no arrival. We see the guru, seated upon a silken cushion, covered with flowers, smiling that ethereal smile of All Love. But we do not see the groveling in our own feces it took to get there. These saintly persons even go to great pains to tell us of their journeys so that we might be encouraged to join them, but we do not hear that; we hear and see only what is there before us, now. No struggle, no suffering, no sacrifice. Just bliss on a pillow.

After some three years of working with my first teachers on a daily basis, I argued with them. It turns out that I was correct in my argument, but they walked out of my life that day. That is how it works. It did not matter whether I was right or wrong; one does not argue with a Teacher. That is, at the least, counter-productive, whether you are learning math, Spanish, or painting. I regret that they gave me no warning, for I would not have displayed my knowledge, monumental ego, and innate wisdom if they had given me a warning. I wept, pleaded, and promised everything, to no avail. Although we remained friendly, we became distant acquaintances. They were not angry, merely aware that I would learn no more from them. They may have been incorrect about that. It doesn't matter. Teachers do not have to be correct, but we still must obey. I have often mused regretfully over what more I may have learned from them.

Life works that way. Shamanism, any spiritual walk, works thus. In all, if we are not walking our Walk *diligently and honestly*, if we are not dedicated and committed, if we argue or drag our feet on this Walk, the journey may be ended at any point *without warning and without reward for works done.*

What is the cause of failed shamans? Ego. Ego and the refusal to release that falseness. To shamanize requires nothing less than ego annihilation. Nothing less. Power never wanted to work with Roberta, only with the shaman. Roberta has to die— mentally, emotionally, and even physically. Not so long ago, a man attending a workshop on spirit journeying came to me, obviously puzzled and concerned. His question was, "How is it you've been willing to sacrifice everything, even physical comfort and love, to be a shaman?"

Sacrifice? This was the first time I'd considered that. I was stunned for a bit. Then I recalled people who have asked about the sacrifices surrounding parenting. When it's your very life, you don't think in terms of sacrifice. It just is.

In tribal days, before we began worshiping individualism, the shaman was helped in her growth and power by all the people. The entire village worked to keep her humble and uncomfortable and off balance. This was also true of the shaman's apprentice—perhaps particularly true. If the shaman did not humiliate the apprentice enough, the village did it. If that was not enough (and it seldom is), life itself humiliated that person. It still works that way, albeit not overtly. Ergo, the apprentice storms out of the Teacher's life and back into ... what? Life? What life?

Academic shamanic literature cites several methods in which life deals with failed shamans. First, they die. Secondly, they die. Thirdly, they die, but they continue to walk around the village and are considered to be someone to whisper about or joke about or to keep one's children away from.

Shamans are despised, feared, and unacceptable within the village; however, failed shamans are an anathema. To everyone. It is a terrible thing for my body and mind to be within the same room with a failed shaman; I am bombasted with the odor of decomposing flesh. My immediate and overwhelming desire is to flee. Those who have failed within my home have been asked to leave quickly. It is exactly like living with a stinking corpse. You may still recognize the features of one you used to know, but the smell is awful and you want them gone right now.

It is true that the failed shaman is now dead. They do die. The persona part may be alive, but the shaman is dead in every aspect of the word. The shaman's light is extinguished, her eyes are flat, there is little intelligence remaining, little judgment. It is hard to function in a logical world—and now, impossible to ever, ever walk the Walk again.

It is over. Done. That is a thing our culture does not seem to comprehend: that often, when a line is crossed, one may not turn back, no matter how passionately one wishes to. We even tend to believe that everything is possible, on a physical level, through modern medicine, with its transplants and medicines—that no matter what, we can be whole again. Not so. We do die. Death has been a natural phenomenon for all time! Death may also represent an end to a certain phase of our lives. An example may be the person who severs his spinal cord and will never walk again, never dance, never drive a car, never even sit without assistance, never make "normal" love. You get the point.

The same is true in any spiritual development. *Do it or suffer the consequences.* Perhaps Power will become disenchanted with our ambivalence and leave. Even if we say we didn't much want to walk with Power anyway, nyah, nyah—yes, we did. Life will be altered in a sad way forever, and we return to the darkest recesses of Plato's cave. Opportunities do not lay stuffed to the brim of a bottomless pit for us to tap into whenever we're in the mood or it is convenient to fit into our lifestyles.

When an apprentice has worked with me in the past, I have given and given. I remonstrate, berate, threaten, and even shout. Most often, they remain within the ego state, clinging to it as to a life preserver. I confess that when it ends, I am relieved; now my life and hers can go forward, separately. There is a time of processing, when I examine the time we spent together to delve up my part in this failure, for it feels as if I have failed also, and I must learn from it. Then I go on. The scars remain. The cosmos is scarred.

The failed shaman's body lives on, but she cannot even return to the person she once was. She must do all she can to carve out a new life for herself. That is difficult, probably more so than the willingness which was required from her by Power in the first place. I believe that, shaman or not, we are all required to be willing. Our own selves require that. The failed apprentice shaman is free from nothing—except great possibilities of dwelling within the All Life and the fulfillment of what we agreed to do in this lifetime. What a great sorrow that is!

As I have lived and observed many failures, I have noted that just as in the Old Times, not only did I provoke and humiliate these apprentices, the future shamans, but so did almost any social interaction they had. So did they themselves humiliate themselves, and so did life. As I observed these acts play out in pain and sorrow, I could see that we are all still treated as we were thousands of years ago. I am sure that today the old shamans and apprentices experience the same hopes, fear, disappointments, humiliations (for the Teacher is also humiliated within this failure), and horror of failure as did our ancestors. Surely, the Old Ones may have comprehended it even as little as I do in the living of it.

A chapter in Joan Halifax's *Shamanic Voices: A Survey of Visionary Narratives* (E.P. Dutton, 1979) is dedicated to this subject. One of her subjects, whom she interviewed, describes his life following his decision to leave apprenticeship in his tribe. He attempts to go back to making a living at fishing, but no one will buy his fish. Other tribal members walk past him without notice. He has become an outcast. It is truly a brutal description of a failed shaman.

What about those who never even try? One woman, upon reading the literature I had suggested describing shamans and their lives, came by and literally threw the book at me. I have it today, to lend to those "eagle eggs" I meet. Her remark was that shamans are dirty and immoral and that the whole thing is disgusting. My, my.

Most, however, simply wish to "put it off as long as they can" because it means giving up control over their (largely uncontrolled) lives. They are buying time. Ultimately, these people are failed shamans— failed from lack of caring. As a friend of mine often says, "the cluephone is ringing, but no one is answering."

Then there is the one shaman who never was. Rebecca and her husband came to me for a healing, referred by a doctor. Seems that Rebecca was weak and ill, and nothing seemed to work. Perhaps she was possessed? They were desperate. They were young. She was not yet thirty.

I had three students with me, including one of my best shamanic practitioners, Chaz. I went into the journey and met Rebecca's soul, and it was immediately obvious that she was a shaman. The soul requested that I identify her and do what I could to get her to practice. We are not called wounded healers for nothing, and it is usually a physical or medical crisis which brings us into our shamanism. I came back from the journey, glanced around the semi-dark room and saw that Chaz knew for sure and that the other two had guessed.

"Rebecca," I said, gently, "you are a born shaman, and all these symptoms are to force you into practice."

"But I don't want to be one," she wailed.

Let me digress a moment: what was going through my mind at this time was that each person in the room had been reporting seeing shapeshifting and other physical phenomena during the journey—most of all, the husband. *All except Rebecca, who reported nothing!*

I told her of the joys of shamanism and how the world needs shamans for balance, particularly now. Her husband was nodding. He could see what I was talking about! He was amazing.

"I just want to get better and have a baby," she whined.

Snarl. Sigh.

After quite some discussion, including a break when the couple went outside and talked in private, she returned and asked if there was anything I could do for her.

"I'm not sure. There is the possibility of draining your power. Healing you of being a shaman, if you will," I said.

"Good. Do it."

"Can we discuss this?" I asked. "I'm not sure about it. It would be meddling with something a lot bigger than all of us here. It seems almost heretical to me. And what if you change your mind later?"

"I won't. Just get this out of me so I can live a normal life."

"It's possible that it won't help," I said.

"Try."

Okay. I began the awful work. Everyone present could see the energy draining down, down throughout her body, and finally out her feet. I took it back to the Source in a sacred, balanced way. I was physically sick.

As I drained her and "healed" her, her husband's ability to "see" anything gradually diminished, until all of his psychic ability was gone. He became increasingly quiet. It was as if his light had gone out as well. After they left, my students and I processed what had happened. In fact, they didn't want to leave. They wept. It was the saddest work I have ever done. Chaz was the most upset. Why on earth was that woman so selfish and blind? This was certainly not what I had hoped my practice would be made up of. And I have only performed one other such: it was to save a failed shaman from certain violent madness, a different kettle of fish entirely.

I have heard recently that Rebecca has never become well and normal. I failed in healing her from shamanism. She is ill, unhappy, and desolate.

Tom Cowan, in his wonderful book about Celtic shamans, *Fire in the Head* (Harper Collins, 1993), describes the failed shaman as the "dysfunctional shaman." He compares the dysfunctional shaman to the legend of the Fisher King and is kind when he suggests that those who fail usually do so out of fear. Cowan goes on to suggest also that the tyro shaman's personality was not shattered sufficiently so that the "shaman's intense and profound vision" could come through and thus overcome that fear. A nicer language than mine, as I refer to this failure as that of the ego staying in charge of the shaman.

Shamans must be equipped with strong egos in order to tolerate being shattered and to tolerate the resultant work in the OtherWorld. However, as with most things we are graced with at birth, shamans must work through that ego, the worldly ego, thus permitting the Shaman itself to move in and live and work. Ego deathing is always excruciating, perhaps more so for one who has a certain innate charisma to begin with and for one who has some power already. Why not use that power without the time, sacrifice, and pain (and terror) involved with killing out one's ego? What we find in that case, for whatever brief period of time there is before the end of any power, is a child run amok, complete with temper tantrums and no control. Not a pretty sight and certainly nothing useful for the Earth and all who dwell here.

The shattering itself is required for the resultant self-discipline and sheer talent to journey into god-knows-what awful places on behalf of others. Yet, most of the "baby shamans" who have come to me for training insist that they be taught how to go there even before they become honest with themselves and allow themselves to become clear enough to do the work. This puts me in mind of giving a madman carte blanche to running the world.

To further quote Cowan, "... He refused to change his life as would be required of someone whose older paradigm of reality no longer explains the universe." However long this failed, or dysfunctional, shaman survives physically, life is over. And there is no negotiation. They are typically neutralized one way or another so that they are unable to wreak more harm than their continued physical existence causes. Their attempts to gain respect and recognition are fruitless and appear to be foolish, even when one does not know the circumstances.

Pat, a skunk who lived with Roberta at RavenHouse.

Chapter 14
Fakes, Frauds, and Fools

He was dressed in what I have come to call the fake shaman uniform: faded jeans, blue workshirt, chukkas, and a leather bag suspended from his belt. He was soft-spoken, self-effacing, and apparently humble in his greeting of a shaman. Showmanship. He was also firmly entrenched in this city, with a mostly female following. And I met one just like him in each city I have traveled to.

There are variations, of course. One such man works primarily with men and boys, presenting them with such things as visionquest-type activities, rites of passage, consciousness-raising, and activities he claims will bring out their feminine, vulnerable side.

One such fraud claims variously to be of several ancestries, but his most fanciful one is his claim that he is Carlos Castaneda's "mentor," Don Juan—who, in all truth, is a fictional character from a completely fictional body of work. This man poses as Don Juan, gathering the gullible about him, imposing peculiar taboos on them, and doing all he can to enslave them to his person.

The women are required to be celibate, but perhaps not so with their "teacher," to whom they must be loyal and above all prove their worthiness in the life. Several women came to me when they found that their lives were no longer livable and had begun to suspect that this Don Juan might not be exactly what he had projected to them. We ended up calling him in a conference phone call and terminating their association with him. I can still recall the threats he shouted over the telephone: they would never know peace, he would track them down in their dreams and attack them as only he could. It interested me greatly. Finally, I spoke up to him, and he disconnected immediately. The women all went on with their lives peacefully, seeking other teachers—hopefully with a little more wisdom and discernment.

There is a fairly well-known man from Southern California who required certain peculiar sexuality from his advanced students in order that they might "prove their love of all mankind." He also falsely claims to be Native American, though he is not.

One man I met claimed to have studied extensively in a Tibetan Buddhist Monastery. It was printed up in his brochures. But he had never been out of the country, and his only connection with Tibetan Buddhism was a meditation bowl he had purchased. This same man made his mark in California by running a series of Tantra Yoga classes, which were neither tantric nor yogic and resulted in a large number of divorces. The man greatly enjoyed his harem for some time until the people there began to catch on.

It is not only men who fake us, but the women seem to be a little less flagrant in their fraudulent claims. Most women who incorrectly claim to be shamans are most likely medicine women, and they simply do not know the difference. They tend to float among us, dressed in airy costumes and lots of beads, just filled with lightness and sweetness. There are, of course, the more infamous shamanic frauds, one of whom is typical, having written an extensive number of purely fictional books and held large seminars to create more shamans. When I read her "autobiography," wherein she relates how she studied with medicine women, I was immediately struck by the fact that she simply could not have learned much since she was most often in a state of being naked and in a faint. She is certainly charismatic and continues to have a fine following, although many periodicals will no longer carry her advertisements. Fewer people attend since her claims were publicly exposed as fraudulent. The shame of it all here is that she did a fine job of raising the consciousness of many women, getting many onto the path of spiritual medicine.

Nearly all of these fakes and fools (they fool themselves most of all) also claim to have Native American ancestry. I met one woman just prior to a lecture I was about to deliver. She stopped me as I entered the hall, gushing admiration for a "fellow shaman" who suffered for the people. What? We conversed. She spoke of studying with me in order to segue into her public work as shaman.

"But what makes you believe that you are a shaman?" I ingenuously asked her.

"Oh, I spent all my childhood on the Lakota Reservation," she replied. "My father was a missionary to the rez."

"And ...?"

"Well, I was with the people, some of them medicine people. I learned a lot, and I understand herbs and plants, and ... well, I just *feel* so *at home* with the *Native ways* ..."

"I am happy to tell you that you are not a shaman," I said, really believing at the time that this news would be gratefully received.

"But I was raised on the reser- ... I am most certainly a shaman!" she stormed.

"Why would you want to be one?" I asked.

"To help people." She was still raging. "I have been born to do something special!"

Nearly everyone I meet feels this way. I think it is a part of being human at this particular time. It is probably true, but most of us do not want to do the special things we are here to do—only those which others are set up to do.

"Why else do you think you are a shaman?" I asked.

"I love everything Indian, and ..."

"Shamans are not Native Americans, and Indians are not all shamans. Only shamans are shamans and that is cross-cultural," I explained.

"But the word itself is Native American," she insisted.

"It is not. It is a Siberian word," I said. "But in fact there are similar words meaning similar things in most languages."

This woman never believed me. And she never spoke to me again. I read about her activities later. She was making up "Indian" artwork for sale and, the last I read, leading "Urban Vision Quests." Sitting and fasting in a parking lot? I wonder what urban quests are.

Another woman came to Arizona to visionquest with me. As I prepared her to quest, she related some "dreams" in which I had played a part, although we had never met. These dreams were also set in the part of Arizona we were to quest in. It did not ring completely true, but people often twist things a bit when they romanticize shamanism. As we were driving back from the quest site to Tucson, she confessed to me that she had confirmed on the quest that she was a shaman.

"What?" I nearly drove off the interstate.

"Oh yes," she said, "I had thought I was, but now I know for sure."

Again, there was a long recitation of peculiarities "proving" her shaman-ness, none of which had any relationship with the shamanic condition.

"And I have been performing quite a few soul retrievals," she went on.

The car veered again. At this rate, I should probably park it in a rest stop until she got all this foolishness out of her system.

"You are not a shaman," I told her as gently as I could.

"And how do you know?"

I explained that I can sense a shaman upon entering any room, that the physicality of a shaman is quite different from others in neurological makeup and electrical energy. There just is no mistaking it.

She was angry.

"Look, why would you want to be a shaman?" I asked. "As a medicine woman, and perhaps shamanic practitioner, you can serve more people, a broader base, than I can. Your work in this life can touch more of humanity than any shaman's. Why on earth would you want to limit yourself?"

"I guess I don't understand," she said.

"A shaman is a specialist; our work is greatly limited," I said. "People must follow their sacred walk, not borrow from someone else's. By doing so, you would become ineffectual at best, dangerous at worst. Don't you see? It is as if I decided I wanted to be an herbalist rather than a shaman. The result of my work would be less than nothing, since I would not be living what I am here to do."

"I guess I know what you're saying," she drawled, "but I still believe that I am a shaman."

"Why?"

"Well, I'm part Choctaw, and ..."

"There are thousands, millions, of Native Americans who are not shamans," I pointed out.

And we went through the usual "Native Americans are special and have the corner on the spiritual market" stuff.

We continued our discussion, going to the subject of her soul retrievals. As she described them, I could see the books she was lifting them from. Being a counselor put her in a position to perform these services, but they were not true soul retrievals, of course. I did point out, however, that often the results of what she was doing were positive, since she was working within a psychological framework. I suggested that she rename these exercises something else in order to create integrity for her work.

By the end of the car trip, intact, she asked me to be her teacher. As I warned her that I am a hard teacher and demand compliance, diligence, and (above all) integrity, I further explained that most people did not like the way I teach and very few remained for long. I warned her as clearly as I could.

She lasted about as long as most and is now continuing to claim that she is a shaman. She still performs soul retrievals—some by telephone!

Fakes and frauds are not always just about people. Well, I suppose they are, but lots of us get fooled and "taken in" by places, too. You see them advertised all the time—power sites you can visit and get all sorts of power from. Here in Arizona, we have a famous site: Sedona. Poor Sedona was once a pristine and beautiful place. It is still lovely, but the town is growing, filled with crystal shops and Tarot readers and tour guides and psychics and shamans. True shamans are not going to be found in crowds or leading tours or in crystal shops.

I once watched a video tape of a fine medicine man discussing Sedona. "Power place?" he laughed. "This place is so noisy with fakery and foolishness that it is like listening to dozens of radio stations all playing simultaneously—with extra static thrown in! This place was powerful when it was natural and still. Just as any part of Mother Earth is powerful when left alone."

He was not a member of the Chamber of Commerce, I assure you. He is right. People have damaged these "power sites" terribly by burying crystals, erecting medicine wheels, defacing rocks, trees, and other natural features with New Age jargon, and even defacing ancient pictographs by stupidity and arrogance. There is such an overpowering noise there that one cannot experience any sort of peace or power. Perhaps it can return to its natural state of power and serenity once people are gone, but it will never be restored to what it was because our traces will continue there forever.

Let me qualify all of this with the fact that many of these fakes are well-meaning people who honestly believe what they are doing is proper and good. Naive fools. You meet with them all the time. I would pity them more if I did not see the messes they create. But then, that is my personal problem, borne out of clearing away those messes when the client comes to me, not only screwed up from the original problem, but having it compounded by foolishness from a healer or psychic.

Since it has become well-known all around the planet that Americans are now "into shamanism" and native ways, you can become besieged with people in other countries claiming to be shamans or to know someone (probably a cousin) who is one. This is becoming a big business in many countries where North Americans frequently travel to experience "sacred power sites." Danger, danger, danger. These people have merely a 1.5 percent chance of actually being shamans. They will offer to take you to "special" mountains, pools, or temples— "because I can sense that you are special and very connected with this secret place." I know of one secret pool where four women I have met have been taken to because they were special. I often wonder if it was the same man who took them there.

Why would they do this? Money. Business. Part of tourism service; give the nice U.S. citizen what he or she wants. Does it end there? No. One woman I know continued communication with her "shaman" via e-mail—until he realized that there was no more money there and that she was becoming a bother.

Are these folks malicious? No again. They are poor and everyone knows that all Americans are rich, right? And it is part of the service, remember. And what does it hurt? (Exaggerated shrug here.) Perhaps they are correct in this. The tourist gets to see the beautiful country and some ruined temples and sacred pools; the home folks get some money they desperately need. Everybody's happy, right? Well, probably, but there are a few cases when the tourist gets hurt emotionally, of course.

And some have to seek spiritual help back home in order to be rescued from what they "picked up" in those sacred places they so naively floated into.

Probably the most important part of spiritual growth is to take along a strong sense of discernment and use that. There is the gentleman seated next to you on the train with whom you converse:

"Oh, you are in our country to seek the sacred places?"

"Yes. I feel so connected here!"

"Would you like to meet a real shaman? I happen to know one."

"Really? Oh yes!"

So ask yourself, is this scenario a coincidence? Did the gods really seat you next to a man who knows a real shaman? Just what is going on here, anyway?

One client who had come to me for healing after a trip to Peru told me that she had experienced the above scenario, and she had gone with this wonderful man. How did she know he was wonderful? Why, he seemed to *know* her! He told her that he had sensed when she sat down that she was very spiritual and had such a pure soul. Yadda, yadda.

"He had to be psychic to know that," she explained to me.

Really? Damn, think of all the money I could make with a couple snappy lines that say nothing.

"Don't you think you looked like a North American tourist?" I asked.

"How would he know that?"

Right.

The sad thing is she ended up staying at his home. While meditating at one of those secret pools with that shaman she was to meet, someone in the family went through her things and ripped off all her money—over five thousand dollars.

"I felt so betrayed."

"But you are planning to return," I said.

"Oh yes. This will be my third trip. It's just so spiritual over there, and I just know I've had a past lifetime there!"

And should it be a real shaman you meet in a foreign country? The key to this is the word foreign. In "Chapter 4: Healing" we explore what has happened to our Vietnam veterans, young men going to foreign, alien places. There is inherent danger here. For example, the psychic surgeons of the Philippine Islands (and other places) are expected to fake healings. Well, let me explain this.

Long, long ago, when a shaman effected a successful psychic operation, the patient—and the village for that matter—expected to see blood and the disease that he/she withdrew from, say, that person's abdomen. In real psychic surgery, one doesn't have that to show, so the old shamans secreted animal blood and parts on them and displayed those as the healing took place. When I perform etheric surgery, I hold my knife in my hand and cause the patient to feel a cut into the area. People around me may even see blood, although I have neither cut into the flesh nor brought blood up. I remove the disease, but it does not appear in yucky form. If I did such trickery in our culture today, people would be put off, and no healing would take place. The culture in many foreign countries still requires this "trickery" for belief, although I do not refer to it in any negative way. It's simply not acceptable here and now.

I once removed a large cyst from someone's hand before several people. I had a piece of owl flesh (the owl had been killed by a car and I buried it) and laid that over the cyst. "Drawing" the cyst by placing my hand over the meat, I then picked up the owl flesh, placed it into a leather bag, held it out for the client, and told her to bury it beneath a tree. Everyone present saw the deep cavity in her hand where once there had been a cyst. I did not need to cut into the hand and pull out a bloody mass. It was obviously gone. And our culture does not require the yucky physical proof.

I inserted this here, not because these surgeons are fakes or frauds, but as an example of how different foreign approaches might be. If they are that different, then they are even more so in perhaps less obvious ways. And those ways may not be compatible with ours.

There is a shaman in a South American country who is often cited in literature for his great healings. However, he effects those healings in an entirely barbaric way: he takes up a guinea pig, breaks its spine, rubs the screaming, agonized creature over the client's body, and then kills the animal. American tourists flock to this man. Is his work compatible with your sensitivity? Consider that. It is difficult for me to view this man as a fellow shaman when I know that one never has to cause pain in any life form in order to heal another. That just does not seem very shamanic to me, especially since shamans are supposed to be created in order to unite humans with all other life.

What maintains my balance regarding this area of life is the fact that I believe that *we all do find the teacher that we deserve and are ready for, be it true or false.* And you must discern for yourself what is truth for you. That must be part of conscious experience and, thus, not wasted time.

Chapter 15
Totems and Power Animals

The owl landed just in front of the pickup on that dark and narrow strip of mountain road. I was on my way to my first visionquest in the Pinaleno Mountains in southeastern Arizona. Since I was moving so slowly, I was able to stop. There was no traffic at all, so I dimmed my lights to park and watched the owl as it watched me back. I've always had this special thing about owls; they speak to me as no one or no animal ever does. This was a real treat. At last, the owl spread its wings, silently floated up over the hood of the truck, and touched my windshield as it flew away, making direct eye contact as it passed me. Goosebumps and glow.

The place I had chosen to fast and pray in was a site in which I had camped alone many times. There was deep forest all about a meadow which ran downhill into more forest. There were raspberry bushes all about and a resident female bear, which always took the food offerings I left when I packed up each visit. She would leave a nice big bear dump in its place. I often heard her, but I seldom saw her since we both were careful of each other's space. She let me know when I inadvertently got too close to her space, and she never entered mine. I also shared this Eden with a large number of squirrels and chipmunks who knew me and my generous handouts of sunflower seeds and peanuts. I have always felt that, if we go into the homes of the animal world, we should leave them something to make up for their being unable to hunt for food during our stay. Laws now insist that we cannot do this, not even feeding birds, citing bear attacks on humans and our causing animals to depend upon us. That is just so much classroom-bound animal husbandry do-do, but we must obey the laws. And I am one of the first to admit that many people are foolish in sharing with animals, even cruel. I know of someone who feeds hot chilies to squirrels to watch them race around, chittering in agony. He sees this as entertainment. And there is no doubt that many so-called hunters set up illegal sites of meat and suet scraps ahead of hunting season to entice bears to their rifles. I bring in the law immediately when I observe such things. Whereas I believe responsible hunting for food is far more humane than eating meat grown, tortured, and butchered domestically, I abhor the beer-can hunters.

Up there, in that magic mountain place, owl chases me. Owl became my totem. So what is a totem? That depends upon whose definition you choose. Here's mine. A totem is the animal essence, personality, or set of attributes that is most closely associated with you. *I feel like an owl.* There are times I feel as if I can fly as they do and can comprehend their language. I have entered the body of a barn owl and eaten a mouse. The texture is peculiar to the human mouth and throat. I feel that I smell like an owl when I work for long periods of time. I sense flight. I call to them, and they reply. I have consummate respect for them and hold them in awe. Larry finds them awaiting him whenever he drives out here at night to our cabin from Tucson and feels that they are greeting his arrival. Practically speaking, of course, they live out here in abundance. To sum up, I enjoy a real intimacy with owl.

When I got my first tattoo, it was owl. Immediately, the intimacy deepened. When you begin to work with your totem, you become it. I *am* owl. In discussing this odd experience with others, we found a definite similarity in our feeling and that experience.

Animals Are Our Teachers

So exactly what is a totem? I define it as the animal essence which chooses us to align itself with. In the old days, we probably inherited a family or clan totem. Today, I believe we must visionquest and fast for our totems to come to us. We have one totem and perhaps several power animals to help us. Totems never change, but power animals may come and go.

So what are power animals, then? I define these as animal essences and personalities which we work with for a long or short time, or for specific purposes. Example: mountain lion works with me in diagnosing illness. We "hunt" together. I "use" her vision to find the problem. She came to me on my second visionquest in a very intense manner. Rattlesnake helps me in protection and in certain healing situations. Her energy, placed on my pickup, for instance, keeps people from touching it. Bat helps me "die" in the shamanic way. In fact, bats also come to me when I stand outside at night. I have often been outside with other people and had bats flying about my head and touching me with their soft wings. Camping, they enter my tent. At the cabin, we feed nectar-drinking bats each summer. It is becoming an attraction for people to join us at night to observe these awe-inspiring creatures.

Raven brings me information. I met a young raven in the Pinalenos when I was camping there once. He still had his baby pinfeathers. I had brought a great deal of good food for him and he brought in the rest of the family: three parents and four other fledglings. But he stayed in my camp and used his wide linguistic abilities on me for five days. Nearly a year later, I traveled back near there to camp. Within minutes, that same raven arrived and after eating (I got out the food immediately), left to bring in his family. When I visionquested others in those mountains, he would fly out and check on each quester, then fly back to my camp and "tell" on them. The questers were sure of that. Each fall, I camped in there and put out lots of bacon for him and his family. Ravens are very familial, and one youngster usually remains with the parents and helps them rear two or three years' fledglings, thereby becoming very successful parents themselves. This was one of those ravens. And each time I was there, he would spend time in my camp, "talking" to me, as I learned from him how to answer back. He was gracious to not mention my poor abilities in raven language.

Then, he began bringing in his mate. She was shyer, of course, but came for the food. And he spent a little less time in camp, chatting. The following year, he brought in three fledglings. Two years later, he showed up, but he was recovering from a wounded leg and was wary of me when people were along. This was also the year that he wouldn't allow his youngsters to play around our camp. Since then, I have not returned to the Pinalenos, but I often wonder how he is doing.

Ravens in other campsites or visionquest sites of mine are willing to interact with me. Usually, it's the male. Most of the female ravens appear to have little patience with this sort of extra communication between species. However, it is a complete high for me to speak with the member of another species in a language they understand and return to me.

I camped often in a box canyon in the Patagonia Mountains of southeastern Arizona. The ravens there were as most are: open and friendly. I brought them duck eggs one time and enjoyed watching them fly up into the blue skies with those great eggs held carefully in their blue-black beaks. Across the stream from my camp was a heavily treed area, which was deep in leaves. One morning, a family of six ravens arrived and, after announcing their intention to use that area, proceeded to play. They romped on the ground, throwing up leaves and sliding on their backs, playing together much as I've seen a litter of puppies do. It was a real treat for me.

Every so often, two of the ravens would fly into my campsite while calling stridently to me, perch in a tall oak, then continue flying up the canyon. It took me years to finally comprehend what these guys were trying to tell me. They appeared thus prior to anyone else entering the canyon! It took that long for me to connect the two occurrences each time. Duh.

A raven *took* me to the grave of a lady shaman in Wupatki (see "Chapter 9: Evil and Shadow"). This raven kept flying over my tent, perched in a nearby tree, and called incessantly to me until I got off my duff and followed it across the valley and up a hill to where it was perched above a grouping of rocks just below the edge of that hill. There I found the grave of a woman and two children below descriptive pictographs. As soon as I arrived, the raven flew off, leaving the dim-witted human in order to do some real raven stuff.

One year, the ravens living near my visionquest site in the Superstition Wilderness taught me how war is sacred and necessary, predicting the onset of Desert Storm not two months later. They also taught me that, despite war and violence, we must maintain our joyfulness. They called to me from the edge of a very high cliff. Once I would look up, they would launch themselves, fly briefly, then turn upside down, flying that way until they would change and begin their rolls and swoops.

So we think of raven as messenger of the spirits and guardian of the sacred.

Rattlesnake teaches us to allow ourselves to shed our skins and change. Serpents do this several times each year, helpless, hungry, and most uncomfortable as they use sticks, stones, and even cacti to rub off the skin of old ways, thinking, and such, so that they might grow. And they do—that new skin is glorious. She also teaches me to lie upon the earth and share Mother Earth's heartbeat. Bear is the symbol of change also, for she "dies" each winter. Bear further teaches us to establish our territorial boundaries and maintain those.

Coyote is my teaching power animal. Coyote is called trickster by many Native American peoples. I suspect that concept was misinterpreted by the untrained anthropologists of the 1700s and 1800s, most of them being missionaries. That is why so many words we have been given for aboriginal words are skewed. But let us use trickster here. Remember that all cultures have relied upon riddles, absurdities, and paradoxes to teach us. Thus Coyote teaches us through such. And so do I. Coyote is so very disliked by ranchers and farmers, but for the most part it is undeserved. I believe that most people do not care for Coyote because he is a survivor; no matter how hard humans have tried to make him extinct, he outsmarts humans, and we cannot handle that. Coyote is a tribal creature, with strict rules of conduct we should investigate more fully. He places the good of the clan before that of any individual—a thing we have forgotten, the we rather than the I. I also believe that many humans dislike Coyote because we perceive that he laughs at us.

Carol came to work with me one summer, and it became clear during our week together that she couldn't say no to her family and just didn't have any boundaries set.

"Let's work with Bear energy," I suggested.

"And how will that help me set boundaries?" she asked.

"Well, the female bear lives in a strictly controlled territory. She may share that with her daughter later on but will always run off her grown son. That is one reason male bears are so much more likely to cause trouble in campgrounds, and their behavior seems so much more erratic to us than their female counterparts," I said. "Lady bear patrols her territory regularly, placing claw marks on trees to notify other bears that this is her land. Only when we relocate bears into strange territories is there real trouble, and the outsider may pay dearly when we plunk him or her down in some other bear's homeland. Bear is adamant about her space. And she takes care of it."

"That sounds like the teaching I need," Carol said. When her Christmas card arrived, there was a note included assuring me that, although she had made mistakes and had to re-vamp her approaches somewhat, Bear was truly teaching her how to set boundaries. Well, I assume that bears need to *learn* the technique of setting boundaries as well.

Protective Animal Essences

Protective animal essences? My personal one is Black Widow. When I call upon her essence, people wish not to be near me. They do not know why. They just realize that being here causes revulsion, and they go away. I have to be careful, however, for I have asked her help in protecting my campsite many times, and we have discovered that people who were to meet me there cannot get all the way in there. They turn around and go home.

Other protective essences may include Rattlesnake, as I have mentioned, bees and wasps, predators, anything with teeth. Let me remind you before you work with a protective animal, however, that you must always treat them with respect: do not overuse them, always say thank you, and never, never harm one. To wit: I feed black widows when I find them and could never kill one, or even put one out in the cold to die. Not that I would, anyway. When I "give" clients a protective animal to work with, I must always consider their inability to respect and live alongside such an animal. Of course, the other consideration is whether or not the animal in question will work with the client. Let's not forget that.

One of the things I had difficulty with as I began to work with power animals was that I was possibly jeopardizing them somehow. Did I really want to place Rattlesnake in a certain canyon to protect it from illegal woodcutters? Then I came to understand more fully that I was working with the human concept and perception of the particular animal. When I ask Rattlesnake to protect my pickup now, I realize that it is not a rattlesnake, but a possible thief's feeling about rattlesnakes which is at work here. There is definitely the energy of a rattlesnake about the truck. Try to touch it. If you have ever been in the presence of an agitated rattler, you know what I mean. You will draw your hand back quickly, just as you would jump aside if you heard and felt that sound on a trail somewhere. So I use the *image* of a rattlesnake.

Upon special occasions, I will "give" a client a power animal. Ordinarily, it is far best to receive them on your own, however. Here's a special case.

Darlene was a little person and a powerful psychologist whose specialty was working with disturbed children—delinquents, if you will. She often had to walk alone through a juvenile facility near Tucson, and the children were larger than she. Naturally, they tried to intimidate her.

"Do they frighten you?" I asked her.

"Well, I hope I never let them know this, but yes," she said.

"Can you not have an officer accompany you when you have to enter those rooms?"

"Sure, but it would let them know that I fear them, and that would be detrimental to my work with them," she said. "And I need to see them alone, for privacy and trust, sometimes."

"I see. Let me journey to find a solution," I said.

In the journey, a large black wolf joined me, walking at my side. Our eyes met, and I knew he was here for Darlene. As I imaged that, he seemed to smile, sitting, exposing his great white teeth, his tongue lolling out. Wow, there's some medicine to cure fear.

"I have a power animal for you, Darlene, to walk with you whenever you must be alone with several of your charges," I said.

"A power animal? What's that?"

I explained. This wolf would walk with her in essence whenever she imaged him. He could stay by her side in her office. He was willing to be her true companion.

"Wow."

"That's what I said, too."

"What do I have to do?" she asked.

"I want you to close your eyes and image a huge black wolf walking toward you," I said. "Now imagine you have some food for him. Roadkill, perhaps. A McDonald's burger. Something. Hold it out in your hand for him to eat, and do so with a sense of respect, gratitude, and awe."

"He's here, and he's eating. He's wonderful."

"Now, feel the request that he walk with you in the deepest sense."

"Oh, he's joining me!" she said.

Weeks later, I saw Darlene at a seminar.

"Wolf has changed my life!" she said. "I'm not afraid anymore, and the kids sense that. I guess they also sense his presence. Immediately upon my return to work after seeing you, their responses to me altered. It has to be Wolf. I'm so grateful to him. It's almost like having a physical friend always with me."

Back to rattlesnakes ... Kathy came to talk to me about her daughter. They lived out here, and it is a long, lonely drive from anywhere to here. Her daughter was working in Sierra Vista until nine at night, then driving home over those dark dirt roads. At least twice a week, she would have to stop and change a tire out there, alone, because they were being stuck with a knife. Just deeply and small enough to get her out of town into the countryside. It was truly scary.

I journeyed. I saw a man we both knew, and I knew he was responsible. Why?

"Kathy, I see Bob doing this," I said. "Do you know why?"

"Oh god," she breathed.

I returned from the journey. "Oh god what?"

"He's found her on that road in the night and stopped to help her. Since then, he has insisted that she use her cell phone to call him whenever she's in trouble. I've been real uncomfortable about it, but she insists that he's never done anything negative."

"Seems to me that he's doing what he can to gain her trust," I said. "I hate to be nasty about this, but this makes me very uneasy."

"Me too. Truth to tell, I have my suspicions but have felt that it was too mean-spirited to dwell upon."

"Okay. Look, I can protect her truck and tires from harm, and that protection can include her. But it would involve an animal people ordinarily fear, and I wonder if she would have any trouble dealing with that."

"What's the animal?"

"Rattlesnake. She would have to come into harmony with that energy, exhibit respect and caring for them, never harm one. Can she do that?"

"I'm going to bring her over here," she said.

The daughter was fine with that. She had just experienced a close encounter with a large diamondback a few days previously and, although frightened, was filled with respect and a sense of wanting to ensure the snake's safety from other humans. Fine.

I went to Grandmother Rattlesnake and petitioned one of hers to protect the young woman and her truck. No problem. I showed both women how to set the protection, how to remove it, and how to approach the truck with the essence set on it.

"Remember, now, that if you have someone with you, they may be troubled about riding with you. If that happens, just image to Grandmother that they are 'with you' in all respects. However, if you are not one hundred percent sure of that person, you may have to forego their company until we remove Her. Okay?"

"Right. Can I tell friends about Her?"

"Not such a good idea. First of all, they will not think highly of your intelligence and sanity. Until you are really close and trust someone completely, you should keep this a secret. You trusted the man in question, and it turns out that he's the perpetrator. Can you really trust your judgment in this? Perhaps, for the time being, it is best to take care of this problem before you worry about friends riding in your truck."

She never had another mysterious flat tire. The man in question never even spoke to her again. Later, she found that he had been questioning the personnel at a gas station about her tires and flat repairs.

Preconceived Notions

We had met north of Tucson, at the desert home of some folks, for a sweat ceremony to be led by a pipe carrier we knew. We had sweated with this man before, and he had invited us to this lodge. Different folks. It might be a great experience. Following each sweat, there is a feast—a potluck meal eaten together in a sacred way, following the suffering and prayers. I found that I could not eat. We were surrounded by "domestic" animals who were not fed, watered, or properly cared for. There was a litter of kittens and their wafer-thin mom all around our legs, begging for food. The pipe carrier noticed my distress and used it to "teach" me which animals are sacred and which not.

"These domestic animals have given up their power by allowing us to enslave them," he said. Was that pomposity?

I did not reply at that time but, later on, re-opened the discussion.

"That sounds just like patriarchal Biblical nonsense," I said.

"No, that's the way of our ancestors," he said.

"Crap," I said. And never sweated with him again.

We rescue abused and neglected "domestic" animals, heal them, and refer to them as our "companion animals." In return, they teach us and charm us and rely upon us for all things. It means that I can never lie in bed in the mornings nor stay inside when it's raining and it's feeding time. It means that if it is cold, I would never be able to sit beside our woodburning stove unless all our companions were also dry and warm.

I meet people and they tell me how much they "love" their dog. In the kitchen (if the poor beast is allowed inside) is a small bowl of dirty water. Some companionship. What about those filthy litter boxes? Love? I think not. Respect? Ha. Most dogs and cats are required to exist on dry kibble. How would you like to live on crackers? These are essentials. Why get a dog or cat and then leave it outside? What is the point of a companion animal when there is so little companionship?

Are domesticated animals not powerful? We have range cattle out here. Let me share with you that the roar of a bull is powerful. We often have five or six bulls meet near our cabin in the mornings and "talk" to one another. It is primordial. A range cow is formidable when she has a calf, although easy-going when she has none. And she grieves terribly when her calf is taken away and sent to market.

Our goats are powerful. The lead doe is Kate, who is half pigmy goat. She rules the roost and has tried (unsuccessfully) to run the lives of our burros. The rest of the goats are all much larger than she, at least a hundred pounds each larger, but she keeps them all in line. She also stands in a protective manner when they are threatened until all are back in their yard. She is last to enter. When we go for walks in the forest here, I observe them for my own well-being. They are relaxed but always alert. I slept with them when two of them were expecting babies one winter. The little barn was warm and filled with alfalfa farts. The goats moved about to keep an eye on me for my prone form was unfamiliar. They do not sleep often (when they do, I fear they've died!). Upon the birthing, the entire herd was excited and wanted to participate in the care of the youngsters. Shy Guy, the dad, is two hundred pounds larger than Kate, but he was there to nuzzle her and her kid gently. I swear he was smiling. These seem to me to be powerful animals.

Chickens? Ever see one kill a field mouse or rat? Our guinea fowl are known for their ferocity in maintaining their territory. They chase large rattlers, and unfortunately, coyotes, who just grab up the manna from heaven. But they let me know when anything at all is amiss around the place.

Burros. These guys have no enemies except humans. In the wild, they survive into age by their ferocity, and yet they quickly become friends with humans or other animals with whom they live. Very protective of us all.

So I have learned that companion animals are also powerful, each in its own way. Animals have not given away any of their power by agreeing to work with us. No, we have *taken it from them.* What we give back is the question here. I suggest that we each look at the world from our companion's point of view and that we treat each of them as we would wish to be treated if we had that physical form and needs. That's all, so simple.

Power animals help us in all sorts of ways. If you seek an animal to work with, however, you should be receptive and entertain few preconceived notions about them. I often tell this story to students who are searching for a power animal.

Nola was learning to spirit journey, and one of the things we do early on is to request the help of a power animal to guide us in the Other-World. She went through the routine for such a quest, and she met up with a deer as she walked through the "forest". Their eyes met, and she received the information that deer was her animal.

"Oh no," she thought, "Deer isn't very powerful."

The deer looked at her long and walked away. By that time, she had considered her reaction and was remorseful.

"Come back. I'm sorry. I wasn't thinking right."

The deer continued to walk away. As it did so, her mind filled with images of how powerful a deer is. Strength and even ferocity when necessary combined with gentleness and grace. She flew after the deer, to no avail.

"Roberta, what should I do?" she wailed. "What a horrible thing I've done!"

I journeyed and located Deer. I offered her food and we sat and ate together by the stream. I explained my student's remorse and imaged how it was that she made such a mistake. We negotiated the deer's return, and it happened.

Nola found some enormous white tail deer antlers which had dropped off not long afterward. She felt she had been forgiven.

Why does this happen? And she's not the only one. It's probably caused by our habit of anthropomorphizing. That means applying human attributes to other species. And it is not only utter nonsense, but it really separates us from them—and excuses our cruelty. I know an environmental biologist who insists that chickens are stupid because they cannot see wire fencing. Really, now. Why would chicken eyes be able to see wire? And what has that to do with intelligence? I hear all sorts of (even) experts refer to certain animals as being more intelligent than others. Ludicrous. How can we measure the intelligence of another species? By what, or whose, yardstick?

Such judgments are so pervasive that, until recently, we were all taught that animals didn't feel pain the way humans do. Isn't that convenient news? They don't use logic the way we do; therefore, they do not feel emotion. Uh-huh. Anyone who takes the time to observe an animal will become quickly aware that the animal thinks and uses *pertinent logic* for its condition and situation. No, they don't worry about the future, for animals remain in the All Life, from whence we all came. That does not mean that they do not fear or hate or love or experience agony.

And of course, it is also true of plants and insects. And stones, if you ever considered a crystal as being sentient. In order for us to work alongside with and benefit from other species, we must relinquish anthropomorphizing. And if you ever find yourself, when thinking of any animal, considering it along the lines of "what is it good for?" ... well, knock it off.

Rather, in shamanism and other earth-oriented spiritualities, we exemplify the other species and contemplate how we can best learn from them.

So there are many ways in which to work with power animals. It seems to add an irreplaceable facet to our wholeness. But do not forget that all-important requirement to do so: respect and receptivity.

A coyote, Roberta's teaching power animal, at RavenHouse.

Roberta with a pair of burros, Clyde and Clementine, in 1997.

Chapter 16
Guilt and Karma

It is something shamans have always done. While soul retrievals are the most dangerous, "karmic healing" is the most painful to shamans. As priests, we frequently are called upon to hear confessions, and people come to us to obtain some forgiveness. Obviously, that is a portion of true healing, but how can one find forgiveness unless one is willing to accept it? Most people I have worked with seek freedom from guilt and karma, but they do not believe that they can obtain that. What to do? Perhaps the answer lies in returning to the time within our genetic makeups where sin as we know it today did not exist. A more innocent time, *the time of the shaman.*

The first shamanic forgiveness I performed was for Paul. He came to me because he felt his life had "become a pile of shit," as he so aptly put it. He had a fine job with tenure, a great salary, a wife and children, and they all got along pretty well. But Paul didn't like people at all, and people didn't seem to like him much anymore. Why? He was also chronically depressed and morose, and he was becoming self-destructive.

"I have just about everything a man could want," he said, "but I'm not happy, and it's beginning to bleed onto my family, as well as my work and my friends, what few I have left."

Bleed? An interesting choice of words. I journeyed for Paul.

"You need forgiveness," I told him a few minutes later. "I see a ... dog? No, coyote. Are you a hunter? You shot a coyote?"

Paul burst into wracking sobs. Bingo. We used tissue, then walked outside in the cool night air to calm him so that we could continue. Ordinarily, I am impatient with outbursts, especially when they seem a little overdone. But in this case, I knew Paul was not emoting and that his tears came from some deep anguish.

"I killed a coyote. I had forgotten it."

"No, Paul, you haven't forgotten it; it is what's killing you today. You may have suppressed it, but the guilt has been eating away at you as would sulfuric acid," I told him. "Let's go inside and get busy on that acid."

Paul had gut-shot a female coyote and, out of curiosity, squatted near her for the several hours it took her to finally die. She was unable to move, her intestines poured out of the wounds, and she died silently and horribly. I empathed the entire incident; even today, my pain and hers are one. The very idea of such a cruel act sickens me—as well it should. Why, then, would I consent to help Paul? Why not let him rot in the hell of his own making? Because shamans exist to serve humanity, even when humans are most inhumane. Would I offer this service to anyone? No. Only when the journey and my spirits command me to do so. When someone sits before me in the sacred way, I am nearly helpless to say no.

In Paul's case, it was simple and straightforward. It was one incident, as opposed to, say, a lifetime of "bad karma." First, however, the covenant, the contract between us must be struck. That is the payment above the greater-than-usual fee for healing or counseling. Paul had rid himself of the shotgun he used on Lady Coyote and swore he would never kill another living being. All fine and well.

"Do you eat meat?" I asked.

"Well, sure," he said.

"Then you must eat no meat, poultry, fish, or dairy for sixty days," I ordered. "If you cannot do this, I will not help you."

"That's hard," Paul complained.

"Not as hard as being gut-shot and dying slowly while flies and ants eat your intestines in front of you, while thinking of your wife and children being alone forever. In the case of the coyote, her pups either had to be adopted by another nursing mother in the pack—and usually there is only one female with pups at a time—or they had to die a slow starvation-and-thirst death while the pack could only look on or leave them to die alone. I think going meatless for sixty days is child's play," I said. "In fact, we will make it ninety days."

"Why? Are you trying to punish me?"

"Well, in a way I'm adding to your penance. But I have set the number of days to correspond with the time it will take me to effect this healing of you," I said.

"I thought you could do it immediately," he said.

"*You* will be healed tonight, Paul," I said, "but I will have the memory, guilt, and empathing the coyote's agony, as well as the anguish of the pack and the slow death of the pups. And that will take time to move on from."

"Oh. My. God," Paul breathed. "That is what you must do to heal me?"

"Paul, do you want to be free of this thing that is robbing you of a full life or not? It is what is separating you from the goodness of living, from your wife and kids, from even having a pet dog at home."

"How did you know about the dog?" he asked, startled. "No, never mind—you know."

"My spirits teach me that the only 'sin' that is unforgivable is the 'sin' of cruelty," I told Paul. "I am also taught that you can be forgiven through the intervention of a shaman, since shamans are here to reunite humanity with the remainder of Life. Perhaps through this forgiveness you will be somewhat reunited with the dog people, at least."

We sat in silence for a few moments.

Paul said, slowly and seriously, "I agree to your terms, both financially and insofar as the meat-free diet. It will no doubt teach me something, if nothing else. Can you really do this?"

"Do you have to ask me that? If I didn't have the ability to free you of this burden, why would I bother to even discuss any of this with you?" I said. "Believe this: your actions with that coyote make me sicker than you can imagine. *And I feel what she felt as she died with her killer squatting there, staring at her. I feel her mind reaching out to you, begging you to end her pain. I feel her longing for her pack and pups. I know her yearning to run and hunt freely with the pack, to have sex, to eat, to howl, to ...*"

"I get the point," Paul cut me off.

"Do you really?" I asked, caustically. "I doubt it, but I can only assume that you get at least enough of it so that we can either do this thing or not."

"Okay, let's do it," he grumbled.

"Sorry, but you're not being nice enough for me to care about." I got up and began to get my things together in preparation to leave the office.

Paul stood up also and left the room, but he returned shortly.

"Please help me. I can't live like this. I believe I feel her pain, too."

I narrowed my eyes at him, speculating. Was he being manipulative? Yes. Some. But he was also being as honest as he was able to be that day. I sat back down, gesturing to him to return to his seat.

Twenty minutes later, Paul was free of his guilt and karma regarding the coyote—and I had made the entire incident my own experience.

Paul reported to me via phone every few days during the ninety-day period. He met the terms of our agreement. He had experienced immediate relief. His nightmares ceased, he was approachable again, his job was fun, he and his family had re-established a good relationship, and he was celebrating the end of the ninety days not by gorging on a big steak dinner, but by bringing a puppy home for his kids. I saw Paul shortly afterward, but I didn't recognize him. He had to prompt me. Appearance does so often mirror our inner health.

Shamans take on physical pain and disease, as well as "bad luck" and guilt and "bad" karma. Those intervening days and nights were pretty bad for me, and they were bad for those close to me. I was miserable; my consciousness filled with anguish and the coyote's experience, as well as the experiences of the pack and pups. It faded over time, and I had freed myself from it within six weeks. All I could tell my students and family was that I was processing through something very nasty and painful and that it would soon be over. I certainly didn't want them to have to share the experience in any detail. It hurt me enough, why sprinkle that pain around on those I care about?

When I take on another's sufferings and "bad karma," it is demonstrated in various physical ways. Over these past couple of years, I've had bloody lesions on my shoulders as the result of such a healing. This is another reason I don't tolerate being touched by others; I require a moment to protect the "toucher" from what I may be carrying.

I met Celeste in the Midwest, while working there. When she walked into the room, I was immediately preternaturally aware of her. There was a certain air about her, and not just her perfume, which I found she blended herself—it was exquisite. No, even more than that, I felt to be in the presence of holiness. I am a holy woman by definition, but this woman was something else. Not quite human. But then, neither are shamans. What then? I would find out soon.

The traditional question: "Why are you here tonight?"

"I'm not sure, because I'm not sick, but it has to do with something more important even than my physical state. I just don't believe I can define it. I guess I just do not know. That's unusual and humbling for me since until today, I have always understood things as they are. But hearing your lecture the other night ... well, I just came away certain that I had to see you." Laughing, she continued, "Even at this ridiculous hour (she had taken the two a.m. slot). Perhaps you will help me understand the reason?"

"All right. You're certainly honest and insightful, and that's refreshing. I'll do an 'exploratory' journey. When I return, we'll discuss the information thoroughly, and then we'll see. Okay?"

"You bet. Whatever you say. Anything you say."

From the beginning of the journey, I could see that this was going to be a very unusual session. By the time I approached the space for potential and probabilities, I wanted to be close to this woman from now on, although I could see that this was not to be. In the space of the Kachinas and Christ, her soul, tall and blindingly pure, danced with them to the beat of What Is—a deep beat from the heart of Mother Earth. I bowed to her and the others in our dancing. It was difficult to tear myself away and continue on the journey, but I went on. Wisdom bowed to her. As I approached her soul at the conclusion of the journey, I asked—as I always do—how I could best serve her at this particular time. The answer was astonishing.

"The subject—that is to say, *we*—are on this earth at this time to *witness what is happening and about to occur*. We are an angel of the Lord upon earth. We are not a famous angel," it chuckled, "but important nevertheless. That is to say, our work, our reason for being here, is essential.

"The persona, Celeste, is not quite pure. She has incurred karma in this lifetime, albeit nothing severe. However, she must be pure for our work, and it is your job, Shaman, to purify her. To reweave her to wholeness to Holiness, if you will. Perform a karmic healing. In turn, we will bless you mightily and you will call upon us one day ..."

I prostrated myself and declared that I would do all I was able to that night.

"That is all we require." The soul prostrated itself before me. Our lights blended and grew. How sweet it was, and how I wished to stay and bask in the holiness there. Work to do!

I brought back the information, fully expecting Celeste to remonstrate with me, or even to walk out, thinking me a charlatan of some sort. After all, how many times does one tell someone that he or she is an angel, for God's sake?

"... and so I must clear you of all personal karma from this lifetime, since you have already evolved beyond prior-life karma."

She took it fine! She wept silently, then said just as quietly, "I know."

Yesss.

This was going to be a real tough nut. Not Celeste—her penance. "I will perform a full karmic cleansing for this lifetime, but you have to do something very difficult in exchange in order to complete the purification," I told her.

"Oh, anything," she began.

"Um-huh. Your soul is making noises as if it were demanding excellence from you," I half-joked. "Your soul demands that you endear many to you and that you separate from many. Are you willing to lose many whom you love?"

Quiet. I waited.

"Well," she murmured, finally, "I can only guess that the manner in which this will take place will be unpleasant for me, right?"

"I'm sure."

Celeste sat up straighter. God, she's tall. She took a deep breath and, bless her heart, said, "I will do whatever it takes, because it seems to me that this is more important than things like depression or happiness."

What a woman! I do admire dedication and courage.

"Celeste, you must make a list of the ten people who are the most important to you in this lifetime. Then you must go to each of these people and tell them that you are the manifestation of an angel."

"Oh." A long silence. "My folks ... my business partner ... my lover ..."

"Yes. Celeste, some of the ten will write you off, laugh, and likely drop you like a hot potato. Some of the ten will follow you like acolytes. Honestly, I'm not sure which is worse."

We both laughed ruefully, then a bit hysterically. My assistant's eyes were barely left in their sockets.

"Celeste, you have ten weeks in which to accomplish this. If you have not done so, all the karma will return to you, added to the karma of what you will have done to me if you fail."

She understood fully.

In a few minutes of drumbeat and shapeshifting, Celeste was cleared and purified, a perfect soul with extraordinary vision—a witness, an angel upon Earth. I was nearly hunchbacked with the burden of her karma, and it wasn't very much karma at that.

We spoke together during the ten weeks, via long distance, although she accomplished her penance in half that time. Her parents thought she should be "put away," but her business partner simply responded with "I know." Today, Celeste realizes that her parents were a distraction in regard to her new "job" and that it all worked out to her highest good. She is an amazing woman, uh, angel.

Re-Weaving the Fabric

Neal was dying. He was only thirty-seven years old and was a part of my extended family, joining the kids and me when he was not quite sixteen. Larry brought out the message to me from my daughter that Neal had just a few days left to live. It was sudden, violent, and awful. The message was simple: please come, you're the only one who can do this.

At the hospital, Neal was restrained flat on his back and had two nasal tubes. Larry had spent the previous night with him, and all he could comprehend from Neal was that his body was in terrible pain from being unable to shift his position. He was restrained because he lost complete control when he was told he had AIDS and only days left to live. It couldn't be much worse for him. The only blood family he had was a rigid aunt who stated that he had chosen his sinful lifestyle and was now paying for it. At least, she had ordered a "no-code" for Neal, allowing him to die without intervention.

I tried to discuss Neal with his physician, that I was his foster mom since he'd been a teen. That cut little ice, although it was decided that I could stay as long as I did not interfere with their treatment of him. I requested the removal of the nasal tubes.

The doctor raged, "No patient of mine will starve to death!"

Uh-oh. I've entered some strange reality here.

Neal's nurse was a fine man, doing what he could to keep Neal in a drugged state of bliss and quiescence. All hospital staff agreed that Neal was incoherent and could make no decisions for himself. According to them, he was comatose.

Not so. I began searching for Neal in this body. I told him I was there, and he responded weakly by clutching at my hand.

"Neal, I'm here to take care of things for you. Trust me now, and we'll get things in order. Okay?"

Pressure on my hand.

What to do? How to start? People kept coming in and out; it was like Grand Central Station here.

"Neal, it's too noisy. I'm going to stay with you and we'll work this out tonight, when things are quiet. Okay?"

Squeeze.

"Rest as best you can, now. I'll stay."

A young man came in shortly after that and leaned quietly against the wall, just looking at Neal. I was drawn to him.

"Hi, are you a friend of Neal's?" I asked him.

"I just met him yesterday. My sister found him and brought him in. She cuts his hair. He seems special, and I found myself coming back today. I don't know why," he said.

"It's nice to have someone quiet here," I said. "Your presence seems to calm him."

"It's odd. When I was here yesterday, he was able to speak a little, and he scared me," he said.

"How did that happen?" I asked. "I thought he was in this state already by then."

"Well, sort of. In and out. At one point, he raised his head up, saw me, and said something really odd. He didn't have the tubes then," he said. "He told me he was really evil."

"Evil? Neal's not evil," I said.

"No, he doesn't seem so to me," he said. "I tried to talk to him about it, but he began raving and laughing some horrible laugh. He said he was satanic, and that there was no hope for him at all. He would go to hell."

Aha. That's what's going on. I thanked the young man for his information. I told him that it would help me immensely to help Neal.

Not long afterward, things got quiet. Dina was there to be with me. We thought we had hours before Neal would die. Larry was on his way with some clean clothing for me. The shift was changing at the hospital. The door was closed. No visitors now.

Neal was born an only child to his parents who were in their late forties when he came to them. His mother was never a well woman, and he was told every day that her poor health, physical and mental, was his fault. In fact, everything was his fault. They told him that he was evil— they used that word—and that he would never get to heaven, would go directly to hell, no doubt about it. Things were compounded when Neal came out of the closet and told them he was gay. She died shortly thereafter, and Neal helped his father die of cancer a few years later, leaving his job, home, and friends to return to Tucson for the months it took. Still, the damage was done.

Neal did have some serious emotional problems, and when he was in one of his episodes, he would absent himself from our lives until it was over. We would just wait for him. But evil? No. From time to time, he would sit and talk with me about how bad he was, and I would always insist that he was not, that he was a fine person.

Well, now that I was up against it, how did I convince him that he was a good person? He could not die in this kind of fear. He needed to find forgiveness of things he had not done! He needed to return to innocence. My mind was whirling.

"Neal, it's Shades (the nickname all the kids used for me when he came to be with us in 1976)." Big squeeze on my hand. We had contact!

"Neal, let's go on a troll patrol," I urged, referring to some of the silliness we all used to do when they were teenagers.

He smiled and grabbed my hand. I spoke as if those days were now. I talked about all sorts of the things we did back then as if it were today. He was with me absolutely. He was a youngster of fifteen again. Innocent.

I entered my shaman form and leaned over his now calm body.

"Neal, it's Nightwing. We're going to walk out of this place together. You will never be alone. I promise you."

He drifted into a peaceful sleep. Ten minutes later, he was dead.

In this case, the healing of Neal has had to continue following his death. He was mentally ill, and although he has shed his imbalanced brain, in spirit form he has continued to grapple with feelings of being a bad person. It gradually got better. Sometimes, I worked with him. Most often, I simply continued to behave toward his spirit as if he were perfectly normal—and good. Without the forgiveness of Nightwing, however, Neal would likely have remained in that body, in those awful conditions, for several more days, out of fear of ... what? Hell? I believe so. In that extreme state of the dying, he was able to receive redemption by going back in time to where he was Innocent.

It was a good death. We walked out of that hospital together.

Pinkie, a cat who lived with Roberta.

Chapter 17

Foreseeing: Predictions and Prophecies

Predictions

I began reading the Tarot cards in 1970, when they were brought to us by some wayfarers who knocked at our door for help after they were stranded in Santa Fe by an enormous snowstorm. They stayed with us for a few days, and the woman brought out her deck of Tarot cards she had just received. Could she practice on us? Sure.

As she laid out the cards, I "saw." I saw things in the background of each card, things which moved and things alive. I was "reading" cards. I sent off for a deck of my own and was soon in business, reading for several people. I was self-taught, using mostly my own intuition about them, but being an observant person, it wasn't long before I was aware of the patterns they presented. I understood the partnership in such a reading: the almost sentient cards, the reader, and the questioner. The patterns were so distinct and solid that it was a balm to my orderly heart. I *liked* the Tarot, at least the deck I have always used, the Aquarian.

What usually comes in card readings is what I call *predictions*, information for individuals, as opposed to, say, the entire planet. It is true, however, that (paradoxes again) the cards, while telling the story of a specific person, simultaneously reveal the future of the planet, since each of us is a living part of it all.

As I teach Tarot students, the cards are alive in that they are always in flux, changing as the world changes, as people change. For example, the card signifying war or violent feelings: this would come up in a reading, say, for a person who was on the brink of divorce—but simultaneously signifying the war called Desert Storm. In this case, predictions and prophesy overlapped, as it does at all times. The cosmos (universe) is reflected in each one of us, showing up in a card reading, or in all parts of our individual lives.

While rational Roberta struggled with believing that a deck of cards could reveal another person's past, present, and future, the shaman within marveled at the orderliness of it all. I was charmed by it while simultaneously trying to figure it out. It simply escaped rationality. As I read for strangers, I found myself knowing ahead which cards they would select from the deck. And I would put the deck away for months. I felt that somehow I was manipulating people to select a card. Now, there's arrogance! It is also another dilemma. Which was easier for me to believe in? That I manipulated people by my thoughts, or that I was able to view their past, present, and future just by them handling these pieces of colored paper and seeing the patterns they fell into? It was too much, so I would "shut down" from time to time. It was years before I realized that it was not necessary to comprehend or explain.

The predictions were unpredictable. I would be left with wondering why a certain person had any need to know that something specific was going to happen to another person. What did it have to do with anything? Jane came in for a reading. The readings took about two hours, and during the course of this one, in the midst of pertinent information for Jane, I came upon this pattern addressing something irrelevant. An acquaintance of hers, a woman she did not know well, would die in the backseat of a car from a sickness which people do not ordinarily die of. She was blonde and young, and I described specific characteristics of the woman so that Jane recognized her.

"What has she got to do with anything?" Jane wanted to know.

"Beats me. I just read the cards," I replied. "I'm mystified, too, but I always promise to tell you everything that appears in readings. It has appeared, and I'm telling you."

Shortly afterward, Jane called me.

"The blonde woman you predicted would die of illness in a car did," she announced. "Her husband and friend took her to the hospital where she was treated for a light case of pneumonia and released. She died in the backseat on the way home. You might recall that the woman is less than thirty years old. No one can figure it out."

So why did Jane get told about her casual friend? They were not close, there was nothing she could do to stop it from happening. Why? I can think of several possibilities, but nothing definitive.

I always cautioned my clients that the predictions were being based upon things the way they were moving *that day,* at the time of the reading. There was always the possibility that they could alter the outcome. I guess that's why people want to know the future, isn't it?

Most of the time, things happened exactly as foretold. In one month, two of my clients were murdered, just as I had forewarned. In fact, in each case, I begged them to alter the conditions in which they were living so as to alter the outcome.

China did that, just as I asked her to. She moved herself and her son from the home where I had seen her husband soon becoming murderously violent. She sent her son to live with friends in another state, and she hid her living place from her husband. She called me. He was, indeed, becoming so violent that she did not recognize him. She was in hiding, and all her friends were doing all they could to protect her.

One night, while we were watching the early evening news, we heard three shotgun blasts. I cried out that it was China. Larry calmed me, saying that it was just so strongly on my mind. It could not be her.

During the late night local newscast, they showed a tape of the restaurant where China waited tables. Her estranged husband had entered during the dinner hour with a shotgun, killed her and then himself. China had altered everything except her job.

Donna had become a friend through repeated readings and counseling sessions. I had observed that the readings revealed an intensified and increasing amount of violence around her coming from her husband Gerald. She was planning to leave him soon, taking her three children. My nervousness increased as the days went by. I advised her to leave the state when she left him, feeling that he was certainly capable of great revenge. She assured me that she would have the support of her family locally and would be "all right." You bet.

Being a medium, I experienced her resultant murder. She was held by Gerald's relative as he stabbed her to death. Her children found her body in the morning.

These two cases occurred within a month. I was surely leaving this sort of work. Of what use was it—or me, for that matter—if it did not prevent such horrors from taking place. Larry came to my rescue, pointing out the obvious: one meets people in trouble in this kind of work. People who are in great shape do not come to a shaman for advice or healing. Thus, I have met, and will continue to meet people who have bad things happening to them. It is not my fault that it happens. By the same token, although I have prophesied tremendous earth changes and profound loss of life, that is not necessarily my fault. Life happens. And we all die.

The purpose of predicting for people is to prepare them so that they can best utilize the choices about to be afforded them.

A fun story. Terri came to me as often as I would allow her to for readings. As for so many, she had the idea that if I read for her often enough, the future she wanted would take form. Well, one evening it did. I saw a man entering the offices in which she worked. For her.

"I see him with the sun behind him, so the front door is eastern?"

"Yes," she said.

"He stands a moment, looking about, then comes past a couple of desks on your right, up to your desk. Is this real estate?"

"Yes. Well, rental locators," she said.

"Okay. He sits and you two talk. He will ask you out, and before two weeks are over, you two will be serious. By the time a couple months have passed, you could be married. That is, if you decide to," I said.

"Should I?" she asked.

I laughed. "How would I know that? Why don't you meet him and get to know him? Then we'll address that question."

Now, I have always made it clear that I only observe the future, that I do not make things happen. And I do so with a little joke that making it happen will cost a lot more money. Yet a couple weeks following this reading, I got a phone call.

"Is this Roberta Lee?"

"Yes."

"I'm a friend of Terri. You read for her a lot, and I want an appointment."

"Sure. When?"

"As soon as possible. She tells us that you can really make things happen."

"What?" I asked.

"You saw a wonderful man coming through the door of our office and told her that soon she could marry him. Well, it happened immediately. They're already engaged!"

Whimper. "I didn't make that happen."

"She says you did."

"No. Really. I just saw it coming. I had nothing to do with it. I just *saw* it."

"I want an appointment."

Predictions are easy for anyone who has the moxie to let go of the preconceived notion of time. Now, let me state that I am a stickler for being on time. Those who aren't and use the excuse that time does not matter are simply rude. When people do not arrive at the agreed-upon time, I consider that an insult, and they had better have a damn good excuse. But for the purposes of this chapter, time does not exist. We get too caught up in the calendar and clock, the 24-hour day schematic which we have created. It surely confines our abilities in the predictions arena.

When I prepare to predict, I almost physically shrug off the idea of time. I image water. I can reach in and pull out anything that has ever happened, is happening, or will happen out of that water. The real trick is interpreting the information, for much of the future is incomprehensible, since it has not taken place yet. As a young woman, the mere idea of a VCR (videocassette recorder), for example, was science fiction. And now everyone is walking around with cell phones stuck to their heads! I ask you, now. So how do you interpret that kind of information? The only errors I have had in predictions have been in interpretation. Oh, and when I have been too much of a wienie to state what I have seen. Predicting is risk-taking. Golly, what if I'm wrong? Doom. But invariably, the times I have "choked" and not spoken of what I have seen were absolutely right on, down to the color of the fingernails.

One of the best students I've had in Tarot, Marthe, observed that the hardest part of reading is exactly what I've so often said: getting the first word out. That old "just do it." The same is true of channeling and healing—and writing books.

Do we need Tarot cards to predict? Naw. Of course not. It helps greatly to use something for focus. Some like a crystal. I have used one to focus my inner eyes upon. With those, I find I work best with something else going on. Like television. I recall working with a piece of crystal, just fooling around to see if it worked well for me. I was watching TV and glancing from time to time into the center of the crystal. If you stare fixedly at it, zip, nada. Suddenly, I saw my daughter. She was sitting in a bus? Like a bus. But outside the windows was dark. Odd. She was reading a book and facing the aisle. She looked up at me, startled. I left just as she made the hand-language sign for I love you.

Less than two hours later, the phone rang. And I already knew it was she.

"What are you doing?" she asked.

"Oh, fixing dinner," I said.

"No, what *were* you doing?" she said.

"Well," I said, sighing, caught, "I guess you're referring to a while ago, when I was fiddling around with a crystal."

"I thought so. You startled the crap out of me."

"Say, just what kind of bus were you on, anyway?" I asked. "The windows were all dark."

She laughed at me. She lived in San Francisco. "That was the BART," she said. "We were underground at the time."

As far as predictions, crystals are not my forte. I use photographs sometimes, but they most often come to me when someone has died or is lost. I seldom see the future in photos, but I do see the past. The same with clothing or jewelry. However, having tactile contact with such items in tandem with a Tarot reading is really useful. And I have the client handle the cards, which is also a tactile contact.

I said for years, when asked, that I did not see auras, until it was pointed out that I certainly did too. Discussing it, I realized that I had seen them all my life and was so used to them being a part of everything that I didn't notice them that much. Still, I react sharply to what I have always called the charcoal cloud which surrounds those within days of being dead. Other colors? I don't know. It's more of a shimmer to me. I have also noted that aura color depends on which "expert" book you read about the subject. However, one can use an aura as a focus for predictions. That must be why I have so often spontaneously predicted for someone, even as I am walking by them. I have even found that I can be aware of what one has eaten just by passing them closely enough. If you use an aura as focus, be sure to look to one side, rather than straight on, for reading and predicting and diagnosing. That would apply to any psychic work.

Around family, I have had to be cautious. Who wants a mother, for example, who not only knows when you lie or what you're doing at any given moment, but who also knows what is *going to happen*? A client of mine sold my daughter her wedding dress. As she wrapped it up, she asked her if I had known of the marriage in advance.

"Yeah," my daughter answered.

"Did she tell you?"

"Not exactly, she just asked me when the lease to my apartment was coming up and suggested that I not sign up for another year."

Well, how do you help your daughter avoid wasting a year's rent money and yet not intrude on her decisions?

On the other hand, this stuff is not an exact science. In assisting a defense attorney with a capital case, I went to the area in which the body in question was found and where it was theorized that the murder took place. It was awful! So many murders. How could I find this one? I did because I have learned to tune in to specific times. I later learned that the site in question was a "favorite dumping place" for murder victims. Going back still further, it was the site for burying bodies of the ancients. Lots of time layers there.

As stated above and as I frequently remind myself and others, prediction is not an exact science. Here's an anecdote about a prediction and warning that was not exact.

Chaz called me one morning and told me that she would not be at one of our classes the following evening. She was going up to Phoenix to visit some friends that afternoon and would not return for two days and nights.

"Don't go this weekend," I said.

"I want to," she said.

"Go next weekend," I insisted.

"I want to go now," she said.

"Okay."

"What do you see?"

"Nothing."

"Am I in danger?" she asked.

"No. I just wish you would wait a week," I said.

"I'm going."

Two days later, she called.

"Why didn't you tell me?" Her voice was edgy with anger.

"Tell you what?" I asked.

"Tell me what was going to happen if I went to Phoenix."

"Well, I didn't tell you because I didn't know," I said. "My god, did something awful happen?"

"My place was broken into and my TV, VCR, and a bunch of other stuff has been taken."

"What about your critters?" I asked. She had a dog, bunny, and bird.

"They didn't hurt them. They were fine, thank god," she said. "But why didn't you tell me? I wouldn't have gone up there if I had known this was going to happen."

"Chaz, honest to god, I didn't know. I just had this strong feeling that you shouldn't go, although I knew it wasn't life or death. That's it."

"Well, you should have known," she said. Grumble.

Of course, one could point out that she should have trusted my caution to her.

I have made plenty of predictions and been off in the time department. Although, as I stated first in this chapter, there is no time. And perhaps that is why I have been off so much. I will explore this further in the section of this chapter on Prophecies. And I have been off many times in descriptions, likely due to interpretation. A great number of predictions regarding people come to us simply from being observant and a student of human behavior. For example, I can "feel" someone who will run a stop sign or pull into me while driving. I don't even have to see them or observe their driving actions. I suspect many of you reading this are capable of the same sort of thing. I do know that people riding with me are aware of my "seeing" the other driver, and most often, I am forcing him/her to stop.

We all know of and have experienced moments when we knew something was going to happen or was happening far away. These are almost always connected with intense emotion, and in fact, emotion really helps in the prediction department. It's hard to read for someone who just doesn't care about anything. Ho-hum. The ability to predict or to "know" something can be governed by anyone. I suggest that, when you feel something is going to happen, you write it into some sort of journal and then check that later. At least, that way you're not taking a risk of people laughing when you're wrong—if you are wrong. Daily meditation is the greatest path to being able to predict. Or to prophesy.

Schlepping Around in the Past

This part probably should be in parentheses, since it is not looking into the future. However, it seems to take the same form, so I will sneak it in here. History has always fascinated me, so returning to the past psychically is a fun part of what I do. When I get outside confirmation, it's a real hoot.

Patrick, Burton, Doyne, and I traveled to Chaco Canyon one spring. This was prior to the place becoming big on the tourist trail, but it did already have some regulations meant to preserve the sites from us. There was only one other group in the canyon while we were there, so we were pretty much able to do as we wished. Arriving mid-afternoon, we wandered around some of the ruins, and by sunset, found ourselves in Casa Grande, the largest standing "town" in the canyon. The kids were tired, so they went to the van to rest while Patrick and I wandered for just a few more minutes. I found myself in the great public courtyard around which the pueblo had been constructed. As I stood there, I felt a sudden rush of many people, as if I were in the midst of a crowd. I stepped back, closer to a wall.

"What are you doing here? Go. This is not your time." An old woman had paused briefly and "spoke" to me. She was not angry, but she was definitely firm on her point.

I called out to Patrick, "Let's get to the van now."

"I want to stay a bit longer, while the light is still available," he said.

"No, let's go. Now." I was feeling pretty anxious.

He began to remonstrate with me.

"No shit, Patrick. Now!"

We began to walk to the van. I ended up nearly running. The kids were watching and threw open the door. They had picked it up also.

Once behind the steering wheel, Patrick started to fuss at me, but I explained my experience to him, and he accepted that, although with a bit of skepticism. He'd had plenty of proof of my psychic stuff, but after all, he hadn't felt or seen or heard anything ...

Well, he would.

From there, we drove to the restrooms, and it was dark as we exited them. Walking through the chamisa to the van, the kids and I clearly heard bodies moving through the brush and "click sticks" and children's excited voices. All around us. Not scary at all, but actually fun.

After a camp dinner, we all rolled into our bags in the van, and we left the sliding door open for the air since it wasn't cold. There was a group of archeological students at the far eastern end of the campground, and we could hear their voices as they settled down for the night, too. As it became quiet, the music and singing began.

It was the same chant over and over. We could identify the voices of men, women, and children. Was it our fellow campers? But the chanting came from the opposite direction! It went on for hours, and soon we were humming along with it. As soon as one refrain ended, another would start up. A celebratory sound. Very pleasant. I fell asleep surrounded by this sweetness.

The next day, around mid-morning, we entered a kiva in one of the pueblos to the southwest of the campground and found the source of our musical evening. The kiva was filled with voices of the people, all singing. And they didn't mind a bit that we were present! We spent some time there, sitting in the midst of that lovely sound from all those unseen throats. Occasionally, there would be some laughter which served as a wonderful counterpoint to the "music."

In the late afternoon, we were exploring a pueblo in the northeastern portion of Chaco Canyon. We had gone from room to room, through incredibly short doors, and had come out into a smaller public courtyard. I sat on the ground, my back against the wall, facing the west, looking up that immense canyon toward the setting sun and breathing in the desert's peace. Suddenly, there were people all about me again, most of them women and most of those working at various things. I found myself inside a young woman who had a child nearby and who was grinding a grain (corn?) on a stone *metate* and whose eyes often strayed to the western end of the canyon. As our connection grew, I realized that she and I were watching for her husband, who had left the previous day with several other men to hunt for meat. They were due back this sunset.

Remarkably, this young woman demonstrated little emotion while I was with her. She seemed almost dull-witted to me, but not. As the men appeared in the distance, her husband among them, she relaxed and continued with her grinding. Her response to her husband's appearance? She would, indeed, require enough grain for three this night. My impression of this communication is that whatever happened was acceptable. If he had died, she would have grieved briefly and likely remarried soon, since she and her child required a man to hunt and work the fields. If her husband had been wounded, the healers and shaman would heal his wounds while she tended him in their apartment. I believe she cared for him, but she was above all practical in her outlook to life. She exhibited no strong emotions to me, but rather an acceptance of whatever life offered.

I further noticed that the children playing and working there in that village plaza seemed to be enjoying themselves, but they were not shrieking as children today might in their play. They were watchful, although I felt that they were secure within the care of the village. Again, this seemed odd to me, since I had expected the romanticized view that early indigenous peoples would behave as innocent puppies.

In that morning, we had hiked up the cliffs and onto the northern plateau rising steeply above the canyon and wandered through a few small ruins. I was drawn to one spot in particular. Seated there, I "saw" people walking close and placing bowls and baskets of food before the "house." What was this? The person who had dwelled there came to me. He was shaman! As such, he was required to live away from the town, although close enough to be summoned easily and consulted frequently by the elders. Of course, he was provided with all the food he needed, as well as clothing and cover. I suspect that whenever necessary, the people repaired his dwelling, although it was made from stone and seemed durable.

Below us, in the pueblo, we came upon one of the apartments which had faded painted designs on the walls. That was odd because, come to think of it, we hadn't seen artwork in this form previously. Again, I sat upon the floor, leaning against the cool wall, and let my mind go free. Ah. An artist. What a strange fellow. At least, that's what the other people thought. Well, all people are accepted for their gifts and foibles. In this case, he had needed a service from the man who dwelled here and "paid" for the service with these homey decorations. Those who lived in this apartment felt that they were nice, although unnecessary, and enjoyed them for their peculiarity. Since this apartment was deep within the pueblo, I wondered how much they could enjoy the colors, since so little light came through. I wondered the same thing about the pots from these towns, which were also painted, but then most meals were prepared and eaten outside.

A few weeks following this fun trip, I mentioned it to Peg, who became excited, telling me that her father was one of the archeologists who had opened Chaco Canyon when she was just a little girl. I must visit him. I was delighted.

I recited my experiences at Chaco to this venerable man. His face lit up.

"Exactly right," he said frequently.

I told him that I found most puzzling the lack of modern emotions I found there.

"But that is what I have always suspected," he said. "They were pretty busy surviving, and I'm sure they simply did not have the energy to put into extra emotion. Not that they were dull people or uncaring, but just that they didn't go overboard in that department."

He went on to corroborate my suspicions about the ruined house above the canyon. "Probably was the shaman or medicine man, although medicine men and women were generally welcome within the towns. Usually, shamans were not—and to this day shamans are not welcome when they are recognized." This was my first exposure to the word "shaman" and to the concept that they were not acceptable persons. I paid it little heed, since it certainly had nothing to do with me! We chatted together for some time, and I got to look at many of the good doctor's treasures from various digs before I took my leave. It's always swell when we get confirmation on a "hit."

What's the point of this one story out of many when I have entered the past? And why would I include it in a chapter about foretelling, when clearly it belongs in "The Dead?" Well, it demonstrates the non-existence of time, I suppose. If one can fore-tell, one can surely "back-tell," right?

If you are interested in this kind of psychic work, I suggest that you go to some historical site or society and look at historic photographs of people. Look into their eyes and allow yourself to enter their memories.

On the other hand, this kind of work can be disturbing. On a trip into Virginia, I was overwhelmed with the human history there. It caused me severe depression and sleepless nights, since my dreams were filled with slavery and civil war. Why so much more there? The atmosphere. All the humidity, the moss-laden trees and grasses—these things "hold" memory much more firmly than does airiness and a dry climate and space.

When entering an area here in the Southwest in which, say, a bloody conflict between Apache and cavalry occurred, I find myself uncomfortable and a bit edgy, but I am able to enjoy the surroundings despite this overlay. In the East, it seems impossible to do so, for I find myself virtually living in the past, as if in a bad dream which I cannot break entirely out of. I can function, barely, but I keep going back to that slavery/civil war imprint. And I must use all my ability—all the time—to continue functioning. I wonder just how deeply living there in that atmosphere affects people in the eastern part of this country.

ROBERTA LEE / NIGHTWING

World Prophecies

World prophecies have been coming in to me since I was very young. But this time, I was going out into the mountains south of Tucson over the Winter Solstice to fast for sixteen days *specifically* for a vision of what is coming for our species and, indeed, the entire world.

A long fast in nature, being on the ground the entire time, grinds one down. I do not recommend it. But I was desperate for insight; I could physically sense that things were rolling to a close for our society, our way of life, our very species' continuity. I needed information. Visions are, for me, visceral and participatory. I am not a spectator; I seldom see pictures in the sky. I become the vision, and that is why I know they are true. One cannot long disbelieve a total experience.

The usual visionquest experiences transpired: ravens came to speak to me of this and that; I went through some mind stuff that had to be endured and finished; Lord Elf came to speak, power animals taught; I had a powerful transformative vision involving some Christ figures (Jesus, Gandhi, Wovoka, Mary Magdalene, the Buddha, and others); some personal work took place. There were only a few days remaining. I was becoming concerned.

Then it came. For two days and three nights solid. No respite. I experienced our species from its inception through its prehistory and history. I saw the first village, which was the beginning of the end. I saw us in harmony with all others, then our separation and aloneness. I experienced the horrors our species has inflicted upon our home planet and those Others we had once been at one with, then how we turned on ourselves. How we are now isolated from our gods and selves, without true pride but filled with despair and hatred and false superiority.

The planet before me, covered with great mushroom clouds. Bombs? I found out that they were not. Great war? No. Enormous planetary cataclysms? Some, of course. Plagues? Yes. Famine? You bet. Slavery? Yes.

Massive death? Yes. People leaving for other planets? Yes. Wait a minute there, what?

Lord Elf led me through much of the planetary history. I walked with Lord Elf among its people, the Old Race, and saw my people as they lived with all life forms in peace and such harmony that there was no division. It appeared that all life forms fed upon some sort of nectar provided by a multitude of flowers, many of which I have never seen or imagined, as well as grains, nuts, and other such foods available to all life. There was no God, no punishments, and little pain. Although all life forms finally aged and died, it was an acceptable, peaceful thing. There was no morality and no sin, no overcrowding to cause psychosis, no mindless taking of Mother Earth's bounty. Then a small number of humans began to want to run things; they wanted to control. They went to a horse and mounted it and made it go where they wanted to go. When it did not, they beat it to cause it to go. These humans began to coerce other humans to their way; they began thinking and using a form of rationalization to place themselves above all other life forms, and this grew and grew as they began feeling apart. If not a part of everything, then superior to all. They stopped coercing and began forcing the other humans to their ways. They formed villages.

"This is where the end began," Lord Elf said.

"Villages? But there still aren't so many humans," I said.

"Look. As soon as people formed villages, they found certain things they deemed to be comforts. They wanted hot baths, indoors, rather than at the hot springs. They wanted what they thought was beautiful, dyed clothing to compete with others. They wanted soft beds. All artificial comforts."

"Weren't they comfortable before?" I asked.

"Yes, Nightwing. But they came to depend upon and demand *artificial* comforts, since the natural ones did not exist in the villages," Lord Elf said. "Once that began, they took and took from nature to provide themselves with ease. They became dependent upon close social contact with large numbers of themselves—herd activity, if you will. Now, they had to go out and harvest nectar to live upon. Soon, some would 'hire' others to harvest nectar and bring it to them. You see, don't you, how all this continues to escalate?"

"Yes, I see it. Lord Elf, they aren't happy any longer." The people were argumentative. I saw a man kick a dog when he was outside his village. I saw families begin to form, whereas previously the children belonged to all and all people were free. Now they were beginning to belong to small groups called families and clans. Jealousy and possessiveness began to take root.

Not all towns evolved at the same rate, but pretty much. Soon, they were harvesting seeds from plants and growing gardens, then capturing animals to feed and slaughter for food. I don't know when they stopped feeding on the free nectar. Enslaving plants and animals for food was part of the power-over movement. Now, villages were fighting other villages, killing each other, taking slaves, forcing other humans to worship the gods each village had created.

The Ancient Race began to drift back into the deepest forests where they watched this strange behavior of an aberrant animal form.

"If only we had put a stop to it right then," Lord Elf murmured. "See how the surface of our Home is? Not scarred, not dug up. Look, Nightwing, see the colors of the waters and skies—even the greens and browns of the Earth are different. Nightwing, those colors are how it used to look, when it was still pure and clean. Before the first village."

"But Lord Elf, can your people not, with their magic and abilities, stop us now? Clear out our great cities and our overpopulation, so that the world can go back to what it was for you and all the other life?"

"No. Your species would simply build another village. They will always want the artificial comforts. They will now always take. There is nothing they can give back.

"Consider, Nightwing. There is nothing your species has or can do to better the perfection that was here. Music? The sound of wind in the trees and water racing over stones is as beautiful as any artificial music. And natural beauty does not require the use of anything else from the planet—no paper, no wood for the instrument. You see?

"Painting? Again, the artist must use materials which are of the Earth to create art. And what does good art do? Many artists in their vanity believe that they are (laughing) *improving* on the beauty of Mother Earth! Impossible! Others are copying Her loveliness. To what end?

"The human species has given nothing and has destroyed all. Nightwing, your people are a deadly virus."

I saw our species and what it has done to the earth and all who live in, upon, and above Her. What a terrible vision! I endured this part of the vision for an entire night and part of a day. I was despairing as much as I can imagine a person to be. What hope is there? None. How do I continue? Even my work is crap in this light. The breath I take is deadly.

I was born loving Mother Earth above everything else. For some reason, I placed animals before myself—and before other people. I hated to step on lawns. Driving a car was misery, for it meant killing untold numbers of insects and even unseeable life. Drinking water is painful. At times, moving about on foot caused me pain for even that means killing other sacred life forms.

But I know that life is about death, and since other animals also move about and thus kill, I was able to live a fairly normal life. I stopped eating my fellow animals, birds, fish, but I had to continue eating vegetables and fruits and grains. I have learned that nothing is perfect, and one simply does one's best and goes on until one finds a better way and does that. This vision, however, was so horrific that I must die.

"No, Nightwing, even the deaths of all human beings cannot either correct the problems or stop atrocities from escalating and spreading," Lord Elf said.

"What?" I almost screamed in my despair. For with these words, came the "pictures" of the mess our bodies will make. And worse.

These are the mushroom clouds I have seen so often in my visions of the Earth. Cities where disease and violence wipe out large numbers of human beings. The souls of these people, in a state of rage, indignation, and terror remain and become congested energy!

"Yes, Nightwing," Lord Elf in my ear, "if these 'soul storms' are not dissipated quickly, they will do more damage than your atomic bomb can. Look at how the clouds whirl about and level trees and buildings and animals. Just like a giant tornado larger than anything known to this planet."

True. In my work with dead folks, I have been impressed with the pure emotional energy they emit. It's that energy which allows us to communicate. What if ten thousand people died within a few hours of one another? What would be left? My jaw drops in awe. One hundred thousand people? What about a place like New York? Mexico City? Tokyo?

"There's enough energy there to tip the axis of the Earth!" I whisper.

"Exactly," Lord Elf agreed. "And that's what will happen. That's what so many of the seers today see covering the continents—soul storms—and they *will tip the axis of this planet*, causing massive natural cataclysms.

"And you have all developed immunizations and medicines for this and that until you have lost your ability to fend off disease in any natural way. It is ironic, Nightwing, that the older people today have more ability to survive sickness because they did so as children and have natural immunities to many conditions.

"Vegetables, fruits, and grains no longer nourish your people because they have little food value since they are grown in depleted soil. Where else would the minerals and vitamins you require come from? So your farmers add synthetic minerals to the soil, which are ineffective. Now, people are taking great amounts of vitamins and minerals and food replacements. And although they tout themselves as being 'natural,' they are not, since where would anything natural come from? Thus, you are starving yourselves and becoming obese as a species since you are constantly eating in an attempt to find food for yourselves."

As Lord Elf continues, I am inside the pictures of these events, experiencing them, participating. I have been leery of the herb industry for some time now, and I can now see why: they often don't work for us—because they are grown in depleted soil and because our bodies have become so unsubtle that herbs just do not affect us as they once did. I see us starving to death, even as we appear large and healthy. I think of all the people I know who are so health-conscious and even afraid of their own bodies or of being uncomfortable. People who exercise too much because they hate their bodies, people who diet to slim down also because they hate themselves. People who will not come into the sweat lodge because it hurts and will do nothing that is uncomfortable because "if it's not comfortable, it's not good for us."

Lord Elf was continuing, "Religions will become increasingly militant and rigid and will ultimately hold actual wars with government over who should be responsible for food and weapons and medicines. There will be localized wars constantly. And before long, your country will decide not to get involved outside its interests. There will be such massive inhumanity that one would be hard put to decide whom to assist in any case. As children begin to die from simple (formerly easy-to-cure) diseases, men will attack medical people and hospitals with weapons, killing all in their way. Violence will be pervasive and will be set off by the other troublesome things going on, Nightwing."

People do have a way of responding to trouble with weapons, I guess.

Lord Elf answered my thoughts, "Yes. Vigilantism will be rampant, and you will be in the midst of some of the earliest and most obvious. It will involve the brown people south of here. No, you will not be a vigilante but will witness it much. You will carry a weapon at all times. People will have an armed friend with them when they shop for food and necessities. Anyplace you go to will be a potential danger to your life. Being aware and alert will separate those living from those dead.

"Which brings me to where all these human souls will go. Nightwing, before your species separated from all the others, no one reincarnated. There was no need, just as the animals have no need to return to improve themselves through varied experience. Their souls return to the Source, just as you once did. You have experienced this Source in your work, and have helped many back into this ineffable Light. It is Home. It is Nirvana. It is also nothingness for many. It may be described as the energy from which this planet creates its lifeforms of all kinds. Thus, when one is a part of this Source, one may 'return' as a molecule of stone, a molecule of tree, and so on.

"There are a very few human beings who have entered the Source or Nirvana and retained their individuality, if you will. Those who do have very little individuality remaining, but there is some scrap of their Selves, and that is expressed in what your Great Teachers refer to as Compassion and what you yourself see as the Christs. Nightwing, long after your death and inclusion into the Source, your passionate love for Mother Earth will glow and retain form. That will be You, whether you ever again take physical form or not. I know your heart, that your only regret about death is leaving your beloved Earth, the tangible part of Her, the touch, smell, sound of Her. You know that you will Be Her, but that is too subtle for your tastes. I tell you, however, that as you have been learning and experiencing, as you Be Mother Earth, you will find that it is very, very tangible, beloved one."

"But Lord Elf," I wept, "I am a part of that awful virus that is humanity, too."

"Yes, and there is no way around that," it said. "All you can do is what you are doing. Living the best way you can, seeking better ways, and loving and having that deep Compassion for Mother and all of us who differ from you. And stay willing to work for Her and us and to rejoin Her and all of us in Nirvana."

"I will be asked this, and I am not sure how to answer. I think I know it from being here right now, but ..." I said.

"No, very few people alive today *deserve* Nirvana in the way they think of it, and a lot of murderers and really bad people will go there also. So why should anyone continue to do their best?"

Ha! I know this one. "Because, Lord Elf, it is what we want to do, to do our best. Because doing our best is there to be done. Why would anyone want to do less than their best? Every soul I have worked with has wanted its person to go the limit, to be willing to do the distance, to walk the walk—in whatever way is before them. Most souls are disappointed though, when their persons just do whatever it takes to get by, or get caught up in some sort of it's-got-to-be-a-big-deal thinking. You know, the more esoteric it is, the better it must be. I have found little willingness out there, Lord Elf. Lots of I'm-willing-but-only-if-I-can-keep-my-nice-house stuff."

You should experience the laugh of a Faire Folke Elf. For a long time, I wasn't sure what it was. Now I'm getting used to it. A little.

"So, Lord Elf, everyone is going to Nirvana? That ought to be good news. If anyone believes it."

"Well, they won't. But aside from that. There are degrees of Nirvana. Well, not really, but this may make it easier to explain. Those who enter the Great All and Great Nothing *consciously and with willingness to be whatever is needed* will retain some consciousness and *be able to return to this Earth in a physical way to help cleanse and build again*."

"I feel a catch in that statement."

"Aren't you becoming suspicious?" It grinned. "But you're right. Those persons who are willing and have that compassion may return in physical form as, say, one of us or one of some other species, some not yet created and some whose forms would appall many at this time. Unrecognizable, perhaps. Frightening to human eyes. But you see, as the differences drop away with compassion in Nirvana, there would likely be no problem. If there were, those would not be souls which would be candidates for regaining physical form.

"Now, Nightwing," and Lord Elf became very serious, "this is important. There are many humans today who believe in extraterrestrial life, 'life on other planets,' which there is, but that has little to do with this. Many of these humans wish to travel to those faraway places. And they can. Once dead now, they can reform on another planet. They can even enter great silver spaceships and fly to those places."

"Imagination! The greatest power and curse of humanity!" I cry.

"Exactly so. These people believe this so deeply that upon death, it can become their truth. Think upon that, Nightwing, the human virus spreading throughout the Universe, to other planets where they will—and many of them righteously—take over and do to them what they have perpetrated here."

Back to the depths of despair with this vision.

"Can't you and your people stop us?" I asked.

"No. Your people can."

"Is there hope, then?"

"Yes," Lord Elf responded, "only your species can stop yourselves. Just as the 'end of the world' for humanity comes from yourselves killing off yourselves, only you can stop yourselves from infecting everything everywhere. Take everyone to the Source!"

I dozed off for a little while and awoke with all of this information as memory within my mind, which was bursting. First, there was the horror that *we are* and how impossible it seemed to stop us, and then the small hope that we truly can stop ourselves from spreading ourselves elsewhere, to other pure planets and lives. And even a chance to start over, consciously in whatever form to do whatever is presented to cleanse and perhaps heal Mother Earth.

I have always held in great contempt those nice, caring fools who have some sort of egotistical idea that they can heal Mother Earth—by sound, crystals (which should have been left within Her where they were!), whatever. How do we have the nerve to believe that we know more than She does about healing Herself?! But here is a real way, one which Mother Earth has given to us.

I began thinking of the Buddhists I have known. I studied a form of Buddhism when I was working with my first teachers, and it is a Way which I greatly admire. It is a Way of Obedience, which comes naturally to me. Perhaps that is why it cannot be my Way at this time. It would be far more comfortable for me than being a shaman. Irony, your name is Life. The Buddha was a man who struggled and worked very hard and attained enlightenment and died and entered Nirvana, just as Lord Elf described, consciously. The Buddha, so complete in his Compassion, lived for us 2500 years ago and could return and live for us again—or for the planet. Perhaps his Compassion causes him to remain in Nirvana to help us all from there. I couldn't possibly know. I do know that we each have the Way we best can use to work through this so that we, too, may enter the inevitable Nirvana—soon—also consciously. We are prepared to then decide how best to work again with things as they are, in *the* sacred way.

When next we met, Lord Elf and I worked on how to get masses of souls over into the Source. I asked about the timing for all of this.

"That really depends. You see, the Earth knows little about your clocks and your sense of what you call time. It also depends upon yourselves, again. How your species responds to what takes place. For example, when the children die, will parents immediately begin shooting at hospital people, or will that begin to occur later on? There are so many of you praying for Mother Earth, that that is slowing down the process.

The best approach here is to understand that everything is working toward one end: the reclamation of the planet. Stay neutral and do your best to maintain a sense of sanctity and awareness that there are matters greater than you and your wants."

"Lord Elf, when will it all be over? Our ugliness? Our killing of Mother Earth and all Her children?" I asked.

Tremendous laughter. Then silence, a sigh. "What would you call over? When the last factory that makes medicine bursts and spills its poisons into the earth and water? The last nuclear power plant blows? Even so-called non-harmful items become poisonous as their chemical structure alters with time. And your nuclear reactors! Without humans around to caretake these things, when will it be done? Probably thousands of your years. Perhaps that is what many of you will do when you reform to come back here—help take care of these things. There is so much that cannot be undone! We recognize that much of the Earth will never be the same as it even is now. It has gone too far. That is another reason the human species must be prevented from traveling to other planets."

"Lord Elf," I said in my smallest mental voice, "people will ask me where they should go during these times to be safe. They have asked Rahotep, and they will ask again."

"Nowhere. There is nowhere safe as you think of it. Except that doing your best and participating in a sacred way is safe."

"Do your people hate mine?" I asked.

"Some do. I have learned, through you, not to hate all of you. It is hard, though, to see all of the death and torture of innocent, perfect beings and then see your species as the perpetrators of all of it and maintain some caring. Some of the Old Race are rampaging now. You know, for I have rescued you from some of them. And you rescue soul pieces from some of them. I restrain."

That is an understatement.

"Nightwing, we are going to take you and your mate to a place for you to live during your last years while this is going on. Safe? We don't do this for your safety; it is simply the place for you to be. The people there will be neither better nor worse than the people in the cities, but it will be easier for you to live there because you will be out of the worst of the noise and chaos and violence. You will empath it and it will intrude upon your life, but you will be able to find some objectivity. This will happen in a way that will baffle you."

Of course.

"Lord Elf, there are many seers who have prophesied about this subject and given us dates—even maps. The dates vary greatly, as do the maps."

"Yes. That is because no one knows the dates. As I have said, the Earth—and we—know nothing about your clocks and calendars and sense of time. You know that time exists, but not as human beings perceive it and wish to conform it. No. As for the maps: you have seen these things on a global basis and are aware that many of the earth-crust changes shown will be similar to their maps. But they have also given dates, which are not germaine. When the soul storms transpire and result in axis tilting, great alterations will take place upon the face of this world."

And since that visionquest, I have seen these and have seen that the etheric body of the planet has already moved in preparation for the non-subtle body to join it, much as your energy hand moves prior to your physical hand.

Postscript

As I have been writing this book, the World Trade Centers have been destroyed and massive life taken by "terrorists." Terrorism continues to unfold each day. I witness many of those visions of 1991 on CNN today.

We see vigilantes here in the Southwest border areas every day as they hunt "illegals," people like you and me who are living in poverty and watching their children die from hunger and absence of medical treatment. People who have made their ways through dire danger into this country, seeking work, only to be held at gunpoint by ranchers and thrill-seekers and hunters, hopefully to be turned over to the authorities and returned to their native countries, rather than be toyed with by less moral vigilantes. People with bigger guns. Every day, reports are made of newer and more terrible diseases especially striking our children. Countries are wiped out by famine and wars. Horrific mass torture by political leaders is reported.

The Centers for Disease Control and Prevention (CDC) has been warning us for several years that the world is overdue for a major plague and that the longer we go without one, the worse it will prove to be when it occurs. This is a natural cycle of a life form, one which humans have side-stepped, at least for a time, with science. But Nature always wins out, and all species are subject to Her Laws concerning overpopulation. Humans are not an exception; they are merely wily enough to forestall those laws for a time.

Mother Earth will heal herself of her worst disease—humanity—and she will live on in whatever form she and her life forms must take on. Each of us has the opportunity to choose how we respond to this. We can continue living blindly and selfishly, or we can cooperate in her healing, living as harmoniously as we can with her.

Chapter 18

The Meaning of Life, the Nature of God, and What Is Prayer

On my way to conduct a Pipe Ceremony in honor of some students who had just completed visionquest, I was driving along Interstate 10, approaching Tucson, and was lightly contemplating a subject never far from my mind: the nature of god. Suddenly, it was there—the answer, the full picture. I quickly pulled off the interstate and was sobbing by the time I had stopped the car. Curiosity kills the cat, I thought. I'd been curious about god and universal meanings, and now I had received the reply. Damn.

Humans created the concept of god.

The meaning of life is to live it with enough excellence that we are prepared to die. Preferably with a great sense of humor and flexibility.

Now what? I was scheduled to lead a prayer circle in about a half hour. This was no way to begin. I didn't have time to fully explore the ramifications of this epiphany. How would I pray in a few minutes? To what or whom would I pray? I certainly could not take this to the fine people awaiting the Pipe and the festivities surrounding the return of four visionquesters. I began to drive again. Thank goodness for habit. I would present a ceremony just like all the other hundreds I had presented. Afterward I would take a hard look at the information I'd just received.

I've always considered myself to be a highly spiritual person. A holy woman, being a woman who is walking her walk and dedicated to living as the Great Mystery would wish. And how about that Great Mystery business? I chose the nomenclature of Great Mystery some years previously when I had concluded that human nature pushed us to discover the nature of gods and goddesses, but when we did discover the nature, our immediate and lasting response to that knowledge was always contempt. Anything I can figure out can't be very powerful or complicated. If I can divine a mystery (and I used to try all the time), then it can't be much of a mystery in the first place. So I called that power to which I prayed Mystery to remind myself not to try to solve it. Leave it alone and let it just be. Walk in harmony with What Is and be just a little humble.

I had removed any idea of a personal god, a grandpa-in-the-sky concept of god, long ago. It didn't make any sense to take life personally. The Native Americans I had associated with referred to "it" as Grandfather. That didn't work either—again, it was just too personal. And my idea of god(s) was too limitless for that. Creator is, once again, sounding like a person-deity. As if the universe needed someone to create it.

Today, I knew. Only humans, of all the species on this planet, needed to believe that someone created all this. Further, human beings are the only species which requires some *meaning to life*. In my close observation and communications with other species, I never heard any of them inquire as to the meaning of their lives. Only humans pray. We even created this god in our own image! For create god we did. Generally speaking, our god was created in the image of what we thought it should be and in the doctrinal form we felt best suited our wants and needs.

I have been blessed with "work" which has required my presence in nature often: visionquesting myself annually for up to twenty-two days and nights, seated on the ground and surrounded by all of Nature, as well as providing visionquests for many others, often as frequently as on a monthly basis, spending six days and nights in a quiet campsite, again on the ground and, once again, surrounded by Nature. This has given me a great deal of conscious experience with other species. I learned to listen to them and realize what their lives were truly like. Recognizing that the other species are my spiritual teachers, I had to question human gods. That led me to this day of realizing there is no god. This opened a huge box. The ramifications of this awareness were far-reaching for me indeed. In fact, it seemed to bend my spiritual concepts out of any familiar form whatsoever. On the other hand, I had found myself increasingly imaging Nature as what I prayed to and with.

Requiring a personal god, particularly one created in our own image, is the ultimate arrogance, isn't it? With such a creation, we found a way in which to control all of our lives. Here was a parent who punished, loved, rewarded, and killed our enemies if we followed him in the manner which he insisted upon. Thus, when things weren't going well for us, it was god's responsibility—and none of us could possibly comprehend god's will for us, right? If there was a famine, it was a punishment laid upon us for something. What? Well, perhaps some sort of sacrifice would propitiate the god. Let's kill animals or slaves—or even our children. That would make him happy with us again.

Or ... if someone is sick with cancer, it is probably because she hasn't been living "right." How many times I have heard even doctors and healers say, "You will be well when you are ready." Ready for what? Does that mean that when I am "ready" I will be a picture of good health and rich beyond belief? To this day, my first knee-jerk reaction when I am sick or in pain is to wonder what I have done wrong! For the past several years, I have learned to move past that reaction quickly. But this has been so drummed into us all that I may never stop that immediate reaction. We have had millennia of this instruction from religious leaders, and most of it is rooted deeply within our DNA, not to mention past-life memories.

The god concept has been used to keep us in line. Well, something had to keep us from being worse brutes than we are. There is a lot to be said for the fear of divine retribution to mitigate our crueler sides. Although let us not overlook the horrors perpetuated on behalf of religion and various god forms. So what would keep us from atrocity born out of a sense of "if it feels good, do it?" For me, freedom from the god thing has caused me to be even more careful of my actions, more responsible for myself. Since there is no one I can blame if I screw up, the responsibility falls to me. The buck stops here. And I find that I actually yearn to do better things now.

It is more exciting to be alive without gods. I feel more intensely alive. Death seems more like a bearable adventure now. After all, there is no Law or god to rule what will occur after my death. It is self-determined only by my belief and even expectation (although we must deal with that old devil ethos).

Going back to the other species, my experience with them is that they do not have an afterlife as we think of it. This is not always true, for I have seen ghost animals, and certain companion animals have essences which seem to remain with us, at least for a time. But I understand that it is mainly due to our demands of these companions. For the most part, animals and plants return to the Source or Nature.

But aren't we special, somehow? After all, we have souls. And many of us believe that our souls reincarnate in new bodies from time to time. Thus, the rules which apply to animals have little to do with us. Right? Naw. That's more arrogance. And fear. If humanity had not broken away from the natural stream of life, we would be living and dying as the other species do. But we set ourselves up to be superior to all other life forms. This separated us from the All Life and made us unnatural. Since that time, we have been striving to return to that perfect existence, which we have named heaven, paradise, and Nirvana.

Everything which drives us is geared toward our return to At-One-Ness with All Life, with Nature, with our own species—and with our selves. Until we relinquish our arrogance, this cannot be accomplished, even to a lesser degree. And we will remain lonely and driven to find that At-One-Ness through drugs, sex, power over others, rage, and religion. But if we move toward At-One-Ness, would we lose our individuality? Sure. God, thy name is Individuality. Heaven or Nirvana is a return to being a part of everything, to releasing the concept of our individual selves and becoming life force itself.

That's the meaning of life.

Almost all the great spiritual teachers I have read of and contemplated have urged us to realize that life is a joke of some sort. I talked for years of starting up a church called the Church of the Cosmic Chuckle. Life is absurd. It is a riddle—and one which remains unsolvable. Isn't that great? Well, I do suppose it means taking responsibility for our own actions, though, doesn't it? What an onus that can be. No "the devil made me do it." It really isn't in god's hands, is it?

How can we take life personally? Life doesn't care about the individual. Life doesn't care about anything. It just is. Nature is. Let's not hear any of this "Nature is cruel" stuff. It isn't cruel; it just is.

But what about those New Age folks who tell us that we can have/be anything we want? "The universe has all you want." Sure it does, but there are an awful lot of people who want it, too. And how about those crippled beggars in India? They want stuff. And they don't get it. They probably live in more harmony with What Is than most of us, since they have no other choice. Is their god less interested in them than ours is in us? Hmmm. We are a blame society, blaming our parents for our adult lives, blaming governments for all social ills, and blaming god for our not having anything and everything we want. A baby dies because it dies. Lots of baby animals die, seedlings die, even stars die. Is the tornado which destroys a town really an "act of god?" Can't it simply be part of the weather patterns which exist on this planet? It is, and has been for a long time now—even before there were humans to blame god for it.

In this book, I have described what takes place following death. It is not pre-determined by a law or god. In fact, god and those laws have been created by people who wanted an explanation for the human experience of life, since humans have to be superior to the rest of Nature. Reincarnation is also not pre-determined, but it is a product of self-determination. At worst, it is the result of self-programming and a desire to return to be with those we crave to be near. We choose situations to return into. Many have chosen the situations which will offer them the best lives to grow within, the most opportunity to evolve. Evolve to what? Back to our beginnings—at one with everything.

Our best preparation for death—and for living—is to have an open mind, to be receptive to learning from the rest of life, our fellow sojourners, of all species. We can begin to drop our limitations, expanding our receptivity to include everything that is. Living as best we can in this way permits us, at death, to continue a limitless existence. Who knows what could happen? Actually, limitations hold safety for us—or at least, we feel they do. We are more comfortable with walls and fences, with myopia. The times when I have been the most uncomfortable—okay, terrified—have been when my defenses are down and I am very receptive. And remember the way to power is through powerlessness.

But recall, also, my story about the dead lady who has her nose to the grindstone in her witless search for the true religion. Who wants to spend afterlife doing that? Let's show a little moxie and allow ourselves to experience everything there is.

Do we need drugs for this? No and no. What I have seen in people who search for "truth" via drugs is that they receive distortion and alter their own peculiar beliefs. We've got to have the guts to drop our limits by ourselves. Can we do this in the comfort of our own living rooms? No again. We need to stretch our limits to the point where we become receptive. Meditation in the living room does not accomplish this, although it is something I recommend fully. To find Truth, we have to suffer a bit. A little—and I stress moderation here—fasting and being in an uncomfortable situation, such as in the wilderness, and experiencing some loneliness and fear can go far in locating Truth for us. Dropping our guards is not easily accomplished, but it can be done if we truly wish to. Being receptive to What Is, rather than what we think it should be, is the key to the meaning of life and all that stuff.

Living in the Southwest, I am most comfortable with much of the indigenous peoples' philosophies. Not necessarily those adopted by the moderns, but those more traditional beliefs and practices. The Navajo believe that Nature is perfect and all we must do in order to share that perfection and joy (Beauty) is to adjust our attitudes and blend in with What Is. For example, a serious drought is considered to be perfect. We must come into harmony with that drought to Walk in Beauty. When a person is chronically sick, physically or emotionally, it is a sign that they are out of harmony with What Is, and a shaman is called upon to bring that person back to Beauty, allowing them to move into the stream of perfection that is Nature.

For gods, I admire the Hopi Kachina gods. There is one to represent every phase of life, every species, every human power and frailty. These "gods" are manifested to the People by men (and sometimes women) who study in the kivas with the elders for years in order to represent a god. On the day that they emerge for the People, they don the mask of their particular god, exit the kiva, the womb of Mother Earth, into the great plaza and dance before those present, providing a corporeal manifestation of those specific attributes. When the mask is placed onto the dancer, he or she becomes that god, those attributes. This resonates profoundly in my visceral being. Here we come face to face with the gods, all the facets of Nature, and it satisfies our desire to come into harmony with All, for we may now dance with Life itself.

Perhaps one of those facets is the *Heyoka* or clown, which reminds us of ourselves and how silly we all are, as well as how funny life is. And this is serious business, this silly life. Life may not be the grand joke, but how we respond to it is. Life happens to us; we determine how we respond to it. Will we accept what occurs with joy, some balance and perspective, or will we go 'round the bend during adversity? There is the riddle and the joke.

Prayer

Returning to my car on the interstate, my own epiphany could wait until tonight. The prayers were sweet, and they further calmed my spirit. Even then the thought slipped in: how could they, when I didn't believe that we prayed to anything?

Over the next few days and nights, as I retreated into the desert, I was helped by my spirits and "voices" to define gods and prayer to the point where I could adjust and balance belief and practice and thought.

Following years of profound communion with plants, rocks, animals, birds, reptiles, and other recognizable species, I could not escape the obvious: only humans have a god. Those other species are our teachers. They are superior to humans by living fully as they were born to. Did they not pray because they didn't need to propitiate gods for their sins, or perhaps because they didn't want anything? Well, the first part of that is overtly true, but we know they want for water when it's dry, warmth in the snow, and food when there is none. What else? When one truly joins in a two-way communication relationship with another species, one first notices the joy of, say, that animal. It seems to run deep and pure. Sure, that animal can, and does, suffer, feel hatred, want revenge, love, yearn, and actually experience an entire range of emotions at times, but there is this joy which one does not always find in human beings.

It seems to be the joy of being fully alive. So is that prayer? Could be. But to whom or what? After years of such observations, I could conclude only one thing, which I shared earlier: humans created the concept of god. We made it up! Something to propitiate through—sacrifice?—when there is famine? That would mean that if there is, say, famine, it is through human error ... sin. That has got to be the penultimate in self-centeredness and ego. Well, and arrogance. But there it is. What else?

So if we made up a god to punish us, it also has to have the facet of approval, right? So we added to this god the attributes involving a loving grandfather who will grant us gifts when we are good. And if we need something, all we have to do is ask. Right? But what about, as I mentioned before, all those very nice people who ask and ask and ask, but continue to be crippled beggars in India? The New Age philosophy tells us that if we are living right, in harmony, and with the proper expectations, the Universe will provide us with all we need and want. Whenever I heard this drivel, I pictured those crippled beggars in India. Aren't they, too, deserving of what the Universe has for them? Is this philosophy only good for wealthy American people who have the luxury of time to ask for them and to "get into the right space" to accept them?

How many times I have been confronted by New Agers who sadly shake their heads at me and tell me that I must not be a very spiritual person since my health is poor and I have no funds. Explaining that a shaman traditionally resides in these states in order to be more one with other sufferers, these good folks look blank and ask why such a thing could be. Try explaining a less than perfect (in whose eyes?) way of living to people like this.

What then am I worshiping? It seems that I find All Life divine. To what, then, do I pray?

For a very long time, I had been imaging Mystery as Nature. Well, that's a fine thing to address prayer to. Okay, but why do I address my needs *to* anything? Even Nature? And what can I expect Nature to do about Roberta and her little desires? This is where I was on that afternoon on the interstate.

Yeah, yeah, yeah, I have heard *ad nauseam* about how all we want and need comes from *within ourselves.* But let's face it, that's not a very satisfying answer to things. I could meditate into the grave and still want and need things, although I might want less since I would be so entirely inside myself as to be drugged. The Lord Buddha taught (and I believe it with my whole heart) that the only time we are unhappy is when we want something. And I use that teaching in my life daily. When I find myself unhappy, I check to see if it is from something I want that isn't important—and weigh it as to just how self-centered I'm being.

The shamanic way of viewing life is that we are to become as closely at one with the rest of Life as possible. I truly empath my environment. I mirror it. I mirror rain, drought, the sun, and the clouds. Of course. And there are times visitors find me to be surprisingly depressed. Well, what kind of holy woman is this? One who shares the depression of the oak trees who lose their leaves in the heat of spring and the animals who have to do without water until the monsoon rains months hence. On the other hand, I'm giddy with ecstasy when the water comes and the leaves return.

This being the case (please stay with me on this, now), I am living what I believe: that we are all part of everything else. Thus, I *am* a raincloud, I *am* the sun and the moon. That's how we can make it rain. Which I don't do very often, believing that Nature seems to know better than I what is best. So to what do I pray? To myself, to all that I am, all that comes into me. To All Life: everything that has ever been, is or will be. The What Is. Why would I pray aloud, in human, English language?

For the images which come with that exercise. And it is imagery, which is power.

Tanya and I had driven ahead of the rest of the group by a couple days to establish a campsite. On our second evening there, I suggested that we each smoke our pipes and pray beneath the incredible stars. We drew our chairs together, loaded our pipes with herbal tobacco, and lit up. Mine was clogged. Drat. I know that when a pipe clogs, it is likely that the person smoking it is clogged. I placed the pipe in my lap, drew out my cleaning materials from the bag and began cleaning it, getting as simple and quiet as I was able, as close to harmony with the pipe as I could. Still clogged. I took the pipe apart, cleaning each piece. Each piece alone was clear: air circulated through them perfectly. Joined together, the pipe clogged. I continued to work on it, staying patient and serene.

Tanya began to squirm.

"How long are you going to work on that?"

"Until it smokes."

"Why don't you wait until tomorrow?"

"Because it's clogged now."

Out of respect and courtesy, Tanya would not leave the "circle" and go to bed. She was pretty restless.

"I have to clear this in order to clear myself," I explained.

I worked with that pipe for over an hour before sweet air moved gently through its entirety. Then, I smoked it.

"Great Mystery, help me to stay unclogged and serene," I prayed. "I have come out here onto this sacred land to renew myself. Great Mystery, I pray for vision. My vision of my work dims and I yearn for that. Please, give me vision."

A long pause in that still, black sky. Then ...

"If not vision, Great Mystery, then I pray for the grace to live without it."

Where did that come from? Oh, my want of vision was a clog!

Even then, there was this part of me which felt quite spiritually noble. I've been humble and asked for grace. So surely I will receive vision. I have done the right thing, after all.

I got the grace to live without it.

That wasn't such a small gift, either. Living without vision is agonizing for me. Why go on? Whine, snivel. The following months were grindingly depressing, but I was able to continue my walk forward somehow. Later on, I could recognize the grace without which I would not have continued my walk.

Living Without a God

It has been very difficult to live without a god. It requires that I accept responsibility for myself in every way. It is also sweet, and I find myself insisting on even more excellence from me. Since there is nothing controlling life and what goes on in it, it goes to us to make of it what it is. How we live life. If we have no rules and regulations from someone else "out there," then we must be stronger in our integrity. It is up to us. And I know that I can punish myself far more severely than could any god or law. As for prayer, the deeper I enter the All Life and become ever more at one with Nature, the more I realize that I *am* prayer. Since my entire life is prayer, it is difficult to extrapolate that for others. It is and I am. We be.

Each night, dreamtime brought me a giant Kachina. It would march in and stand before me, huge and masked, expressionless. It was all white and gold. The Sun Kachina, but without the traditional colors. Then this Kachina began appearing in some of my journey work. It came to me in the sweat lodge. I would awaken at night and there it was, standing in the corner of the room. Soon, I could feel the earth tremble as it appeared—its marching, its dancing. I began noticing the power lines as I drove along the interstate, the towers supporting those lines looked like Kachinas. They marched, they danced, they were showing me something, but what? Their moods seemed to shift. At times, they seemed intent and solemn, other times they felt almost playful. What was this?

Clair called me from California about a disturbing dream.

"There is this great cloud of dust, and I know it's from horse's hooves. It's night, but I can see. Moonlight. Then, out of this dust and crowd of unseens rides this Native American man on a horse," she described.

Oh no, not more Wannabe stuff. Everybody wants some great Indian chief, complete with medicine bonnet trailing in the dust.

"He's huge. Dressed all in white. Feathered bonnet all the way to the ground."

Um-hum.

"And his horse is white. They stand before me. He stares deeply into me as if he's expecting something. Then it disappears."

"Clair, it sounds like too many books and movies," I said.

"No, I thought of that. It's something more. The man—who is not really a man at all—wants something. What could it be?"

"Too much pizza," I insisted. Nothing about this reminded me of the Kachina experiences I had been having for years.

"Please, I know it's important," she said. "Please journey for me and call me back."

I did. The man in white appeared in the journey immediately ... *with my Kachina!* Then the Kachina dancers emerged from a limitless *kiva* and I danced with all of them. As we danced: joyfully and sadly and with pain, holding little children and alongside crippled men and women—with every aspect of life, I was informed of the meaning behind Clair's dream and my experiences.

"We are the Christ Consciousness. We are representations of that Christ which is you. As humans become increasingly conscious in their lives, we appear to them, to encourage and goad them to excellence."

"Are you part of us?"

"Yes. And also from without. We are composed of that powerful energy which bathes the earth each Winter Solstice—the Christ. Another word is Buddha. These words describe those of you who have consciously returned to this planet in human form to live and teach and heal and give."

"I'm no Buddha. I'm not even a very nice person."

Rumbling laughter. "Shamans aren't usually nice people. But you are living the life you chose to best give yourself to Nature and the What Is. And since we are here, it means that *you* lack the perfection *you* demand prior to accepting buddha-hood."

Long pause while I digested this. I found that I was still dancing with them. I looked back up into their faces.

"Since I am dancing with you, that must mean that I am one with you?"

"Good."

"So I am a part of that Christ energy?"

"Yes, you are in it, of it."

"And Clair?"

"Yes."

"Why does this appear to her in the form of a Plains Indian?"

"It is what resonates with her. She views the Plains Indians as being perhaps more naturally spiritual than other peoples"

"What about those power line towers alongside the highway?"

"Ha. They are real. They do speak to you in their energy emissions. And you comprehend their messages. You are in a time—and going ever more deeply—of tremendous change and intensity. They show you war and strength and sternness, but they also dance love and joy and the comedy of life."

"Please, before you go, tell me about prayer."

"Your dance of life, with life, is prayer, the only prayer worth anything. You must dance the What Is in order to transform. Only when you accept where you are right now can you be ready to change. That is what dancing with us is, and that is what prayer is."

"Shall we continue to smoke the Pipe and pray aloud?"

"Oh yes. Spoken prayer not only helps you but helps those present. It is a gift to be shared with all. And it is effective. Not those limited "gimme" prayers, but those limitless paeans which arise from those praying in a circle around a sacred Pipe. Help those who fear to pray aloud and with others to speak out. It is only your culture which has taught those shy ones not to speak aloud to the gods of Nature and self."

The journey ended. Sort of. It seemed to go on—and still lives with me today.

I called Clair and explained the journey to her. She had a little trouble with the word Christ, confusing it with Christianity. But after some discussion and a couple of books I suggested she read, she understood. She continues to have the dream, particularly at times of transformation, when things are edgy and tough, and it encourages her to go forward. This experience has also expanded her limits greatly.

Nancy has her great white Snowy Owl which represents her Christ. Ed has his enormous white man.

I was in some deep trouble financially. I journeyed about that. This is the vision.

I am at/in a traditional Sun Dance. Many people. Because I am here to pray about my financial problems, I am pierced and attached by leather thongs to the pole. We dance for four days, all day, in the extreme heat, with no water under the blazing sun, blowing our eagle-bone whistles for strength to continue. Each day I dance, trying to break my flesh and thus free me from that pole. Each dusk, I am brought a small cup of water as I sit in the deep dust, weary to death from dancing. All night I sit in that dust, attached to the tree/pole by those thongs fastened into my flesh. Each evening, I notice that I am older. My suffering is tremendous.

The fourth day dawned, and we begin dancing again. As I move about the circle, I notice friends, students, and family in the shade of the arbor around us, cheering me on, encouraging me in my striving to break free of the thongs holding me to that tree. Only with their encouragement may I continue. That night, I still haven't broken free. I am in desperate physical condition, very weak. It is even hard to breathe, and I am hungry and thirsty. My throat is dusty, my eyes coated with dust. I sit at the end of the thongs, facing the tree, praying wordlessly. My friends are present, still quietly encouraging me. I stand and begin to dance again, barely moving but unable to do anything else. Then I see the faces of my friends. They are looking beyond me. I look behind me.

There is the Great Kachina moving slowly toward me. How humiliating that I cannot even suffer properly. I do not want to call upon it since I am such a complete failure in this sacred dance. And there it is, coming into the Circle. Once again, I pull hard against the thongs. To no avail. I sink to my knees in weakness, finally and forever giving up.

I feel myself being lifted gently. Onto the Great Kachina's lap. It wipes my face. It removes the thongs from my body. It gives me water.

"When you surrender, I will save you."

Recently, I was asked how I pray. My formal prayers are with the Pipe, and this is good because once I have smoked, I shift into a finer space. And my prayers, although often for myself, are not of the gimme genre. Here is an example.

"Great Mystery, you who are all things and nothing, it is I, your servant and holy woman, Nightwing (we always give our sacred names back in prayer, and doing so reminds us of who we are and where we exist in the Great Scheme of Things), praying in this sacred circle and with this sacred smoke.

"Great Mystery, I pray for all the four-leggeds, the two-leggeds, the winged ones, those who creep and crawl, those who swim, the sacred plant people, and the rock beings. May we all recognize them and rejoin them in a union of grace and love.

"Great Mystery, I pray that I become more in harmony with All Life. I ask that my eyes become more seeing, my ears more listening, my heart gentler, and my mind more open to what is placed before me to better myself.

"Great Mystery, I offer thanksgiving for What Is, for all the beauty and even the grief and pain around me. Help me remember gratitude more often. Stop my steps that I may commune with All Life. Great Mystery, I beg that I walk more gently upon our blessed Mother Earth, that I become more aware of my footfalls and more fully notice how my shadow caresses or disturbs her and my fellow beings here.

"Great Mystery, thank you for the simple blessings of the Pipe and the fellowship of like-minded people. As I smoke, I am reminded of the Circle of Life and how that grows and encompasses all else. I ask that I might be reminded of that more often, so as to keep that image before me always."

"Great Mystery, I give thanks that I have such a profound love for Mother Earth within me, that I am willing to do anything which will help Her. Help me to become ever more willing. Help me to be willing to be willing to walk my walk in all ways ..."

And so on. This is a typical prayer of mine. The student who asked me how I pray suggested that most of us pray when we are in desperate needs or straits, or are in terrible fear. Pause for thought. Ye-es, I used to pray that way: o god, let me survive this, and I will be a better person. I promise. Um-hum. Then, the crisis over, I would bit-by-bit slip back into my old self-ness.

I have not prayed that way in over fifteen years! And I hadn't even realized that until Ed asked the question about prayer. Celebrate! When in dire straits or danger, I simply become more alert and try to learn from the experience presented. I hope that when the time comes for my crossing to the next phase of life (death), I will continue in this habit.

"How do you pray for others?" Ed asked me.

I do pray for others. Long ago, I would sort of "wrap" them into a "bundle" and then place it before the Great Mystery, realizing that the Great Mystery knew what was best for all of us more than I did. It was a matter of presentation and trust. Well, that wouldn't work very well once I left the concept of a personal god, would it?

"Ed, when I tell someone that I will pray for them, I sort of take them and their situation into myself and then work on it sometime, usually during the quiet night hours," I said. That is not exactly correct, but it is as close as I can describe it. And people know that they can call upon me at any time and know that I will be there. My daughter was being harassed and frightened by another driver on the interstate between Tucson and Phoenix. Recalling my word to her that anytime she was in danger that all she had to do was to image me or call my name and I would take care of it, she did so. The driver pulled immediately off the highway, and she drove home in peace. This type of assistance occurs often. Each time, it feels to me as a hand caressing me.

So I do believe that we can pray to and petition other humans, spirits, and even power animals for help. I call upon Lord Elf when the problem involves something to do with Other type beings. And it always joins me when I travel to the OtherWorld for soul retrievals and other life-threatening work. When I ask. I call upon my totem, Owl, to enhance my "owl eyes," which is to say "seeing" that which is non-physical, using my non-corporeal vision. All of these techniques are obviously some sort of prayer.

I most often pray for grace. Just to handle life more graciously. Since I mirror life around me, my environment, whatever that may be, I usually need that grace. So many times I would have quit had it not been for the grace to continue, which is granted to me from without. Who grants that? I believe it is drawn from all the life that is, has been, or will be. As we unite ourselves with the collective consciousness, we become the prayer and are now able to accomplish more.

"What about meditation?" Ed asked.

Meditation

Well, if you consider attending one of the hundreds of seminars and classes that are constantly presented to teach people how to meditate, then give me the money you would spend on it here and now. Meditation is not difficult, nor is it esoteric. It is simply moving into receptivity. Meditating is best done on a regulated basis, at least at first. The self-discipline of that is most useful. Then, keeping in mind that, above all, we are not meditating to "get" anything and that there is no right or wrong way to do this, we can relax a bit and just "be there," which is mostly what it's all about.

We are admonished to "empty our minds" in order to meditate. Balderdash. As soon as one is told to empty one's mind, the super-ego takes over and spins full speed. My first teachers instructed me to simply be there, at attention, for whatever may or may not occur. I was warned that expectations would bar any positive response to my being there. I have certainly had proof of that, since it is human nature to expect something from everything we do. It has gotten much better. Their directions worked for me. I found myself physically being in a chair, listening to the electric wall clock and refrigerator hum, each day at the same time. After just a couple weeks of this "exercise" (for that is what it is, exercise), I found myself looking forward to those ten minutes each day. It caused me to feel more comfortable in my life. A little self-discipline is a good thing for us, and our consciousness responds to it eagerly.

During several months of my ten minutes of daily attention, I found myself becoming far more peaceful internally. And lo and behold, something happened! My Voice came to me to teach me. I began my mystical work. Only a couple years later, I entered my first shamanic trance state, and I believe it happened so naturally because of the meditation I was practicing.

Practicing? Don't we get it right? Remember, there is no right or wrong way to meditate. It's easy. Just be there and be receptive to the potentials and possibilities. I recommend to my students to start off with five or ten minutes. Those who begin with a half-hour space are courting failure, and most will quit meditating in short order. How can anyone maintain a space of receptivity when the kids are banging on the door, the phone keeps ringing in the other room, and the dog begins barking furiously outside? Impossible. And you will quickly skip a day, then two, and then ... well, as with any exercise, missing even one day can stop us from doing what makes us feel better.

Receptivity is a bit tricky. It takes real practice. I missed the greatest impact of my first visionquest because I had been expecting something other than what was presented for me. Only when I shared my experience with some others did I recognize the wonder of what had happened out there. Many of the people I have visionquested have "missed it" also. We expect a vision, for example, to come within a certain form, and when it doesn't, we disregard what is given to us. Expectations become a wall erected between us and the possibilities presented to us. Opening our minds and dropping our limitations can result in some astonishing information.

Rosie was out on her second visionquest. Her first had been very powerful, although she hadn't seemed to have realized that. This time, she declared, she would have a *bona fide* vision. During the first days and nights of her quest, I could feel her groping toward an experience, yet missing it. I knew it was there for her, because I could "see" it all about her as she sat within her sacred circle there in the mountains. Finally, on the third day, I went out to her to counsel.

"Nothing's happening!" she wailed.

"Yes, it is, Rosie, I can see it," I said.

"Well, I can't!"

"Listen, just relax and be here. Watch what is happening all about you. I believe your vision will come from the east there. Just pay attention, and drop your expectations."

During the night, I felt her "get it." In the morning, I heard her whistle blowing in signal for help. What on earth? I didn't feel that anything was going wrong for her. She seemed to be perfectly safe. And she had experienced the presence of the Great Mystery and the spirits that previous night. But I hauled myself out to her circle.

"I want to come into camp," she said. She had already packed up her frame pack and was ready to go.

"Why? Everything seems okay here. You're not sick, are you?"

"No, but I can't stay out here any longer."

"Why not?"

"Well, last night, there were Kachinas dancing all along that cliff edge. They scared the crap out of me. I can't be here tonight."

"Rosie, that was your vision," I said. "The gods came to you and danced for you to impart some information. It's what you wanted."

"Not like that. It scared me. I want a nice vision of a goddess figure in the sky which will teach me and comfort me and be with me."

"But that's not what has happened."

"No, and that is why I want out of here," she said.

"Rosie, your expectations and demands for what you want and how you want it are keeping you from your vision. Please stay and give it up and receive what is being given to you. Let go of your preconceptions and open your mind and heart to what is here," I urged.

After some more of this, Rosie stayed for the last day and night. But she let herself sleep that final night so that she wouldn't have to see the scary stuff. Later on, she told some of the others that visionquesting was not all it was cracked up to be, and that having gone out twice, she still got nothing.

Become receptive and allow What Is to spread through you—even when you may not understand its meaning at first. That is power.

I went into Transcendental Meditation during the late 1960s. That's a state in which you are way tranced out. People were mightily impressed with me when I did that. But to what end? The Lord Buddha encourages us to remain present always, even during meditation. Trancing out is not being present. When we try to block our thoughts, they become more insistent and we find ourselves in a no-win battle. Being receptive is a simple, non-combative state. With practice, one may attain receptivity easily and with little distraction.

"But," say some people, "if you are receptive, how do you know that what you receive is appropriate and not from the 'dark side'?"

Oh, come on. Unless you suffer from schizophrenia or other serious mental ills, you can tell the difference. Refer to "Chapter 8: Danger, Judgment, and Protection." If a "voice" suggests that you kill someone or cause harm to anything, you can have a good idea that this came from some consciousness that you don't want to associate with. So don't. Once you gain some information, write it down and refer to it later to see if you can divine its meanings. In the meantime, practice your meditation exercise.

What about aids to meditating? Some people recommend chanting mantras or gazing at a special object or picture. Sogyal Rinpoche, in his book *The Tibetan Book of Living and Dying* (Harper, 1994), gives many good recommendations for meditating and is well worth reading. If I find myself distracted, I may well turn on a tape of drumming or chanting. I do not use soft tinkly music because that either makes me nervous and edgy or I fall asleep. I can also attain a state of receptivity simply by looking at my inner wrist. Nothing very esoteric. I have heard from people who went to a woman who teaches meditation. She didn't seem to charge too much for the weekend. Well, until she "created" your specific mantra, which was an extra charge. Really. Just what part of becoming receptive is so impossible?

One way to slip into a meditative state is via contemplation. In contemplation, we take a topic and consider it from all angles. Let's use an example here: say you want a new house. Begin contemplating that home: what does a home mean to you in the spiritual sense? After all, one's environment is pretty important. Contemplate how the animals create and care for their homes: nests, dens, and hollows in the earth. Look at your home and all it means to you in all ways and from all directions. Let's keep this viewing on a spiritual level as much as possible. Consider a hut with very few belongings. Consider the simplicity of living in a small cave. Don't forget to consider just how important—or non-essential—a house really is for us. Contemplate where you now reside. Is it adequate?

Contemplation allows us to begin thinking and then gradually enter receptivity by giving those thoughts our attention and letting them move on out of our space. Thus, we are not fighting our thoughts, but perhaps harnessing them and using them to segue into a state of meditation.

Let us not confuse contemplation with mind games, however. Those quickly become an exercise in futility. On the other hand, fighting our thoughts is also worse than useless. On one of my visionquests, I was having real difficulty stopping my mind chatter about a problem which had raised its ugly head in the hours just prior to leaving home. It went on for a couple days and nights, and instead of being receptive and *there*, I was going over and over this stupid problem.

"Don't worry about it, Nightwing," said Lord Elf.

"But I don't want to waste all this precious time letting my mind block me," I said.

"You aren't wasting time, you are spilling your problem-thoughts out into the ether," it said. "You recommend to people to truth-speak about things that bother them in order to get those truths out of their bodies, right?"

"Yes. When people suppress stuff, their bodies absorb the junk and stress."

"Same with thoughts. Don't suppress these troubling thoughts; allow them to come up into your consciousness and then out of you."

"Oh."

I was able, at last, to turn the thinking into some contemplation, thereby placing this problem into a more positive space. I began viewing it from all sorts of angles and seeing the possibilities and potentials for growth there. Within hours, I had moved on into my desired state of receptivity and the problems I had been wrestling with were safely placed into their proper perspective.

What's another way to begin contemplation? Let's begin at the beginning. By prayer. Pray, then contemplate your prayer, then ease into meditation. Become one with All That Is, even if it doesn't overtly feel like that. Perhaps one day, someone will ask you about prayer, and you will search your memory and realize that your prayer life has altered greatly into a state of comfort and ease and inner richness.

Bonus Content
Walking Hawk

I am Walking Hawk, and I shall be speaking through you for a time. You and I have a strong history. Through our work together, you will come to know it and will write about it. First, let me show you my history with Red Deer and the People.

Red Deer stood at the cliff's edge, watching the sun begin its ascent. He looked down upon his village, then to the birthing lodge. Moon Laughter was giving birth to the son of his creche brother, Tall Spine. This child was the son of their lodge, but that lodge included Red Deer, by right and responsibility of the creche, the group of young born within approximately one year of one another. All children born within the same time frame were considered to be siblings of a sort which matched and, in some cases, superseded that of blood relationships. Thus, Red Deer had slept with all creche members, and the child could have sprung from his loins, although that was neither known nor important. Moon Laughter and Tall Spine had formed a lodge union which he, himself, had blessed formally and publicly. He was still a part of their family and would spend the night there with them from time to time, all of them sleeping in a heap, much as puppies would do. As far as this new life entering the world was concerned, it would be precious to them all, no matter the paternal ties. In any case, children belonged to the mother, since they lived for so many moons within her and drew first nourishment from her.

Red Deer had crept down to the birthing lodge under the cover of darkness to sit by it and touch it, just to be near and to try to draw off some of Moon Laughter's pain. It would not do for anyone in the tribe to see him so by daylight. But he thought she knew. Tall Spine would understand the love of a member of the creche. He could see a small group of people waiting outside the lodge, tending a small fire, awaiting news; these were all his special brothers and sisters. They all shared one another's pains and joys. Because of Red Deer's position as shaman of the village, he must stand up here awaiting the breaking sun, aloof and holy, for all to see, doing his job of welcoming the life-giver. He felt a slight irritation as his gaze moved down to that little grouping of people. It would be much nicer there, with them.

As the sun broke over the next ridge, almost blinding him, Red Deer saw two things at one time: a red-tailed hawk leaping off the cliff-top to soar in the warming air and a woman emerging from the birthing lodge. The child was born. He could tell from her gestures that it was a boy. They all had a fine son. And Red Deer knew his name would be Red Hawk.

Red Hawk grew and thrived amidst his lodge family, his parents' creche family, the extended aunts, uncles, cousins, grandparents, and the tribal family. It was warm and secure; he was never alone, never knew loneliness or any kind of separateness. He had his own creche siblings, too, with whom he played and became educated on the important ways of the People. They would play until it was time to eat, run to whichever lodge was closest, fill their bellies, play some more, then fall and sleep wherever they lay, snuggled up together.

Through these days and nights, Red Deer walked among the lodges, alone and sensing the safety and comfort of the People. He was required by his position to live outside the village, but he was very aware of every nuance and altering of breath of his people. When they had need of him, they came to his lodge and sought him out, and he would enter the village to tend to the sick or fearful if necessary. When the leaders wished to consult him, they most often came to his lodge and would seat themselves before it and talk. A few people approached him as family and friends—Tall Spine, for example—but even they took care that they not intrude upon his solitude, which was essential for his work.

At one time, Red Deer would occasionally enter the lodge of one of his creche siblings, eat, and perhaps spend the night. Sometimes, he found solace in the body of a creche sister. But that had ceased now that the power had come down upon him. He simply had no urges in that way any longer. And that was as it should be—shamans stayed to themselves for the most part. Sharing physical love with another could cause that partner harm.

He especially enjoyed watching the youngsters at play. It was rough and tumble, preparing them for a rough and tumble life. The People did not hunt much; when they did, it was seasonal. When there was an overabundance of rabbits, for example, the People hunted them out before they died of starvation. In this desert, there were few fish, and those which did survive in the nearby streams were held in a sort of awe by the People. Fish and toads lived in the in-between world and were therefore teachers of what was possible. This part of the desert was high enough to be fruitful with walnut trees, oaks, junipers, manzanita berries, and gramma grasses, whose seeds were ground up for a rich flour, as were mesquite beans. Some years ago, the council had agreed to experiment with limited irrigation, so there were small fields holding squash, corn, pumpkins, and beans. There was some concern lately that these fields were expanding more than needed. The old ones suggested that the tribal membership had grown as a result of so much easy food. Certainly, it was true that the village was nearly half again larger than it had been when they were children. Perhaps it was the easy food. That was when the rabbits over-populated and then must be rubbed out. In all things, one must seek balance.

Red Hawk raced past with his creche. As the rest of them continued to run, Red Hawk stopped and took Red Deer's hand, looking up into his face. What did Red Deer see in those eyes? Just a glint, quick and then gone, just another dirty little boy again, face smeared with grease and honey. Red Hawk raced off, leaving his uncle/father to ponder what it was that the boy had. So familiar, yet so different from the others ...

Red Deer stopped at the lodge of Moon Laughter and Tall Spine. As expected, he was handed a bowl of soup as he sat down. He made the polite eating noises, demonstrating how good it tasted and how it fed his body and soul. Then he rinsed his mouth with water and spat, clearing himself so that he would not offend those close to him, and leaned back on the wooden framed seat and sighed. Tall Spine was working on a short spear he used for throwing and glanced at his brother.

"And? It is good to see you, Brother. Is this social?"

"To tell the truth, Spine, I did not plan this stop. I just felt the desire to sit with my brother and sister for a time."

"You grace our lodge," said Moon Laughter. "And I am glad to see that you can still gobble up a great load of food."

This was the woman who he had rolled in the dust wrestling with when they were children. She would seldom be in awe of him, and even then only when he worked. This was real comfort.

"I just got run over by a pack of wild children, and it seems to me that one of them resembled Red Hawk," he drawled.

"He is the worst of the lot," said Tall Spine, "and he is taking over the position of the leader and trouble-maker. He is able to think up pranks none of us ever considered."

"Ah, not so, Spine. It seems that I can recall some wild things you got us into," Red Deer said.

"We were tame compared to the children of today," Tall Spine insisted.

"My mother tells me that each creche is worse than the last," chuckled Moon Laughter. Her voice reminded Red Deer of water bubbling over smooth stones.

"Well, and my old teacher often told me that I was a much lazier apprentice than he ever was," said Red Deer. "And he was sure that I would never stand up under the power when it came upon me. I guess that is part of getting older."

They were quiet. Not one of them felt he or she was aging in any way. Actually, they wished to be racing around the village just like the creche was.

Red Deer stayed with them until after the evening meal, when Red Hawk came home from his rampaging. He observed the boy as he was checked over by his mother to see how well he had bathed in the river before he was allowed to sit upon the pallets in the lodge. It seems he passed her scrupulous inspection. She did make him go outside, rinse his mouth well, and chew some mint leaves. Then, when he sat by her, Moon Laughter combed his matted hair and looked through it for insects.

"We will wash this tangle of hair tomorrow," she said sternly.

"Mother, I have to meet the creche at ..."

"No, that is when we will be washing your hair," she said.

"But ..."

"Red Hawk," said Tall Spine. And there was a comfortable silence once again.

"I shall be meeting with your creche starting with the moon of rain to begin your instruction," said Red Deer. "Do I need to talk with each family, or will you tell them for me?"

"I will tell them, Uncle," said Red Hawk. "What will you teach us?"

"Haw. If I told you tonight, you would go to your creche and teach them and I would have nothing to do with all my time," Red Deer said. "No, you must wait. But be sure that all your creche is there on the day, down by the tall rock at the river, and ... be clean."

Red Hawk opened his mouth slightly, as if to ask why or to argue, but clicked it closed again when he saw the look in his mother's eyes. "We will all be there and we will be clean, Uncle."

"Good. I must go to my lonely lodge now." Red Deer was rising as he spoke. There was something almost disturbing about this boy. Not bad. He was very intelligent and was from intelligent parents. His mother was looked up to by the village as an example of good housewifery and mothering. Tall Spine was held in respect for his counsel. But there was something else, too. Again, he saw glimmers of it only a few times in the evening. Well, he was but a child yet, and it would doubtless become clear before his initiation into adulthood. That was, what—five years away? Yes. Boys became men of the People when they had attained twelve years. Until then, children were unformed and easily influenced. The People did all they could to stand back and allow their children to form themselves, insisting only that they be clean, healthy, and courteous. The rest was up to the child. And the spirits.

Red Hawk grew within the People and with his creche. As they grew older, the games became a little rougher, the hunting a bit more serious, and the girls began to spend more time apart with girls' pastimes, playing with dolls, helping with younger siblings, learning to cook. Still, they all romped together often during the days and nights there on the floor of the high desert. They were as free as little animals until the time came for them to take their places in the village as young adults.

When Red Hawk was nearly eleven years of age, the creche began taking instruction for adulthood from several of the People. Various responsibilities were taught, and they began performing small jobs at the gardens, bringing water to those who worked, sharpening tools at the teaching of adults, learning which plants were ready for harvest, learning how to water and when, learning what were weeds and what were not. They were present at the erection of new lodges to learn as they fetched items. More often, now, the boys and girls were separated for teachings to prepare them for their initiations into adulthood.

Red Deer was a frequent teacher of both the boys and girls, educating them regarding the various spiritual aspects of nature and the proper ways in which to conduct themselves in their lives in order to stay in harmony with life. As he did so, he observed them closely, always seeking the ones who might become healers, and perhaps even the one who might become the shaman to follow him. In this venue, Red Hawk seemed merely another little boy, polite but ever ready to leave the classes and play with his fellows. Nothing special there. Or was there? And what special thing was Red Deer looking for? Was he special when he had eleven years? Actually, he recalled that his young years were spent with him behaving as normally as possible. He observed his friends and matched his behaviors to them. Is that what this lad was doing? *No, he's just a normal little boy who will grow up to be a normal member of the tribe*, Red Deer thought to himself. And why would he want the child to be a shaman anyway?

One morning, the creche was dashing through the village, kicking up dust and knocking over seats and racks. At least, at this age, they often stopped to restore their damage and apologize. They were, after all, courteous and decent youngsters. But they were also enjoying what they knew to be the last few months of childhood freedom. The game they were playing was rough, and they were intent on winning. The game was one with a ball roughly the size of a human head and sticks, which each child had found and worked until it was exactly the right shape and smooth to the hands. Whichever team got the ball to the river first won, and there were no rules.

Red Deer heard the cry all the way up in his lodge on the cliff and knew it was serious trouble. He started hurrying down to the village immediately, passing the herbal woman on the way. He looked for the bone setter as he strode swiftly among the lodges toward the people crowded around the still form lying upon the earth near the river. He heard the cry of Moon Laughter and knew. Oh gods, no.

Red Hawk lay crumpled where he had fallen, his head bleeding where it had been smashed by a playing stick. One eye was open, the other closed. Already, his right arm and leg were curling up toward his center as Red Deer had seen on old ones who never walked nor spoke well again. The herb woman cleaned away some of the blood from the boy's head, enough to see the white bone showing through. The bonesetter looked, but she shook her head. She could do nothing with a break of this kind. All eyes turned to Red Deer. Moon Laughter came to him, grasping his arm, tears streaming down her lovely face. Behind her was Tall Spine, his eyes pleading with Red Deer.

One boy was standing near, weeping and chanting over and over, "I didn't mean to hit him so hard." The rest of that creche had closed their ranks, comforting one another, but this boy was alone. All these things Red Deer took in immediately. That boy had to be helped, too.

Crossing to the boy, he said, "Badger, go quickly to your father and mother and have them pack enough supplies for five persons for many days. Bring robes and extra sandals. Water for a day's travel. Then get Widow, the one who cares for me, and have her prepare to join us. Fast, now. And ask your father to join us, as you will, on this journey."

He looked at Tall Spine. "Stay here with Moon Laughter and trust me in this matter. If there is any chance our son will live, it is where I go. If all is well, we shall all return in several days."

"Red Deer, brother, you will need help," started Moon Laughter, "and I can manage without Spine. Let him help you. He needs to."

"No, you have your young ones to think of, and Spine can help you. Truly, I think it best that it is done in this way. There is a thing here that does not seem apparent at once. My heart is certain that the boy will live. And Badger and his father need to help in the healing so that they, too, may be healed."

All was ready within a very short time, and Red Deer lifted Red Hawk into his arms. The four of them began walking northeast out of the village, across the great basin in which they lived. Red Deer was on the trail which would take them to the place a day's journey away where he made his sacred medicine, and there he would place Red Hawk upon his holy stone and bring his spirit back into his body. All that day, they walked, stopping briefly to drink and eat a handful of grain or so. Red Deer and Badger's father took turns carrying the boy, and they all carried whatever of the supplies they were able. The way was rough, most of it up over mountain ranges and through cactus forests, the trail often so narrow that it did not allow for error in placing their feet. At last, near sunset, they arrived at the sacred place.

"I will carry Red Hawk to the top of the rock myself," said Red Deer. "None of you will come up there, but stay down here and set up camp and cook us some nourishing soup. There is plenty of water in a stream about one hundred yards west of here. Be sure that all our water containers are kept filled. As soon as I set the boy down up there, I will return for two robes and a gourd of water, and some food for myself. Pray always."

Widow had accompanied Red Deer to this place before, so she was able to show the others where things were and direct Badger to the stream for water. Soon, a fire was set for the soup, robes were laid down for the night, and she had uncovered the cache of supplies that was always left there. They were ready.

On the great rock, Red Deer laid the boy down on a robe. He'd had to cover his face and head in order to keep his right eye closed. He put water into the eye whenever they had stopped, and he did so again. He could bind that eye closed now with a strip of yucca cloth, soaked in water. The eye showed little color, just the black cave in which the spirit lives. But there seemed to be nothing living in Red Hawk's eye. From the first moment in which he had looked upon the bloody body of Red Hawk in the village, Red Deer knew that this was a holy wounding. If he survived, Red Hawk would be shaman, the one to walk in Red Deer's footsteps.

Four days and five nights passed as Red Hawk lay unconscious. Red Deer was able to trickle drops of water into his mouth and kept his lips moistened. He prayed constantly, sang his songs, and poured sacred juniper smoke over the child to keep purity. During the third night, Red Hawk began thrashing about from time to time, muttering strange sounds, some of them animal words. At one point, the boy suddenly sat up and sang the sunrise greeting very clearly, then collapsed again, still unconscious. A fever ravaged his body during the days, and Red Deer poured cool water upon him and fanned him with his sacred eagle feathers. Red Deer pinned the edges of the terrible wound together with cactus thorns, and it healed well and clean.

Red Deer waited. He knew that the boy was far away in dreamtime, in the sacred land of the "Others," where shamans were taken and where they chose whether or not to walk in the way that was chosen for them. It was a fearful place, and all there were terrifying. What would Red Hawk decide? If he were to choose not to be shaman, he likely would live out his life as a drooling cripple. And the tribe would care for him with tenderness, as one in a sacred space. But he would not know that during these days that he was away in that place. He would have to make his decision with very little information, just what the spirits chose to reveal.

Oh, if only he had known before this accident! If he had been able to prepare Red Hawk for this decision! Of course, that was nonsense;

shamans were never prepared. They must accept their walk with no notice and accept it with no information. They had to trust those very spirits which seemed so terrifying. All Red Deer could do right now was to keep this beloved body alive and look for the spirit of Red Hawk to return to it.

Just at the earliest gray light of dawn on the fifth day, Red Hawk spoke. "Uncle, I thirst for water. And then, if I could, I hunger for food."

Red Deer's heart nearly leapt from his body. Red Hawk's spirit had returned. Whole. As he bent to pour water into the cup for the boy, he prayed thanksgiving.

"Widow, heat some soup for this boy up here," he called down. "He has decided to wake up and join us again!" he called out.

Below the rock, he could hear three voices sing with rejoicing. Looking over the edge of the rock, Red Deer was able to see Badger dancing a dance of triumph. That was a good thing, for such an accidental death could have placed deep scars upon the young man.

As the day progressed, Red Hawk gained strength and consciousness. Red Deer carried him down to the others so that they could see and touch him. Then, they returned to the rock, and Red Hawk began to question his uncle.

"Why can I not walk? What has happened? There is pain in my head, and I slept poorly, Uncle, for I had very strange dreams ... and where is this place? My parents?"

"During a game, Badger struck you upon the head with his stick. Do you remember that?" asked Red Deer.

"Yes, some of it. I remember the game, and then nothing. We were about to win, but Badger jumped right in front of me, and ..."

"Well, your head was cracked open, my son. Your mother and father feared you would die. All did. So Badger, his father, Widow, and I brought you to my secret holy place to heal you. It has been five days, now, since the accident, so you are naturally weak ..."

"Uncle," Red Hawk whispered, "it is more than weak. I cannot make my arm or leg do anything I tell it to. And there is this thing over my eye ..."

"Yes, son. I have placed a wrap over your eye because, while you slept a long sleep, it would not stay closed. I have seen this before when people do great harm to their heads. You may get your strength back little by little."

There was a long pause.

"And I may not?" Red Hawk's voice was small.

"And you may not," Red Deer conceded. "It may be that the spirits have a use for you that requires that your body be slowed down in this way. Your dreams ..."

"Oh, they were terrible, Uncle. More terrible than anything I have ever dreamed or thought. There were creatures there which were not of this land. And they spoke to me in pictures. And things were never what they seemed to be. And then they changed back into things I knew, and even that was a lie. I suffered greatly in those dreams, Uncle."

"I know, Red Hawk, for I have those dreams also, and often they are not dreams," said Red Deer. "Now that I am older, I go to that dream place on purpose on behalf of the People."

There was no more talk until that night. Red Deer had propped Red Hawk up against an outcropping of stone, and they sat side by side, looking at the stars. Red Deer had prayed his sunset prayers and saw that Red Hawk followed them silently. Now, their eyes followed the trail of a shooting star as it crossed the sky, leaving a long white and gold stream behind it. They sighed together.

"Uncle, what has happened to me?" Red Hawk asked.

"My son, you were born and then reborn to be a shaman. You accepted that in your deep sleep that was not a sleep, and now you must begin training for your role as shaman to the People. It is hard to accept, but you were brave enough to do so. I know these things, for I too had the choice and chose to live as I do. I did not have the injury you have; I had a bad sickness from which it was thought I would never recover."

"Uncle, it seems to me that I shall always be crippled as I am. My heart hardly beats for that knowledge. Why must I drag myself through life like this? Shall I ever be able to close my eye? Is my face ugly? It feels ugly. Will people run from me after seeing how ugly I am?"

"I do not know. I know so little. Why must you go through life slowly instead of quickly, as others do? Perhaps you were meant to walk instead of fly. Yes, people will be uncomfortable with you, especially as you come into your power, but that would be also true if you were beautiful. And, Red Hawk, if your eye does not close of itself, we shall get the bone setter to stitch it closed so that the light will not cause you pain.

"My son, do not spend much time feeling sad about yourself, for you can eat and think and speak. You are valued by the People, and will be even more so once they learn of your future. As for being beautiful, you will always be handsome if you are so inside. Your face will droop, but your spirit is great, and it is that which the People will notice above all. You must decide again how you will live now. Will you hide yourself in a darkened lodge for all time or will you live in the sun and beneath these sacred stars and give yourself to the People? As you give yourself, you will forget about the small things such as how you walk or speak or how you look. And so will others."

"Uncle, I will try to understand these things. Uncle, I want a woman and my own lodge and children."

"And you know that as shaman," Red Deer said, "you will not have these things."

"I know," he whispered. It was still. He was asleep.

After three more days of resting and eating and drinking and praying, the little group began their return to the village. Again, it took nearly a day, although this time it was downhill most of the way, and they had left the robes and certain foodstuffs in the cache. Red Hawk still needed to be carried, and he was truculent about it at times. But when he realized that it made Badger feel worse, he showed a happier face. After all, he really was glad to be going home to his parents' lodge. Being at Red Deer's sacred rock was pretty exciting, though. Only Widow had known where it was before this.

The village people saw them coming while they were still quite a way off, and many men came to share the burden of carrying Red Hawk. It surprised him that they seemed to consider it an honor and that they wanted to carry his broken body. Soon, he was brought to his mother's lodge, and there she was, tears streaming down her face. Tears of joy. He realized that she didn't even notice that he was now ugly. She was only happy that he was alive and returned to her arms. He forgot his advanced age and held her as close as his left arm would permit.

That night, there was a feast to honor the return of the wanderers. During the feast, Moon Laughter and Tall Spine gave many gifts to Badger, his father, Widow, and Red Deer. Then, Red Deer called for quiet.

"Red Hawk left this village as a boy. A wounded boy. He was healed in a sacred place. During his healing time, his spirit traveled very far away, and while on that journey, he met spirits which are not human and not animal, but others. He was given a choice about his life among us. And he chose to live in this village as shaman. His new name is Walking Hawk."

From the time I was struck upon my head, life changed for me. Greatly. I could no longer run or participate in any way with my creche. They tried to include me, but how could they, when I had to drag my right side about with me? Oh, my heart could soar, but my body limped. As time went by, my right hand turned into a hawk-like claw, and my face took on the appearance, on the right side, of an aged man. There was a white streak in my hair which grew out of the scar the wound left.

No, I did not blame Badger. We were playing as all boys do. Yet, I believe he may have blamed himself the rest of his life, for he often avoided me afterward. The bonesetter and herb woman did their best to improve my life and ease my pain, but my body was wracked with pain from any movement until new muscles took over the burden.

I am ashamed that I fled into my parents' lodge, into the darkness there, and hid. Red Deer allowed this for a time. My mother and father were patient, despite the lump which dwelled within their home. Moon Laughter even spoon fed me when I refused to eat myself. But then, one day, Red Deer came to our lodge in his full authority as shaman, and I needed to obey.

"Red Deer approaches the lodge of Moon Laughter and Tall Spine," the village crier called out. We were required to respond with respect. My parents went out of the lodge. I stayed within, but sat up and brushed the matted hair from my face.

"Where is your son?" Red Deer inquired of my parents.

"He is within the lodge," Tall Spine said.

"Why does he not display respect to his shaman?" asked Red Deer.

"He ails, Shaman, as you know, and we cannot force him from his bed," Moon Laughter said.

Red Deer's head appeared inside our door flap. He looked about the lodge, and his eyes fell upon me. His head disappeared. I was safe.

"All I see in there is a sickly pup," I heard him roar outside. "You should club him and put him out of his misery. It stinks in there."

"No, Shaman, please ... he is our only son," Moon Laughter cried.

"That cannot be Walking Hawk, who has been chosen to follow me as shaman of the People," Red Deer said. "He would be outside, helping me and greeting the sunrise each day. No, that is but a sickly pup. It looks to be in its last hours and should be clubbed to death to save it and you more trouble."

I called out. "Shaman, it is I, whom you have named Walking Hawk. I am in great pain to move, thus I keep to my bed until I can once again walk well."

"You see? I hear the pup yipping in pain and the grief of impending death," said Red Deer.

"No," I called out. "It truly is I, Walking Hawk."

"Then, boy, why are you not walking?" roared Red Deer.

"I am in much pain," I whimpered.

"You do not yet know pain," said Red Deer. "When you meet pain, you will not curl up and whine like a dying pup."

"What would you have of me?" I cried out.

"Be at my lodge when the sun is mid-heaven. Be clean. Be alone." And he took respectful leave of my parents and walked off.

When Mother came back into the lodge, I asked her to help me clean up, but she would not. She pretended that I was not present. I began to realize that my parents were fine actors and that this had all been put on for my benefit, to shame me before the village. I was angry and felt sorry for my situation. But anger won out, and I began to drag myself from my bed, gathering clean clothing and headed for the river to wash.

That took some time, for I had not yet learned to walk and refused the aid of a stick my father had prepared for me. Sometimes, I was nearly on my belly, worming along like a bug we used to stomp. "Maybe someone would come along and stomp me, and my troubles would be over," I thought. But I made it to the river and shouted at some girls there to leave so that I could bathe. They left, all right, for they could well see that I was black with anger. It took some work to get the mats cleaned from my hair and to make myself presentable. I would not go to Red Deer without being my best, not after he had made sport of my weakness. It was not my fault that my body was thus!

Taking my filthy clothing back to my parents' lodge, I took the stick my father had made for me and started off to Red Deer's lodge. So far!

He lived up on the edge of the cliff overlooking our village. Why couldn't he come to our lodge? Step by step, I crept up toward his lodge, even though it seemed to move farther off with each step I took. Then, as I approached, I could hear him chanting. As I remembered our days on his sacred rock, I gathered my last strength and came to his door.

"Who is at the door of Red Deer's lodge?" came his voice from inside.

"Walking Hawk," I called out as strongly as I could.

"This is not the trick of an ailing pup is it?"

"No, Shaman, it is I. I come to you clean, walking alone all the way, as you ordered," I said.

"Then enter."

I stooped and entered his lodge. He was seated at the back, directly across from the door. There was a seat placed close to the door, and upon a small fire was heating the most wonderfully scented soup I have ever smelled. I set down my gift to him, a pot of gelled soap my mother had made and packaged for me to bring to him. One never approaches a shaman without some gift in hand. He nodded.

"Moon Laughter makes my favorite soap. You are fortunate to have access to such a fine thing and should use it more often," he said.

This would be one of the first scoldings and teachings he presented to me during our long (but not long enough) time together. I made note of it and would remember to bathe more often.

"My parents are the finest of the People," I said, "as are all their creche siblings." Perhaps that would flatter him.

"Haw," was all I got from him.

We ate of the soup.

"Widow is a fine cook," Red Deer commented as he belched his appreciation. "We have a good friendship, and this is a great benefit of being shaman, that there is always a widow woman who will care for us in return for us caring for the People. She is a good woman."

"I recall her cooking for us when I was upon the sacred rock," I ventured. "I thought then that it was almost as good as my mother's."

"There, you are already learning to be a shaman. Diplomacy and tact are essential, even when we must be harsh. Do not forget that, Hawk."

That began my apprenticeship with Red Deer, to become a shaman of the People. It was grueling work, and he never let up on me. Each day I would traverse the difficult trail up to his lodge, and I learned to rise earlier and earlier, so that I would arrive before he was impatient to begin. Most of the time, I cleaned his lodge and cared for his various feathers and bones and items he used in healings and seeings. It was long before he allowed me to care for his best implements, for I had to earn his trust. I was to accompany him to consult with the leaders and to counsel with the People who asked him for help in making decisions. I was present when he sat in judgment over certain disagreements and when some of the clans had conflict. Of course, I was in attendance when he healed the people, stepping in when the bonesetter and herb woman finished their work, when he would heal the unseen wounds to all involved. I attended during all rites and ceremonies. And always, I was behind him.

"Learn to be unseen," he advised. "Shamans are invisible except to their enemies. Our foes see us well enough, and often we wish to be hidden to them. It is also good to show a silent and serene face. You see, the People fear us enough. We do not wish to cause them more fear. They must feel they can approach us. Be self-effacing and courteous and kind, for when we work, we are not. When we take on our presence of Shaman, we are pitiless and not of the same flesh."

At first, I understood this to mean that I should behave as all others did, but I soon found what Red Deer meant for me by trial and error. When I tried to be as my creche siblings, they all thought of other places to be until I was once again alone. I noticed as I hobbled through the village that women took their young ones inside their lodges. People would greet me, but then they passed me by. All those things hurt as much as the pain of my body. I sought counsel of Red Deer.

"Yes, those things hurt the human part of you," he mused. "As old as I am, it still does. Your parents are the only ones who still treat me as one of them, and I am grateful that there are those two. I am fortunate. And I think of that each day.

"Walking Hawk, it is not that the People dislike you. It is that they do not comprehend who or what you are now. There is this thing about you, since you have been named shaman, which causes them discomfort. They do not know how to converse with you or how to behave in a respectful but friendly manner. Do not expect too much of them! They are good people, but confused. Especially your creche siblings: they remember Red Hawk, but you are no longer that young man. Have you looked upon yourself? You appear different, you are named different—and, boy, you are a different person.

"It is important that you remain compassionate toward all of these people. But know that it is unlikely that you will be able to be close with any of them ever again. Well, you may be close, but they will not be. Do you understand that?"

"Yes, Teacher," I replied. It was the first time I had used that nomenclature for Red Deer, although I thought of him that way. Today, I truly became his apprentice and humbly accepted my place there.

Well, no. I did, but the road was rough for us, for my great pride often provided the rocks in that road which many times we had to dismount and remove from our way. It was a long process, the tearing down of my humanity in order that the shaman might inhabit the lodge that was my body and mind. Red Deer had his hands full.

Spending most of my time with Red Deer, I had little spare time on my hands, but I did manage to lurk around, watching my creche siblings at play. By now, they were flirting with one another, and that awakened *within me the desire to be looked upon in favor by a girl. They imitated our elders in many ways, thus learning how to establish adult relationships when the time came. No girl looked well upon me. I remained alone. They were also preparing to go out on visionquest, where they would learn of their special places within the People. But not I. Whining to Red Deer was useless. He just reminded me that I had already had my quest on the sacred rock. But that seemed to me to be by default. I had not had the chance to prove my manhood by moving through the fear the other boys/men would face. I was just unconscious. Telling Red Deer this was even worse, for he lost his temper and railed against me.*

"*Boy, you faced fear worse than any they could even imagine! You traveled to the OtherWorld and back. They never will. Stop your sniveling and apply yourself to growing into your place within the village!*"

References

Anaya, Rudolfo A., *Bless Me, Ultima*. TQS Publications, 1972.

Cowan, Tom, *Fire in the Head: Shamanism and the Celtic Spirit*. Harper Collins, 1993.

Eliade, Mircea, *Shamanism: Archaic Techniques of Ecstasy*. Pantheon, 1994.

Halifax, Joan, *Shamanic Voices: A Survey of Visionary Narratives*. E.P. Dutton, 1979.

Harner, Michael, *Way of the Shaman*. Bantam, 1980.

Huxley, Aldous, *The Doors of Perception*, Chatto & Windus, 1954.

Kalweit, Holger, *Dreamtime and Inner Space*. Shambhala, 1988.

Kalweit, Holger, *Shamans, Healers, and Medicine Men*. Shambhala, 1992.

King, Serge, *The Urban Shaman*. Simon & Shuster, 1990

Rinpoche, Sogyal, *The Tibetan Book of Living and Dying*. Harper, 1994.

Strieber, Whitley, *Communion*. Avon, 1987.

Strieber, Whitley, *Transformation: The Breakthrough*. Avon, 1989.

Vallee, Jacques, *Dimensions: A Casebook of Alien Contact*. Ballantine, 1989.

About the Author

Roberta Lee / Nightwing

Roberta Lee, C.Ht. is a traditional shaman of Anglo/Celtic origin, a healer, seer, and dedicated pipe carrier. She was born a shaman into a straight-laced Methodist family and later attended college on a journalism scholarship. She had two children whose father died in 1969 and the single-mother went on to work a series of traditional jobs—including working as an astrophysicist's technical writer, a political consultant, a funeral counselor, a home health care supervisor, and an office manager for both a criminal lawyer and a private investigator. In 1986 her shaman-side required she shift all of her attention to doing the work of a shaman so she did and, among other things, traveled around Canada and the USA teaching and healing. Lee's shamanic services and activities have been successfully integrated with the services of psychologists, medical doctors, chiropractors, kinesiologists, naturopaths, 12-step counselors, therapists, ministers, and priests. In 1996 she retired to a one-room cabin, RavenHouse, in a remote wilderness area of southeastern Arizona to be in nature and stillness to continue her service. She lived there with more than 90 rescued animals—from finches to burros to emus—which she considered her teachers. She returned to civilization in 2012 and currently lives in Tucson, Arizona. Watch for the release of Roberta's next book, *Sacred Wheel of Our Ancestors*.

www.ingramcontent.com/pod-product-compliance
Lightning Source LLC
Chambersburg PA
CBHW062145080426
42734CB00010B/1574